Evangelicalism and Fundamentalism

Evangelicalism and Fundamentalism

A Documentary Reader

Edited by Barry Hankins

NEW YORK UNIVERSITY PRESS

New York and London

NEW YORK UNIVERSITY PRESS
New York and London
www.nyupress.org

Library of Congress Cataloging-in-Publication Data
Hankins, Barry, 1956–
Evangelicalism and fundamentalism : a documentary reader /
Barry Hankins.
p. cm.
Includes bibliographical references (p.   ) and index.
ISBN-13: 978-0-8147-3716-3 (cl : alk. paper)
ISBN-10: 0-8147-3716-1 (cl : alk. paper)
ISBN-13: 978-0-8147-3717-0 (pb : alk. paper)
ISBN-10: 0-8147-3717-X (pb : alk. paper)
1. Evangelicalism. 2. Fundamentalism. I. Title.
BR1640.H366   2008
277.3'082—dc22   2008023039

New York University Press books are printed on acid-free paper,
and their binding materials are chosen for strength and durability.
We strive to use environmentally responsible suppliers and materials
to the greatest extent possible in publishing our books.

c 10 9 8 7 6 5 4 3 2 1
p 10 9 8 7 6 5 4 3 2 1

For my sisters: Bobbie Green and Bindy Peters

* * *

Contents

* * *

Acknowledgments

I would like to acknowledge the fine work of my research assistant, Steele Brand, who faithfully tracked down texts and addresses of copyright holders and did a number of other important yet mundane tasks necessary for this book to come together. I would also like to thank a number of friends who study American evangelicalism, all of whom suggested various texts that ought to be included in the book. I fear I was unable to include every recommended text, but I took the suggestions very seriously. These colleagues include: Margaret Bendroth, Michael Hamilton, Darryl Hart, Rick Ostrander, and Bill Trollinger.

I would also like to thank Byron Johnson and Baylor's Institute for Studies of Religion for a summer stipend to support the book, as well as Baylor's history department and chair Jeff Hamilton for general support and working conditions conducive to scholarly endeavors.

At NYU Press, editor Jennifer Hammer enthusiastically supported the book when it was merely an idea. Sometimes known as "Jennifer THE Hammer" (at least by me), she checked in regularly with encouraging words, prodding me along so the book would be completed in a timely manner. Authors who accept too many writing projects at one time need this sort of encouragement, and I greatly appreciate the entire editorial staff at NYU Press.

* * *

Introduction

A Brief Overview of American Evangelicalism

This book is a collection of primary texts from American evangelicalism during the twentieth century. The point of the book is to give readers a sense of the range and diversity of viewpoints that evangelicals have held as well as to show that there are common themes that make evangelicals an identifiable subculture of Americans, diverse though they may be. The book is designed to be used as a text in courses of study on modern American history and religion in America. It is hoped that having read the selections, readers will have a sense of what constitutes American evangelicalism.

A Brief Description of Evangelicalism

There is a sense in which evangelicalism traces its history to the Protestant Reformation of the sixteenth century. Martin Luther, John Calvin, and even the left-wing groups of that era emphasized the primacy of scripture and salvation by faith. *Sola scriptura* and *sola fides* were the great Reformation protests against the theology of the Roman Catholic Church. Often called "evangelicals," sixteenth-century Protestants believed that salvation came to individuals by faith alone, not by faith plus participation in the sacraments, as the Catholic Church taught. Likewise, on the issue of scripture, Protestants taught that the Bible alone was authoritative, not scripture plus the church, as Roman Catholics believed. More directly, for our purposes here, American evangelicalism was shaped decisively by the revivals of the First Great Awakening of the eighteenth century. In addition to the twin pillars of *sola scriptura* and *sola fides*, the revivals emphasized the conversion experience and an active life of faith that resulted in evangelism and social reform.

Historian David Bebbington has developed a quadrilateral that brings these elements together as biblicism, conversionism, crucicentrism, and activism. Biblicism is another name for the Reformation Protestant doctrine of *sola scriptura*. Evangelicals believe that the Bible stands above all other authorities in matters of faith and Christian living, and many evangelicals ascribe even historical and scientific authority to scripture. Conversionism is essentially the doctrine of *sola fides* with a revivalist twist, which is the belief that one must experience a personal conversion, usually in an instantaneous moment of decision to accept by faith the free gift of salvation that comes to human beings by the grace of God. There are some nonrevivalist evangelicals today who believe that one grows gradually and steadily in the faith as one is catechized by the church, but most evangelicals can identify pretty nearly the day and time they were converted. Even those who cannot point to such a specific experience nevertheless testify to an assurance that their sins have been forgiven.

The evangelical conversion experience is made possible by the crucifixion and resurrection of Christ, which Bebbington labels the crucicentrist plank of modern evangelicalism. While many liberal Protestants (to be discussed and defined below) point primarily to Christ's life as an example of faithful living, evangelicals are more apt to emphasize His death on the cross as the sacrifice for the sins of humankind and Christ's supernatural resurrection as the hope of everlasting life with God. This is all possible because for evangelicals—as for Roman Catholics, Orthodox Christians, and other types of traditional Christians—Christ is believed to be the son of God. Like liberal Christians, evangelicals also see Christ's life as an example for living, but the Christlike lifestyle is something that follows conversion made possible by the crucifixion. Even if it were possible, living a Christlike lifestyle would not make one a Christian aside from conversion made efficacious by Christ's sacrificial death. So it is, argues Bebbington, that evangelicals are crucicentrist; the crucifixion is central to their view of conversion and Christian living.[1]

Christian living is the activism plank of modern evangelicalism. Evangelical activism entails evangelism, the sharing of the faith with others in hopes that they too will convert, and also social reform. Evangelicalism from the nineteenth century to the present has produced many social reformers emphasizing everything from antislavery to antiabortion. Jesus taught his followers that they were to be salt and light in a world that was decayed and darkened. In addition to evangelistic efforts to win others to Christ, evangelicals also emphasize personal morality and social justice.

An Overview of Evangelicalism, 1877 to the Present

There is fairly wide agreement among historians that nineteenth-century American culture was dominated by Protestantism and that American Protestantism was at that time pervasively evangelical. The so-called mainline churches—Baptist, Methodist, Presbyterian, and Congregational—for the most part taught something like Bebbington's quadrilateral, and there was a strong wing of the Episcopal Church that was evangelical as well. Whether a higher percentage of Americans actually converted and attempted to live a Christian lifestyle in the nineteenth century as opposed to today is questionable, but only a small minority of Americans would have intellectually challenged the tenets of evangelical Protestantism before 1877. The majority of Americans took the truth of the Bible for granted whether or not they attempted to live out its teachings.

The dominance of evangelical Protestantism was challenged in the late nineteenth century by the rise of theological modernism within the mainline Protestant denominations of the North. Modernism was the attempt to adjust Christian theology in light of modern ways of thinking, in particular, romanticism, evolutionary science, and higher criticism of scripture. Modernism would eventually become known as theological liberalism, and for the purposes of this book, theological modernism and theological liberalism are synonymous. While evangelical thinkers were not uniformly antievolutionist immediately on the appearance of Charles Darwin's *Origin of Species* in 1859, modernists enthusiastically embraced the evolutionary model not only for biology but also for virtually all other areas of human knowledge as well. Applied to Christianity, the modernist position meant essentially that the Bible was not necessarily authoritative for modern Christians. Rather, scripture represented the earliest and most rudimentary form of Christianity. The faith had evolved over nineteen centuries into a much more advanced experience with God. Modernist preacher Henry Ward Beecher put it best when he said that the oaks of civilization had evolved over time. He asked, therefore, why we should "go back and talk about acorns?" The acorn was the ancient faith from which had grown the oaks of modernity.[2]

This evolutionary view of the Christian faith directly challenged the biblicist notion that scripture was authoritative. Instead, the Bible was the fallible record of how first-century humans experienced God. Modern humans, living in light of modern science, would experience God in modern ways. Romantic religious experience became the centerpiece of modernist theology, which meant that particular doctrines such as the virgin birth of Christ, Christ's literal resurrection and ascension into heaven, and His predicted Second Coming were no longer essential. Rather, they were dismissed as merely the language or even superstitions of ancient Christians. The core of the Christian faith for the modernist was an experience of God that was natural and made possible because God was immanent, meaning very near to human beings. Moreover, individuals had within them a natural capacity for experiencing God and needed no supernatural conversion made possible by the crucifixion. For this reason, modernists emphasized the incarnation, the idea that God was in Christ, more than the crucifixion, and they believed that God dwelled in all humans in much the same way God lived within Christ. Christ was merely the best model of what all humans could be.

In addition to the evolutionary model of modern science and a romantic experience of God, modernist Protestants also adopted critical literary methods. When applied to the scripture, this form of textual analysis became known as higher criticism of scripture. Essentially, higher criticism was the application of the same literary, textual criticism to scripture that was used in studying other ancient texts. Rather than evangelical biblicism with its emphasis on the uniqueness of scripture as the inspired word of God, the Bible was studied from a critical perspective that held all questions open for investigation, including authorship of various books, dating of historical events, and ultimately even the question of whether historical events recorded in scripture actually happened.

The application of the evolutionary model, romantic experience, and higher criticism of scripture directly challenged at least three of the four components of Bebbington's quadrilateral. The Bible's authority was rivaled and often replaced by the centrality of religious experience; conversion was unnecessary because human beings possessed a natural capacity to experience God; and the crucifixion was no longer central, as it had been overshadowed by the incarnation. As liberal theologian Horace Bushnell put it, Christ's death was "not a sacrifice in any literal sense."[3] Moreover, in one of Bushnell's earliest books he argued against revivalist conversion, saying instead that children could be nurtured in the faith throughout their lives. On the issue of the resurrection, some modernists taught that Christ rose spiritually, not physically, while others said that the resurrection was merely the memory of Christ in the minds of the apostles.

As one would expect, there was a vigorous response to the rise of theological modernism, and that response shaped twentieth-century evangelicalism. The traditionalists and conservatives become known as "fundamentalists" in 1920 when a Baptist preacher and magazine editor coined the term. Curtis Lee Laws of the *Watchman Examiner* said that a fundamentalist was one who was ready to do "battle royal" for the fundamentals of the faith. Presbyterian conservatives at Princeton University and Seminary had first attempted to identify the fundamentals of the faith in 1910 in response to modernist attempts to change the Westminster Confession of Faith, which was the doctrinal creed of Presbyterians. The Presbyterian five points were: (1) the inerrancy and full authority of the Bible; (2) the virgin birth of Christ; (3) Christ's substitutionary atonement; (4) the bodily resurrection of Jesus; and (5) the authenticity of miracles. In the 1920s, many fundamentalists changed the authenticity of miracles to the more specific doctrine of Christ's literal second coming.[4]

In between the Presbyterian effort to identify the fundamentals of the faith and the full flowering of fundamentalism in the 1920s, two California millionaires sponsored the publication of twelve pamphlet volumes of theology known as *The Fundamentals.* They were mailed to virtually every Protestant preacher, youth leader, and YMCA and YWCA director in the country, and in the words of historian George Marsden served as early fundamentalism's "tour de force." The wide-ranging pamphlets dealt with issues of evolution and higher criticism of scripture, the relationship of evangelical Christianity to science more broadly, daily Christian living, evangelism, missions, and so forth. Moreover, the volumes popularized the term fundamentals, leading to Laws's coining of the term "fundamentalist" a few years later. Several of the selections in this book come from *The Fundamentals.*

The battles that took place in northern denominations in the 1920s came to be known in American history as "the fundamentalist-modernist controversy." In the Northern Baptist Convention and the northern Presbyterian Church U.S., the modernists won, largely because a group of centrists sided with the modernists in believing that the denominations could tolerate both liberals and fundamentalists. In the twenties and thirties, fundamentalists were of two minds on how to respond to modernism. Many took a separatist position, believing that it was theologically necessary to separate from denominations that had become liberal or modernist. This group tended to be militant defenders of the faith. In his 1980 book *Fundamentalism and American Culture*, Marsden wrote, "Fundamentalists were evangelical Christians . . . who in the twentieth century militantly opposed both modernism in theology and the cultural changes that modernism endorsed."[5] This is still the standard scholarly definition of fundamentalism.

Others stayed within the mainline, liberal denominations attempting to assert an evangelical influence. By the 1940s, many of the conservatives on the fundamentalist side of Protestantism grew weary of the fighting, especially as separatist fundamentalists tended to split not only from liberals but then also from each other. Moreover, most of the separatists were heavily into the end-times prophecy known as dispensational premillennialism that appeared to more centrist evangelicals as almost cultic in its fascination with "signs of the times." For these reasons, a group of centrist evangelicals attempted to demarcate a difference between fundamentalism and evangelicalism. Hoping to recapture the positive and culturally engaged spirit of nineteenth-century evangelicalism, this group formed the National Association of Evangelicals in 1942, Fuller Seminary in 1947, and *Christianity Today* magazine in 1956. They took the name neoevangelicals.[6] By 1960 or so, those who continued to espouse fundamentalism tended to be separatist and premillennial as they militantly fought to defend the faith, while neoevangelicals sought to engage culture from an evangelical perspective.

Fundamentalists today make up the right wing of evangelicalism. All fundamentalists are evangelicals, but most evangelicals are not fundamentalists and resist being called fundamentalists. That said, there is no clear marking where fundamentalist evangelicalism ends and the broader evangelicalism begins. The key difference is that fundamentalists are more militant and separatist. For example, when one encounters an evangelical who will not participate in evangelical enterprises such as Promise Keepers, InterVarsity Fellowship, or Campus Crusade for Christ because to do so would be to participate with evangelicals who have not separated from liberals, one is usually speaking to a fundamentalist. When in doubt, one need only ask because most fundamentalists will gladly use that self-designation. The entry of evangelicals into politics in the form of the Christian Right from 1980 to the present has blurred neat distinctions between fundamentalism and evangelicalism. This is because many Christian Right activists retain the militant, fighting spirit of fundamentalism, but they are anything but separatist. Not only do they engage culture politically, they also cooperate with nonevangelicals and even non-Christians in doing so. In light of the difficulty in defining evangelicalism and fundamentalism, scholars have joked that an evangelical is anyone who really loves Billy Graham, while a fundamentalist is an evangelical who is angry about something. Indeed, from the 1950s into the twenty-first century, Graham has been the symbol of the neoevangelical brand of evangelicalism. Biblicist, conversionist, crucicentrist, and activist, he nevertheless has been very much in the culture, even if not of it. Moreover, he has cooperated with every kind of Christian—liberal or conservative, Protestant, Catholic, or Orthodox—in his crusades. It is worth noting that from the 1950s forward, some militant fundamentalist leaders have been highly critical of Graham and at times have attacked him viciously.

To summarize, evangelicals are Protestant Christians who affirm the authority of the Bible, insist on the necessity of a conversion experience made possible by the crucifixion and resurrection of Christ, and attempt to live a holy and active life of faith, sharing the gospel with others in an attempt to win them to the faith. Beyond this, they are quite diverse, as the selected texts in this book will show.

A Word about the Organization of the Book

The chapters of the book have been organized topically to address theology and the Bible, the fundamentalist-modernist controversy, end-times prophecy, science, politics, race and gender, and evangelical attitudes toward Catholicism. There are two chapters covering evangelicals and evolution and two covering evangelicals and politics. The evolution chapters are broken into "before Scopes" and "after Scopes," while the politics chapters cover "before 1980" and "after 1980." Within each chapter the selections are arranged chronologically to show change over time and the diversity of viewpoints within evangelicalism. I have tried to keep the selections short enough to hold readers' attention but long enough so that the arguments make sense. Each section, and sometimes specific selections within it, has a brief introduction that will allow readers to pick and choose specific texts and still have some sense of the context for each selection.

* 1 *

The Bible and Evangelism

The Bible

EDITOR: *At the center of evangelical belief is the authority of scripture. This does not mean that evangelicals agree on the Bible's teaching in all or even most matters. In fact, the importance of scripture almost assures that evangelicals will disagree over biblical interpretation because so much is at stake. Generally, evangelicals believe the Bible is the product of special revelation and contains what God intends for humans to know about sin and redemption. Beyond this, many evangelicals and fundamentalists believe the Bible is inerrant in matters of history and science as well as theology and Christian living. To say that all evangelicals believe that the Bible is authoritative above all other teachings is something of a truism because scholars define evangelicals historically as those who hold to the authority of scripture above all other teachings and also believe in a life-transforming experience of salvation made possible by the death and resurrection of Christ. This belief in the authority of the Bible, along with a belief in the necessity of conversion through Christ's redemptive work on the cross, constitute the core of what it means to be an evangelical.*

Below are two selections from The Fundamentals, *which were several volumes of articles compiled between 1910 and 1915 and published as the tour de force of early fundamentalism's battle with liberal theology. The range and diversity of* The Fundamentals *was remarkable, with virtually all of the entries intended to answer certain challenges posed by the rise of liberal Protestantism. Liberal Protestantism was called "modernism" during the first quarter of the twentieth century and was generally an attempt to modernize Christian thought in light of new modes of thinking, particularly evolutionary science and literary criticism of ancient texts. Modern literary criticism applied to the Bible was called "higher criticism."*

Evangelicals and fundamentalists believe that the Christianity found in the Bible is the purest and most developed form of the faith known to humans. The Christian faith of the Bible is something people should return to. Beginning in the late nineteenth century, modernists tended to believe that the centerpiece of the faith should be Christian experience, not ancient scripture and the doctrines found therein. For modernists, the Christianity found in the Bible was a rudimentary form of the faith that had evolved over two thousands years into its more highly developed form in the late nineteenth and early twentieth centuries. Where evangelicals wanted to return to the Bible, modernists wanted to transcend it by using modern ways of understanding to experience God in a way not possible for ancient people. Evangelicals and fundamentalists, therefore, squared off with liberals or modernists not just over the meaning of scripture but even over what the Bible actually was. Was it the timeless and authoritative word of God or was it an ancient book that gave us merely a glimpse of how ancient people interpreted their experiences with God, not necessarily authoritative in a modern age that has evolved over the course of two thousand years?

The two passages below argue for the traditional, evangelical view and roundly condemn liberal views of inspiration and biblical criticism.

Gray, James M. "The Inspiration of the Bible—Definition, Extent and Proof." In *The Fundamentals*. Edited by R. A. Torrey, A. C. Dixon, and others. 1910–15. Reprint, Grand Rapids: Baker, 1970.

In this paper the authenticity and credibility of the Bible are assumed, by which is meant (1), that its books were written by the authors to whom they are ascribed, and that their contents are in all material points as when they came from their hands; and (2), that those contents are worthy of entire acceptance as to their statements of fact. Were there need to prove these assumptions, the evidence is abundant, and abler pens have dealt with it.

* * *

I. Definition of Inspiration

1. *Inspiration is not revelation.* As Dr. Charles Hodge expressed it, revelation is the act of communicating divine knowledge to the mind, but inspiration is the act of the same Spirit controlling those who make that knowledge known to others. In Chalmer's happy phrase, the one is the influx, the other the efflux. Abraham received the influx, he was granted a revelation; but Moses was endued with the efflux, being inspired to record it for our learning. In the one case there was a flowing in and in the other

a flowing out. Sometimes both of these experiences met in the same person, indeed Moses himself is an illustration of it, having received a revelation at another time and also the inspiration to make it known, but it is of importance to distinguish between the two.

2. *Inspiration is not illumination.* Every regenerated Christian is illuminated in the simple fact that he is indwelt by the Holy Spirit, but every such an one is not also inspired, but only the writers of the Old and New Testaments. Spiritual illumination is subject to degrees, some Christians possessing more of it than others, but, as we understand it, inspiration is not subject to degrees, being in every case the breath of God, expressing itself through a human personality.

3. *Inspiration is not human genius.* The latter is simply a natural qualification, however exalted it may be in some cases, but inspiration in the sense now spoken of is supernatural throughout. It is an enduement coming upon the writers of the Old and New Testaments directing and enabling them to write those books, and on no other men, and at no other time, and for no other purpose. No human genius of whom we ever heard introduced his writings with the formula, "Thus saith the Lord," or words to that effect, and yet such is the common utterance of the Bible authors. No human genius ever yet agreed with any other human genius as to the things it most concerns men to know, and, therefore, however exalted his equipment, it differs not merely in degree but in kind from the inspiration of the Scriptures.

In its mode the divine agency is inscrutable, though its effects are knowable. We do not undertake to say just how the Holy Spirit operated on the minds of these authors to produce these books any more than we undertake to say how He operates on the human heart to produce conversion, but we accept the one as we do the other on the testimony that appeals to faith.

4. When we speak of the Holy Spirit coming upon the men in order to the composition of the books, it should be further understood that the *object is not the inspiration of the men but the books*—not the writers but the *writings*. It terminates upon the record, in other words, and not upon the human instrument who made it.

To illustrate: Moses, David, Paul, John, were not always and everywhere inspired, for then always and everywhere they would have been infallible and inerrant, which was not the case. They sometimes made mistakes in thought and erred in conduct. But however fallible and errant they may have been as men compassed with infirmity like ourselves, such fallibility or errancy was never under any circumstances communicated to their sacred writings.

* * *

5. Let it be stated further in this definitional connection, that *the record for whose inspiration we contend is the original record*—the autographs or parchments of Moses, David, Daniel, Matthew, Paul or Peter, as the case may be, and not any particular translation or translations of them whatever. There is no translation absolutely without error, nor could there be, considering the infirmities of human copyists, unless God were pleased to perform a perpetual miracle to secure it.

But does this make nugatory our contention? Some would say it does, and they would argue speciously that to insist on the inerrancy of a parchment no living being has ever seen is an academic question merely, and without value. But do they not fail to see that the character and perfection of the God-head are involved in that inerrancy?

Some years ago a "liberal" theologian, deprecating this discussion as not worth while, remarked that it was a matter of small consequence whether a pair of trousers were originally perfect if they were now rent. To which the valiant and witty David James Burrell replied, that it might be a matter of small consequence to the wearer of the trousers, but the tailor who made them would prefer to have it understood that they did not leave his shop that way. And then he added, that if the Most High must train among knights of the shears He might at least be regarded as the best of the guild, and One who drops no stitches and sends out no imperfect work.

* * *

IV. Difficulties and Objections

That there are difficulties in the way of accepting a view of inspiration like this goes without saying. But to the finite mind there must always be difficulties connected with a revelation from the Infinite, and it can not be otherwise. This has been mentioned before. Men of faith, and it is such we are addressing, and not men of the world, do not wait to understand or resolve all the difficulties associated with other mysteries of the Bible before accepting them as divine, and why should they do so in this case?

* * *

1. *There are the so-called discrepancies or contradictions between certain statements of the Bible and the facts of history or natural science.* The best way to meet these is to treat them separately as they are presented, but when you ask for them you are not infrequently met with silence. They are hard to produce, and when produced, who is able to say that they belong to the original parchments? As we are not contending for an inerrant translation, does not the burden of proof rest with the objector?

But some of these "discrepancies" are easily explained. They do not exist between statements of the Bible and facts of science, but between erroneous interpretations of the Bible and immature conclusions of science. The old story of Galileo is in point, who did not contradict the Bible in affirming that the earth moved round the sun but only the false theological assumptions about it. In this way advancing light has removed many of these discrepancies, and it is fair to presume with Dr. Charles Hodge that further light would remove all.

2. *There are the differences in the narratives themselves.* In the first place, the New Testament writers sometimes change important words in quoting from the Old Testament, which it is assumed could not be the case if in both instances the writers were inspired. But it is forgotten that in the scriptures we are dealing not so much with different human authors as with one Divine Author. It is a principle in ordinary literature that an author may quote himself as he pleases, and give a different turn to an expression here and there as a changed condition of affairs renders it necessary or desirable. Shall we deny this privilege to the Holy Spirit? May we not find, indeed, that some of these supposed misquotations show such progress of truth, such evident application of the teaching of an earlier dispensation to the circumstances of a later one, as to afford a confirmation of their divine origin rather than an argument against it?

✷ ✷ ✷

3. *There is the variety in style.* Some think that if all the writers were alike inspired and the inspiration extended to their words, they must all possess the same style—as if the Holy Spirit had but one style!

Literary style is a method of selecting words and putting sentences together which stamps an author's work with the influence of his habits, his condition in society, his education, his reasoning, his experience, his imagination and his genius. These give his mental and moral physiognomy and make up his style.

But is not God free to act with or without these fixed laws? There are no circumstances which tinge His views or reasonings, and He has no idiosyncrasies of speech, and no mother tongue through which He expresses His character, or leaves the finger mark of genius upon His literary fabrics.

It is a great fallacy then, as Dr. Thomas Armitage once said, to suppose that uniformity of verbal style must have marked God's authorship in the Bible, had He selected its words. As the author of all styles, rather does he use them all at his pleasure. He bestows all the powers of mental individuality upon His instruments for using the scriptures, and then uses their powers as He will to express His mind by them.

Indeed, the variety of style is a necessary proof of the freedom of the human writers, and it is this which among other things convinces us that, however controlled by the Holy Spirit, they were not mere machines in what they wrote.

Consider God's method in nature. In any department of vegetable life there may be but one genus, while its members are classified into a thousand species. From the bulbous root come the tulip, the hyacinth, the crocus, and the lily in every shape and shade, without any cause either of natural chemistry or culture. It is exclusively attributable to the variety of styles which the mind of God devises. And so in the sacred writings. His mind is seen in the infinite variety of expression which dictates the wording of every book. To quote Armitage again, "I cannot tell how the Holy Spirit suggested the words to the writers any more than some other man can tell how He suggested the thoughts to them. But if diversity of expression proves that He did not choose the words, the diversity of ideas proves that He did not dictate the thoughts, for the one is as varied as the other."

William Cullen Bryant was a newspaper man but a poet; Edmund Clarence Stedman was a Wall Street broker and also a poet. What a difference in style there was between their editorials and commercial letters on the one hand, and their poetry on the other! Is God more limited than a man?

4. *There are certain declarations of scripture itself.* Does not Paul say in one or two places "I speak as a man," or "After the manner of man?" Assuredly, but is he not using the arguments common among men for the sake of elucidating a point? And may he not as truly be led of the Spirit to do that, and to record it, as to do or say anything else? Of course, what he quotes from men is not of the same essential value as what he receives directly from God, but the *record* of the quotation is as truly inspired.

There are two or three other utterances of his of this character in the 7th chapter of 1 Corinthians, where he is treating of marriage. At verse 6 he says, "I speak this by permission, not of commandment," and what he means has no reference to the source of his message but the subject of it. In contradiction to the false teaching of some, he says Christians are permitted to marry, but not commanded to do so. At verse 10 He says, "Unto the married I command, yet not I, but the Lord," while at verse 12 there follows, "but to the rest speak I, not the Lord." Does he declare himself inspired in the first instance, and not in the second? By no means, but in the first he is alluding to what the Lord spake on the subject while here in the flesh, and in the second to what he, Paul, is adding thereto on the authority of the Holy Spirit speaking through him. In other words, putting his own utterances on equality with those of our Lord, he simply confirms their inspiration.

* * *

Time forbids further amplification on the difficulties and objections nor is it necessary, since there is not one that has not been met satisfactorily to the man of God and the child of faith again and again.

* * *

Johnson, Franklin. "Fallacies of the Higher Criticism." In *The Fundamentals*. Edited by R. A. Torrey, A. C. Dixon, and others. 1910–15. Reprint, Grand Rapids: Baker, 1970.

The errors of the higher criticism of which I shall write pertain to its very substance. Those of a secondary character the limits of my space forbid me to consider. My discussion might be greatly expanded by additional masses of illustrative material, and hence I close it with a list of books which I recommend to persons who may wish to pursue the subject further.

DEFINITION OF "THE HIGHER CRITICISM."

As an introduction to the fundamental fallacies of the higher criticism, let me state what the higher criticism is. . . . The higher criticism has sometimes been called the "documentary hypothesis." But as all schools of criticism and all doctrines of inspiration are equally hospitable to the supposition that the biblical writers may have consulted documents, and may have quoted them, the higher criticism has no special right to this title. We must fall back, therefore, upon the name "the higher criticism" as the very best at our disposal, and upon the definition of it as chiefly an inspection of literary productions in order to ascertain their dates, their authors, and their value, as they themselves, interpreted in the light of the hypothesis of evolution, may yield the evidence.

"ASSURED RESULTS" OF THE HIGHER CRITICISM.

* * *

While some of the "assured results" are thus in doubt, certain things are matters of general agreement. Moses wrote little or nothing, if he ever existed. A large part of the Hexateuch consists of unhistorical legends. We may grant that Abraham, Isaac, Jacob, Ishmael and Esau existed, or we may deny this. In either case, what is recorded of them is chiefly myth. These denials of the truth of the written records follow as matters of course from the late dating of the books, and the assumption that the writers could set down only the national tradition. They may have worked in part as collectors of written stories to be found here and there; but, if so, these written stories were not ancient, and they were diluted by stories transmitted orally. These fragments, whether written or oral, must have followed the general law of national traditions, and have presented a mix-ture of legendary chaff, with here and there a grain of historic truth to be sifted out by careful winnowing.

Thus far of the Hexateuch.

The Psalms are so full of references to the Hexateuch that they must have been written after it, and hence after the captivity, perhaps beginning about 400 B.C. David may possibly have written one or two of them, but probably he wrote none, and the strong conviction of the Hebrew people that he was their greatest hymn-writer was a total mistake.

These revolutionary processes are carried into the New Testament, and that also is found to be largely untrustworthy as history, as doctrine, and as ethics, though a very good book, since it gives expression to high ideals, and thus ministers to the spiritual life. It may well have influence, but it can have no divine authority. The Christian reader should consider carefully this invasion of the New Testament by the higher criticism. So long as the movement was confined to the Old Testament many good men looked on with indifference, not reflecting that the Bible, though containing "many parts" by many writers, and though recording a progressive revelation, is, after all, one book. But the limits of the Old Testament have long since been overpassed by the higher critics, and it is demanded of us that we abandon the immemorial teaching of the church concerning the entire volume. The picture of Christ which the New Testament sets before us is in many respects mistaken. The doctrines of primitive Christianity which it states and defends were well enough for the time, but have no value for us today except as they commend themselves to our independent judgment. Its moral precepts are fallible, and we should accept them or reject them freely, in accordance with the greater light of the twentieth century. Even Christ could err concerning ethical questions, and neither His commandments nor His example need constrain us.

The foregoing may serve as an introductory sketch, all too brief, of the higher criticism, and as a basis of the discussion of its fallacies, now immediately to follow.

* * *

SECOND FALLACY: THE THEORY OF EVOLUTION
APPLIED TO LITERATURE AND RELIGION.

II. A second fundamental fallacy of the higher criticism is its dependence on the theory of evolution as the explanation of the history of literature and of religion. . . . . "The nineteenth century," [Professor Jordan] declares, "has applied to the history of the documents of the Hebrew people its own magic word, evolution. The thought represented by that popular word has been found to have a real meaning in our investigations regarding the religious life and the theological beliefs of Israel. Thus, were there no hypothesis of evolution, there would be no higher criticism." The "assured results" of the higher criticism have been gained, after all, not by an inductive study of the biblical books to ascertain if they present a great variety of styles and vocabularies and religious points of view. They have been attained by assuming that the hypothesis of evolution is true, and that the religion of Israel must have unfolded itself by a process of natural evolution. They have been attained by an interested cross-examination of the biblical books to constrain them to admit the hypothesis of evolution. The imagination has played a large part in the process, and the so-called evidences upon which the "assured results" rest are largely imaginary.

But the hypothesis of evolution, when applied to the history of literature, is a fallacy, leaving us utterly unable to account for Homer, or Dante, or Shakespeare, the greatest poets of the world, yet all of them writing in the dawn of the great literatures of the world. It is a fallacy when applied to the history of religion, leaving us utterly unable to account for Abraham and Moses and Christ, and requiring us to deny that they could have been such men as the Bible declares them to have been. The hypothesis is a fallacy when applied to the history of the human race in general. Our race has made progress under the influence of supernatural revelation; but progress under the influence of supernatural revelation is one thing, and evolution is another.

* * *

THIRD FALLACY: THE BIBLE A NATURAL BOOK.

III. A third fallacy of the higher critics is the doctrine concerning the Scriptures which they teach. If a consistent hypothesis of evolution is made the basis of our religious thinking, the Bible will be regarded as only a product of human nature working in the field of religious literature. It will be merely a natural book. If there are higher critics who recoil from this application of the hypothesis of evolution and who seek to modify it by recognizing some special evidences of the divine in the Bible, the inspiration of which they speak rises but little higher than the providential guidance of the writers.

The church doctrine of the full inspiration of the Bible is almost never held by the higher critics of any class, even of the more believing. Here and there we may discover one and another who try to save some fragments of the church doctrine, but they are few and far between, and the salvage to which they cling is so small and poor that it is scarcely worth while. Throughout their ranks the storm of opposition to the supernatural in all its forms is so fierce as to leave little place for the faith of the church that the Bible is the very Word of God to man. But the fallacy of this denial is evident to every believer who reads the Bible with an open mind. He knows by an immediate consciousness that it is the product of the Holy Spirit. As the sheep know the voice of the shepherd, so the mature Christian knows that the Bible speaks with a divine voice. On this ground every Christian can test the value of the higher criticism for himself. The Bible manifests itself to the spiritual perception of the Christian as in the fullest sense human, and in the fullest sense divine. This is true of the Old Testament, as well as of the New.

FOURTH FALLACY: THE MIRACLES DENIED.

IV. Yet another fallacy of the higher critics is found in their teachings concerning the biblical miracles. If the hypothesis of evolution is applied to the Scriptures consistently, it will lead us to deny all the miracles which they record. But if applied timidly and waveringly, as it is by some of the English and American higher critics, it will lead us to deny a large part of the miracles, and to inject as much of the natural as is any way possible into the rest. We shall strain out as much of the gnat of the supernatural as we can, and swallow as much of the camel of evolution as we can. We shall probably reject all the miracles of the Old Testament, explaining some of them as popular legends, and others as coincidences. In the New Testament we shall pick and choose, and no two of us will agree concerning those to be rejected and those to be accepted. If the higher criticism shall be adopted as the doctrine of the church, believers will be left in a distressing state of doubt and uncertainty concerning the narratives of the four Gospels, and unbelievers will scoff and mock. A theory which leads to such wanderings of thought regarding the supernatural in the Scriptures must be fallacious. God is not a God of confusion.

* * *

NO MIDDLE GROUND.

But might we not accept a part of this system of thought without going to any hurtful extreme? Many today are seeking to do this. They present to us two diverse results.

1. Some, who stand at the beginning of the tide, find themselves in a position of doubt. If they are laymen, they know not what to believe. If they are ministers, they know not what to believe or to teach. In either case, they have no firm footing, and no Gospel, except a few platitudes which do little harm and little good.

2. The majority of those who struggle to stand here find it impossible to do so, and give themselves up to the current. There is intellectual consistency in the lofty church doctrine of inspiration. There may be intellectual consistency in the doctrine that all things have had a natural origin and history, under the general providence of God, as distinguished from His supernatural revelation of Himself through holy men, and especially through His co-equal Son, so that the Bible is as little

supernatural as the *Imitation of Christ* or the *Pilgrim's Progress*. But there is no position of intellectual consistency between these two, and the great mass of those who try to pause at various points along the descent are swept down with the current. The natural view of the Scriptures is a sea which has been rising higher for three-quarters of a century. Many Christians bid it welcome to pour lightly over the walls which the faith of the church has always set up against it, in the expectation that it will prove a healthful and helpful stream. It is already a cataract, uprooting, destroying, and slaying.

* * *

EDITOR: *By the 1970s, evangelicals and fundamentalists were debating among themselves just how far one could go with higher criticism of scripture and still be an orthodox evangelical. Conservative evangelicals and fundamentalists charged that many evangelical scholars and institutions were losing their emphasis on the inerrancy of scripture and adopting modern scientific and higher critical views that modernists of the late nineteenth and early twentieth centuries had utilized to challenge orthodox positions. Harold Lindsell's 1976 book* The Battle for the Bible *was a bellwether call for the return to biblical inerrancy.*[1]

In response to the argument that Lindsell and others made, the Chicago Statement on Biblical Inerrancy was formulated by a group of evangelical leaders meeting at the Hyatt Regency O'Hare Hotel in Chicago in 1978. This meeting was sponsored by an organization called the International Council on Biblical Inerrancy. Lindsell was one of the statement's three hundred signers. The International Council on Biblical Inerrancy disbanded in 1988. While it is probably safe to say that most evangelicals and all fundamentalists in America hold to some version of the inerrancy of scripture, there is a substantial minority of evangelicals that does not. Moreover, there are many different ways to interpret what inerrancy means, which allows for some diversity among inerrantist evangelicals. Some inerrantists are biblical literalists, while others believe that the Bible never errs in what it teaches but some passages are meant to be taken figuratively. There are even inerrantist evangelicals who believe in evolution. The division among evangelicals over gender (see chapter 8) cuts right through even inerrantist evangelicals.

International Council on Biblical Inerrancy. "Chicago Statement on Biblical Inerrancy." http://www.reformed.org/documents/icbi.html.

Article I

WE AFFIRM that the Holy Scriptures are to be received as the authoritative Word of God.

WE DENY that the Scriptures receive their authority from the Church, tradition, or any other human source.

Article II

WE AFFIRM that the Scriptures are the supreme written norm by which God binds the conscience, and that the authority of the Church is subordinate to that of Scripture.

WE DENY that Church creeds, councils, or declarations have authority greater than or equal to the authority of the Bible.

Article III

WE AFFIRM that the written Word in its entirety is revelation given by God.

WE DENY that the Bible is merely a witness to revelation, or only becomes revelation in encounter, or depends on the responses of men for its validity.

Article IV

WE AFFIRM that God who made mankind in His image has used language as a means of revelation.

WE DENY that human language is so limited by our creatureliness that it is rendered inadequate as a vehicle for divine revelation. We further deny that the corruption of human culture and language through sin has thwarted God's work of inspiration.

Article V

WE AFFIRM that God's revelation in the Holy Scriptures was progressive.

WE DENY that later revelation, which may fulfill earlier revelation, ever corrects or contradicts it. We further deny that any normative revelation has been given since the completion of the New Testament writings.

Article VI

WE AFFIRM that the whole of Scripture and all its parts, down to the very words of the original, were given by divine inspiration.

WE DENY that the inspiration of Scripture can rightly be affirmed of the whole without the parts, or of some parts but not the whole.

Article VII

WE AFFIRM that inspiration was the work in which God by His Spirit, through human writers, gave us His Word. The origin of Scripture is divine. The mode of divine inspiration remains largely a mystery to us.

WE DENY that inspiration can be reduced to human insight, or to heightened states of consciousness of any kind.

Article VIII

WE AFFIRM that God in His Work of inspiration utilized the distinctive personalities and literary styles of the writers whom He had chosen and prepared.

WE DENY that God, in causing these writers to use the very words that He chose, overrode their personalities.

Article IX

WE AFFIRM that inspiration, though not conferring omniscience, guaranteed true and trustworthy utterance on all matters of which the Biblical authors were moved to speak and write.

WE DENY that the finitude or fallenness of these writers, by necessity or otherwise, introduced distortion or falsehood into God's Word.

Article X

WE AFFIRM that inspiration, strictly speaking, applies only to the autographic text of Scripture, which in the providence of God can be ascertained from available manuscripts with great accuracy. We further affirm that copies and translations of Scripture are the Word of God to the extent that they faithfully represent the original.

WE DENY that any essential element of the Christian faith is affected by the absence of the autographs. We further deny that this absence renders the assertion of Biblical inerrancy invalid or irrelevant.

Article XI

WE AFFIRM that Scripture, having been given by divine inspiration, is infallible, so that, far from misleading us, it is true and reliable in all the matters it addresses.

WE DENY that it is possible for the Bible to be at the same time infallible and errant in its assertions. Infallibility and inerrancy may be distinguished, but not separated.

Article XII

WE AFFIRM that Scripture in its entirety is inerrant, being free from all falsehood, fraud, or deceit.

WE DENY that Biblical infallibility and inerrancy are limited to spiritual, religious, or redemptive themes, exclusive of assertions in the fields of history and science. We further deny that scientific hypotheses about earth history may properly be used to overturn the teaching of Scripture on creation and the flood.

Article XIII

WE AFFIRM the propriety of using inerrancy as a theological term with reference to the complete truthfulness of Scripture.

WE DENY that it is proper to evaluate Scripture according to standards of truth and error that are alien to its usage or purpose. We further deny that inerrancy is negated by Biblical phenomena such as a lack of modern technical precision, irregularities of grammar or spelling, observational descriptions of nature, the reporting of falsehoods, the use of hyperbole and round numbers, the topical arrangement of material, variant selections of material in parallel accounts, or the use of free citations.

Article XIV

WE AFFIRM the unity and internal consistency of Scripture.

WE DENY that alleged errors and discrepancies that have not yet been resolved vitiate the truth claims of the Bible.

Article XV

WE AFFIRM that the doctrine of inerrancy is grounded in the teaching of the Bible about inspiration.

WE DENY that Jesus' teaching about Scripture may be dismissed by appeals to accommodation or to any natural limitation of His humanity.

Article XVI

WE AFFIRM that the doctrine of inerrancy has been integral to the Church's faith throughout its history.

WE DENY that inerrancy is a doctrine invented by Scholastic Protestantism, or is a reactionary position postulated in response to negative higher criticism.

Article XVII

WE AFFIRM that the Holy Spirit bears witness to the Scriptures, assuring believers of the truthfulness of God's written Word.

WE DENY that this witness of the Holy Spirit operates in isolation from or against Scripture.

Article XVIII

WE AFFIRM that the text of Scripture is to be interpreted by grammatico-historical exegesis, taking account of its literary forms and devices, and that Scripture is to interpret Scripture.

WE DENY the legitimacy of any treatment of the text or quest for sources lying behind it that leads to relativizing, dehistoricizing, or discounting its teaching, or rejecting its claims to authorship.

Article XIX

WE AFFIRM that a confession of the full authority, infallibility, and inerrancy of Scripture is vital to a sound understanding of the whole of the Christian faith. We further affirm that such confession should lead to increasing conformity to the image of Christ.

WE DENY that such confession is necessary for salvation. However, we further deny that inerrancy can be rejected without grave consequences both to the individual and to the Church.

Article XX

WE AFFIRM that since God is the author of all truth, all truths, biblical and extrabiblical, are consistent and cohere, and that the Bible speaks truth when it touches on matters pertaining to nature, history, or anything else. We further affirm that in some cases extra-biblical data have value for clarifying what Scripture teaches, and for prompting correction of faulty interpretations.

WE DENY that extrabiblical views ever disprove the teaching of Scripture or hold priority over it.

Article XXI

WE AFFIRM the harmony of special with general revelation and therefore of biblical teaching with the facts of nature.

WE DENY that any genuine scientific facts are inconsistent with the true meaning of any passage of Scripture.

Article XXII

WE AFFIRM that Genesis 1-11 is factual, as is the rest of the book.

WE DENY that the teachings of Genesis 1-11 are mythical and that scientific hypotheses about earth history or the origin of humanity may be invoked to overthrow what Scripture teaches about creation.

Article XXIII

WE AFFIRM the clarity of Scripture and specifically of its message about salvation from sin.

WE DENY that all passages of Scripture are equally clear or have equal bearing on the message of redemption.

Article XXIV

WE AFFIRM that a person is not dependent for understanding of Scripture on the expertise of biblical scholars.

WE DENY that a person should ignore the fruits of the technical study of Scripture by biblical scholars.

Article XXV

WE AFFIRM that the only type of preaching which sufficiently conveys the divine revelation and its proper application to life is that which faithfully expounds the text of Scripture as the Word of God.

WE DENY that the preacher has any message from God apart from the text of Scripture.

✳ ✳ ✳

EDITOR: *In addition to the Bible and conversion, evangelicals are generally evangelistic. While the words evangelism and evangelical are related, they are not synonymous. Evangelical, as mentioned above, is a theological position marked by belief in the authority of scripture and the necessity of conversion. Evangelism is the act of spreading the gospel in an effort to see others converted. The vast majority of evangelicals and fundamentalists believe they have a duty to share Christ with others. Below is a typical how-to essay on evangelism from* The Fundamentals. *While there are all kinds of strategies for how to best share Christ with others, this one is fairly standard whether one is considering the early twentieth century or the present. Note that nothing Stone says is a direct response to modernism. This essay could have been written before the rise of modernism, and it shows the continuity between nineteenth- and twentieth-century evangelicalism. In other words, while twentieth-century evangelicalism was shaped in part by its encounter with modernism, evangelicalism is not merely a response to modernism.*

> Stone, John Timothy. "Pastoral and Personal Evangelism, or Winning Men to Christ One by One." In *The Fundamentals*. Edited by R. A. Torrey, A. C. Dixon, and others. 1910–15. Reprint, Grand Rapids: Baker, 1970.

The story of evangelism is the specific history of the Cross of Christ. Great movements and revivals have made up much of its general history, but slowly and quietly through the years and centuries the Evangel has won, as men and women have led their fellow human beings to repentance and have by precept and example followed in the footsteps of their Lord.

✳ ✳ ✳

The Almighty could have so arranged His Divine plan that He Himself, without human help, might arrest and enlist followers as He did with Saul of Tarsus, but this was not His plan. By man He would reach men. Human mediums of power must do His wondrous work. Man must go, in the power of His Spirit "into all the world, to preach the Gospel to every creature." And His promise was sure and permanent: "Lo, I am with you always."

GOD'S HOLY SPIRIT

The first requisite in winning men to Christ must be the presence and power of the Holy Spirit. "It is expedient that I go away from you, for if I go not away, the Holy Spirit will not come." With His presence "greater works" than the works of Christ "shall ye do." "Ye shall receive power when the Holy Spirit is come upon you, and ye shall be witnesses." To live in the power of God's Holy Spirit, and to know that He is present and will lead, is in itself an assurance of a joyful and successful service. The Spirit will constantly "call to our remembrance the things of Christ," and hence we may not be anxious as to the words we are to speak, for He will direct us and speak for and through us.

So many times we are fearful and embarrassed, but this will not be the case if we are under the influence momentarily of God's Spirit. "He will guide us into all truth." "He will not speak of Himself," but will glorify Christ. That which we say in weakness He will use with power, and "His word will not return unto Him void, but will accomplish that whereunto it was sent." We may always take for granted His preparation, for He does not send but calls us. His word is not "Go," but "Come." Thus we will always be on the alert for opportunities to speak the things He would have us, and our words and thoughts will be those which He suggests and honors. We will be nourished constantly by His Word within, and equipped with His sword for sustained protection and aggressive attack. If His Word abides in us, we will never be weak in body, nor unprepared and weaponless. His Spirit will also give us courage and endurance, and the fearless one who has stability and patience need not fear the unexpected nor the aggressive opponent. The Spirit of God also prepares the one whom we must approach, and is working in his heart as well as with our words. Prayer is also a real factor in our lives, and we live in His presence by the true conversational method of association. As God speaks to us through His Word, so we talk with Him in prayer, and the place and surroundings are of little relative importance, as we are always with Him and He with us.

* * *

THE BIBLE

A second most necessary element in winning men to the Master is a knowledge and appropriate use of God's Word. We must be workmen who need not to be ashamed, who can rightly divide the Word of Truth. The use of the Bible is the greatest advancing weapon for Christ. The worker who knows his Bible will constantly read it for strength and apply it in dealing with the unconverted. He will not argue with men, nor talk about God's Word, but he will explain with it, and repeatedly refer to it. An open Bible before and with an inquirer almost always means conversion and spiritual growth to follow. When dealing with your subject, ask if he has ever considered what the Bible says on the point under discussion. For instance, a man tells you he does not take much stock in what you have been saying about the necessity of the Cross; it seems somewhat foolish to him. Do not be angry, but reply pleasantly that you do not blame him a bit, in fact, Paul himself writes, in his first letter to the Corinthians, that men will feel exactly that way. Tell him you appreciate his frankness, and meanwhile pull your Testament from your pocket or take it from the table, and turn to the passage in First Corinthians, one, eighteen; or better still, hand him another copy of the Bible open to the place, and read from your own copy: "For the preaching of the Cross is to them that perish foolishness, but unto us which are saved it is the power of God." Then, before he is angered or troubled about that word "perish," ask him to notice in the same connection the twenty-first verse, just below: "For after that in the wisdom of God the world by wisdom knew not God, it pleased God by the foolishness of preaching to save them that believe." These passages will at least arrest his attention, and unconsciously interest him somewhat in reading the Bible himself.

* * *

PRAYER

We do not estimate the place and power prayer has in winning others to Christ, prayer for others in intercession, and prayer with others as we take them individually into the very presence of God.

First, pray for them. No matter what your method or lack of method may be, take those for whom you are working up to God in prayer. Pray for them by name; pray that you may approach them aright and appeal to them with Divine wisdom. Pray that you may be able to put yourself in their place, and be patient as well as wise with them. Pray that you may turn to the right Scripture, and use the appropriate illustrations, to help them. Pray that you may lead them to Jesus instead of talking with them about Him. Pray that they may be responsive and willing. Pray that their sins may not hinder them from giving their best selves to the consideration of this all-important subject. Pray that they may see in you that vital interest and real sincerity which will actually arouse them. Pray that their companions and surroundings may not prove a barrier or hindrance to them. Pray that you may converse with them on the essentials and not spend the time on unimportant and relative matters.

Pray that you may not be timid or careless, but fearless, clear and exact. Pray that human sympathy and love may influence you to show your heart and soul to touch and melt their hearts. Pray that just the favorable opening may come to you, and that you may be ready to use it. Pray most of all for the Holy Spirit's power with you.

Then secondly, pray with the individual. After Scripture has had its chance, and decision should be reached, get your friend on his knees, and ask him to decide after you have poured out your heart to God for and with him. I have known more men who have yielded on their knees than anywhere else. At just the right time, when genuinely prompted by loving impulse and sincere motive, your hand placed upon his shoulder may help him make the decision. To let one know you love him for Christ's sake breaks many a heart. When thus praying, no matter how cold your heart may have been, you will feel three are present rather than two, and the third is the Saviour of men.

* * *

Recently, when a man yielded to Christ, he replied, when told by his friend he had long prayed for him: "Well, I knew something was influencing me, for I have felt unhappy and dissatisfied until now, and it was not natural for me to be troubled about myself." Prayer is, then, a most effective and powerful agency in winning others.

* * *

METHOD AND MEANS

We must now take up the subject of method and means. The method is, after all, secondary, and if it becomes too set and orderly, it will be self-destructive, for as soon as one sees your method, the heart and mind are steeled against it, and there is little or no interest. When God's Spirit leads, we are responsive to all kinds of openings and ways. Instead of studying approach we simply advance as the plan opens before us, and we find ourselves doing in an unexpected way the very work we have always hoped to do. A revival of God's Spirit means the disregard of former ways and means, and an initiation of new and untried channels. We regard and value less the method, and seek only for the result.

It is wise and right for us, however, to consider methods and means. Christ Himself began His work with reaching individuals and training them to work for others.

* * *

One of the most efficient means some have used is that of training men and women to call upon those in their neighborhood and personally invite them to services—not a formal invitation, but a call in which they may get acquainted and feel at home with one another; one call followed up with another until a friendliness springs up and there is a response.

* * *

This little handbook is thus sent out to assist in meeting that need, that the hundreds of young men and young women already won may become winners of others. . . . In connection with this same little volume, there are certain practical notes which we would also give to you:

"One cannot use God's Word without studying it.

"You cannot win others to Christ unless you believe in Him and keep near Him yourself.

"He must work through you. 'Apart from Me ye can do nothing.'

"Prayer must be a reality and a power to you. 'Ask, and ye shall receive.'

"Confidence in Christ's power must attend your effort. 'I can do all things in Him which strengtheneth me.'

"Common sense means putting yourself in the other man's place. Do not merely argue. Use the Word of God.

"Do not do all the talking; win the confidence of the one for whom you are working, and let him tell his story.

"Do not be in haste. Remember 'God's delays are not denials.' Work and wait. Be patient and persistent.

"Pray with your man as well as for him. Don't be afraid of falling on your knees in the presence of another.

"Get him to pray for himself.

"Learn to pray anywhere and in any posture in an office or an automobile, in a quiet spot on the street, standing, sitting or kneeling, but always reverently.

"Get your man alone. Do not present the matter when another is present. (Exceptional cases may occur, as at times when talking with husband and wife).

"Study your case beforehand (when possible).

"Do not approach your case with fear but with prayer and faith. 'It shall be given unto you. . . . What you shall speak.'

"Learn how by doing, and gain confidence through experience.

"Remember you are not only Christ's representative but that God's Holy Spirit is working through you. The power is His.

"Approach and do your work with a happy heart and with joy. Always show that 'the joy of Jehovah is your strength.'

"Beware of the temptation to postpone. The evil one prompts such suggestion. Many a man is never asked to give his heart to Christ because a good impulse was averted by indecision and the false plea of 'a better time to speak.'

"If you fail, do not be discouraged, but determine to get nearer to God and to gain more power through your apparent failure. Write a good letter to the one you have failed to reach or failed to find after repeated calling. Many have been won by correspondence. He knows you are interested very definitely if you write.

"Win back to service the Christian man who has lost interest, and lost touch with Christ and the Church." Robert Speer has well said, "When we love men for what we know Christ can make them, we shall go after them for Him." We might add, "To persuade one soul to lead a better life is to leave the world better than you found it." God has certainly a very definite work for individuals to do in His Kingdom, and the Christian worker needs to realize that his duty is to set people to work and to train them in this service.

Another very effective method is by correspondence: So many times when we do not find people at home, or when we are not able to approach them as we desire, if we would sit down and write a direct and personal letter, it would have its weight and influence. . . . The ways and methods for reaching others are manifold, and thank God they are as diversified as the personalities and training of those who are workers. God has new methods and ways to use constantly, but we must be alert in this great work, and reach out in faith and in earnestness. One of the best means of reaching others is to be able to put one's self directly in the place of another, to feel his temptations, to understand his difficulties, and to be willing to meet him upon his own ground and with his own needs. If we can establish this human sympathy, we have gone a great way toward reaching others.

Another most effective way must be through the Sunday School and through the regular channels of active association. Whatever we can do to bring to others the positive need of settling this question for one's self, communicants' classes, catechetical classes, individual pastor's classes, all such methods should be used. A pastor should get into the public and private schools of the boys and girls of his own parish, to know where they live and what their work is and what their problems are, and then he should plan in some way to meet them individually. A pastor should go to the various Sunday School classes in his own Sunday School, not regularly or at stated times, but sometimes informally or by definite arrangement with the teacher, thus getting into touch with the scholars and meeting them upon their own ground. He should also arrange special classes, to meet them and talk over their relationship to Christ. All through the church, he should have those who are so interested in individuals that they will take to him the special cases and refer them to him.

But after all, the greatest method in the world, the greatest means of all in winning others to Christ, is that of persistent, patient, faithful prayer. This, followed by action and associated with all the details of service, will be rewarded. Times of revival will spring up. Others will wish for special services and methods and will suggest them, and before we know it our churches will be alive with a newness of material, and we will find that men and women are not only crying out, "What must we do to be saved?" but "How may we win others to the Master?" We will all become "workmen who need not to be ashamed, rightly dividing the Word of Truth," and we will realize that God's Word shall not return to Him void, but "shall accomplish that whereunto it is sent."

Surely, "He that winneth souls is wise."

EDITOR: *The next text is a tract that was created in 1956 by Bill Bright of Campus Crusade for Christ. The tract has been widely used by evangelicals and fundamentalists in their efforts to win others to Christ. Millions have been handed out across the globe during the past half-century, and the tract is now available online in more than 150 languages. The website edition of* The Four Spiritual Laws *pamphlet is prefaced with the words, "Just as there are physical laws that govern the physical universe, so are there spiritual laws that govern your relationship with God."²*

Bright, Bill. *The Four Spiritual Laws.* Orlando: New Life Publications, 1956.

1. God loves you and offers a wonderful plan for your life. (John 3:16, John 10:10)

2. Man is sinful and separated from God. Therefore, he cannot know and experience God's love and plan for his life. (Romans 3:23, Romans 6:23)

3. Jesus Christ is God's only provision for man's sin. Through Him you can know and experience God's love and plan for your life. (Romans 5:8, I Corinthians 15:3-6, John 14:6)

4. We must individually receive Jesus Christ as Savior and Lord; then we can know and experience God's love and plan for our lives. (John 1:12, Ephesians 2:8,9, John 3:18, Revelation 3:20).

EDITOR: *One of the key doctrines that developed within fundamentalism and one that the neoevangelicals of the 1940s and 1950s rejected was separatism. Fundamentalists believe that one must separate from liberal Christians and also from other evangelicals who will not separate from liberals. Separatism also has cultural implications. Fundamentalists generally attempt to separate as much as possible from secular culture and politics, while evangelicals since the 1940s have sought cultural engagement and political activism. This neat division between culturally engaged evangelicals and separatist fundamentalists began to breakdown in the 1980s when Jerry Falwell and some other fundamentalists became culturally and politically engaged. Historian George Marsden has written recently that perhaps such Christian Right figures should be called "fundamentalistic evangelicals," since they are militant like fundamentalists but culturally engaged like evangelicals.*

Below is an article by one of Falwell's former associates, Edward Dobson (not to be confused with the more well known James Dobson). He explains what biblical separatism means for fundamentalists. Dobson's interpretation of separatism is quite moderate, and his tone is far more irenic than some mid-century fundamentalists such as Carl McIntire and John R. Rice. It is worth noting that Dobson, like many others, began to think of himself as an evangelical in the 1990s. Today, hardly any evangelical espouses separatism, but many fundamentalists still do. Separatist fundamentalists not only eschew political engagement beyond mere voting, they will not even participate in an evangelical movement such as Promise Keepers (see chapter 8) because to do so would be to enter into a relationship with nonseparated evangelicals. Although this text comes from the 1980s, it is included here because it is representative of the type of separatism that emerged from the fundamentalist-modernist controversy of the twenties.

Dobson, Edward. "Does the Bible Really Teach Separation?" In *Fundamentalist Journal*, May 1985, 12–13.

Great confusion exists today in Conservative circles over the issue of ecclesiastical separation. There are those who argue that any who do not accept their criteria for associational purity are guilty of compromise. Some have gone as far as to raise their own personal preferences to the level of doctrinal absolutes. Their quest for absolute purity has often divided them from other true believers and driven their ministries into total isolation.

On the other hand there are those who, in the interest of absolute unity, have promoted an individualism that accepts others for fellowship regardless of their doctrine, practice, or lifestyle. They are quick to argue that ecclesiastical separation is judgmental in nature and violates the unity of the church and the love of Christ for all men. They further contend that separatists deny the individual leading of the Holy Spirit and confuse the unsaved public with their constant internal bickering. Their hesitance to draw any lines of demarcation has left them susceptible to gross doctrinal error.

Goal of Separation

Taking a stand for an issue of separation is one thing, but remembering why that stand has been taken is another matter altogether. The scriptural goal of separation is reconciliation of a wayward or errant brother (Gal. 6:1). Even Paul's severe "deliverance, unto Satan" of Hymenaeus and Alexander (I Tim, 1:18-20) was done in the hope that if they were genuine believers, they would repent. Paul's goal in separation was always reconciliation. In 2 Thessalonians 3:14-15, he instructs believers to have no company (fellowship) with those who disobeyed the teaching in his epistle. Yet: he continues, "count him not as an enemy, but admonish him as a brother."

Those who refused to respond to church discipline after the second admonition were to be rejected (Titus 3:10). Thus, the biblical balance is clearly stated in regard to the goal of separation. Our first admonition is to confront and restore those who are in error as brothers in Christ. Every attempt at total reconciliation should be considered. However, when those confronted persist in hardened unbelief or disobedience, we are to separate ourselves from them in hope that even the act of separation will bring them to repentance and restoration.

Many of us would do well to ask ourselves if we really want to see people with whom we disagree restored to fellowship. All too often a "stand" is taken against a brother on an issue and no effort is ever made to reconcile. "Writing off" someone is always easier than restoring him.

Means of Separation

The local church is the only institution in Scripture given the mandate of separation. No school, magazine, or parachurch organization has been given the authority of church discipline and separation. While such organizations ought to reflect a church position on these matters, they have no right to dictate standards of ecclesiastical separation to autonomous local congregations.

In matters of personal offense, Matthew 18:15-17, instructs us to follow three levels of confrontation:

Personal—"If thy brother shall trespass against thee, go and tell him his fault between thee and him alone" (v.15).

Plural—"But if he will not hear thee, then take with thee one or two more, that in the mouth of two or three witnesses every word may be established" (v. 16).

Public—"And if he shall neglect to hear them, tell it to the church: but if he neglect to hear the church, let him be unto thee as an heathen man and a publican" (v. 17).

Matters of personal are to be resolved personally if at all possible. When such is not possible, the final authority for discipline (including excommunication and separation) is the local church itself.

Every passage in the New Testament that deals with the issue of separation does so in light of the context of the local church. The church is the guardian of doctrine (1 Tim. 4:13-16; 2 Tim. 2:24-25) and the only place given in Scripture for dealing with a disobedient elder (1 Tim. 5:17-20), an unrepentant brother (1 Cor. 5:10-11), or idle brothers (2 Thes. 3:1-15). The church is to reject false teachers (2 Tim. 3:1-9; Titus 1:10-16; 2 Peter 2:1-15). The local New Testament church is the ultimate authority in the exercise of separation and discipline.

Biblical Basis for Separation

The Bible clearly opposes false teaching and theological error. Those who argue that doctrine is not important to God have simply never read the Bible. The resurrected Christ said to the church at Pergamos, "So hast thou also them that hold the doctrine of the Nicolaitans, which thing I hate" (Rev. 2:15). If Christ Himself hates false doctrine it must be a serious issue! The Word of God continuously reinforces this position on false doctrine.

Old Testament. Throughout the Old Testament, the people of Israel were commanded to be a holy people and a separate nation (Lev. 1:45; 20:22-26). Three New Testament passages (2 Peter 2:15; Jude 11; Rev. 2:14) refer to the false prophecy of Balaam in Numbers 31:16, with glaring condemnation.

Message of Jesus. In dealing with the Samaritan woman at the well (John 4:22), Jesus confronted her wrong theology and rebuked her: "Ye worship ye know not what: we know what we worship: for salvation is of the Jews?" Thus, our Lord was not only concerned with her conduct but also with her theology. Christ continually rebuked the Pharisees for their hypocrisy, legalism, and theological error, even calling them "children of hell" (Mark 23:15). Concerning the wrong doctrine of the Sadducees, He said, "Ye do err, not knowing the scriptures, nor the power of God" (Matt. 22:29).

Writings of the Apostles. Everywhere in the New Testament Epistles there are warnings against false teaching: "Mark them which cause divisions and offenses contrary to the doctrine which ye have learned; and avoid them" (Rom. 16:17); "If any man preach any other gospel unto you . . . let him be accursed (Gal. 1:9); "Be ye not unequally yoked together with unbelievers . . . come out from among them, and be ye separate" (2 Cor. 6:14,17). Believers are even warned not to bid the false teacher "God speed" lest we become a partaker in his "evil deeds" (2 John 11). False teachers are referred to as those who "live in error" (2 Peter 2:17-22) and as "raging waves of the sea" and "wandering stars" (Jude 12-13).

Criteria for Separation

One of the most frequently quoted verses on separation is 2 Cor. 6:17 "Wherefore come out from among them, and be ye separate, saith the Lord, and touch not the unclean thing; and I will receive you." The verb translated "separate" means "to mark off from others by boundaries, to limit, or to separate." It is utilized to describe the separation of the wicked from the righteous (Matt. 13:49); the separation of the nation at the end of the age (Matt. 25:32); Peter's refusal to eat with the Gentiles (Gal. 2:12); and Paul's separation unto the gospel (Rom. 1:1). The root of this compound verb is *horos*, meaning "a limit or boundary." The underlying concept is that separation is predicated upon specific boundaries or limits. When discussing ecclesiastical separation one must be careful to establish the biblical boundaries that govern such a separation and not one's personal bias. The boundaries are clearly identified in Scripture.

Personal Offenses. In Matthew 18:15-17, Jesus explains how to deal with a brother or sister who has sinned against us. The first level of confrontation is private. If unrepentance persists, it is to be followed by confrontation with two or three witnesses, to guarantee that both parties are acting fairly and honestly. If this fails, the matter of ultimate discipline is to be exercised by the church.

Doctrinal Disputes. The local church is the repository of doctrinal truth and is to be the sole guardian of that truth. The essential, nonnegotiable, fundamental doctrines of the church are to be held as standards of absolute authority. Thus, each church has the responsibility to settle matters of doctrinal dispute within its own congregation.

Disobedient Elder. First Timothy 5:17-20 refers to dealing with an elder of a local church who has sinned. Because of the unique position of the elders, they are to be treated with respect and honor. No accusation against them is to be entertained unless it is brought by two or three personal witnesses. Public rebuke, if necessary, is to serve as a warning to others that they not fall into the same sin.

Unrepentant Believers. In I Corinthians 5 we have an example of unrepentant immorality. While any sin may be repented of unrepentant sins (fornication, idolatry, drunkenness, etc.) are to result in excommunication ("not to keep company"). Such separation has a twofold design: 1) to keep the church pure, 2) to urge the unrepentant to repentance and reconciliation.

False Teachers. God clearly warns the church to separate from false teaching and doctrinal error (such as denying the deity of Christ or the doctrine of salvation by grace, etc.). False prophets are described as "denying the Lord" (2 Peter 2:1) and those that "serve not our Lord Jesus Christ" (Rom. 16:18). The church is clearly commanded to separate from every teacher who denies the deity of Christ and the gospel of Christ (Rom. 16:17). Any teaching that is contrary to Scripture is not to be tolerated within the church, so that the truth of Scripture is preeminent.

An Appeal

Does the Bible really teach separation? The obvious answer to that question is an emphatic yes! However, the practice of separation should be guided with the advice of Paul to speak the truth in love (Eph. 4:15). To practice the truth of separation without a genuine demonstration of love is to reduce that doctrine to a pharisaical legalism that divides and destroys the body of Christ. To practice love for everyone without the truth of separation is to reduce the doctrinal purity of the church to that which is not even Christian at all. The mandate of Scripture is to practice the truth in love. May God help us do it!

* 2 *

The Fundamentalist-Modernist Controversy

EDITOR: *The first third of the twentieth century was marked by fierce fighting between fundamentalists and modernists. This controversy is known as the fundamentalist-modernist controversy and was particularly heated in the twenties in the Northern Baptist and northern Presbyterian denominations. The term "fundamentalist" was not brought into common use until 1920. For the next two decades, virtually everyone on the traditionalist or conservative side of the fundamentalist-modernist controversy was known as a fundamentalist. In the 1940s, many of these so-called fundamentalists grew weary of the militant and fighting spirit of their own movement. These moderate fundamentalists sought to recapture the more irenic name "evangelical," and they tried to reengage culture rather than separate from it as had been typical of the more militant fundamentalists.*

The texts below are representative of the arguments of the fundamentalists, with the Fosdick selection added to show the modernist, or liberal, position. Note that among the views represented here, Riley was a popular Bible teacher, while Machen was an erudite scholar. Both were militant defenders of the faith, but their approach was very different. Still, for a time during the 1920s, they found common ground in the battle against modernists such as Fosdick.

Riley, W. B. "The Faith of the Fundamentalists." *Current History*, XXIV (June 1927): 434–40.

A DOZEN years ago a great layman, Lyman Stuart [sic] of Los Angeles, placed in the hands of a competent committee a fund of $300,000, requesting that the money be used to publish a series of books dealing with the Christian fundamentals, and that the entire Protestant ministry of the world be made a present of them. The inspiration for this undertaking Lyman Stuart [sic] received as he listened to a great sermon from the lips of Dr. A. C. Dixon, then pastor of the Metropolitan Tabernacle, London, England. The publication and distribution of these books had been completed when Dixon and the writer were thrown together for days at the Bible Conference at Montrose, Pa. After long periods of prayer and conference, we agreed to call the initial meeting that brought into existence the World's Christian Fundamentals Association.

At its first meeting in the last week of May, 1919, in Music Hall, Philadelphia, over 6,500 Fundamentalists gathered from different States, provinces and continents. Additional auditoriums had to be employed to accommodate the crowds, and at the end of the week the organization was a completed fact, a volume, *God Hath Spoken,* was ready for the press and the Fundamentalist movement was a new-born infant, but a lusty and promising one. . . .

What is Fundamentalism? It would be quite impossible, within the limits of a single article, so to treat the subject as to satisfy all interested parties. There are too many features of this Christian faith for one to attempt a delineation. But there are at least three major propositions that must appear in any adequate reply, and they are these: It is the Christian Creed; it is the Christian Character; it is the Christian Commission.

THE GREATER CHRISTIAN DOCTRINES

Fundamentalism undertakes to reaffirm the greater Christian doctrines. Mark this phrase, "the greater Christian doctrines." It does not attempt to set forth every Christian doctrine. It has never known the elaboration that characterizes the great denominational confessions. But it lays them side by side, and, out of their extensive statements, elect nine points upon which to rest its claims to Christian attention. They were and are as follows:

1. We believe in the Scriptures of the Old and New Testaments as verbally inspired by God, and inerrant . . . , and that they are of supreme and final authority in faith and life.

2. We believe in one God, eternally existing in three persons, Father, Son and Holy Spirit.

3. We believe that Jesus Christ was begotten by the Holy Spirit, and born of the Virgin Mary, and is true God and true man.

4. We believe that man was created in the image of God, that he sinned and thereby incurred not only physical death, but also that spiritual death which is separation from God; and that all human beings are with a sinful

nature, and, in the case of those who reach moral responsibility, become sinners in thought, word and deed.

5. We believe that the Lord Jesus Christ died for our sins according to the Scriptures as a representative and substitutionary sacrifice and that all that believe in Him are justified on the ground of His shed blood.

6. We believe in the resurrection of the crucified body of our Lord, in His ascension into Heaven, and in His present life there for us, as High Priest and Advocate.

7. We believe in "that blessed hope," the personal premillennial and imminent return of our Lord and Saviour, Jesus Christ.

8. We believe that all who receive by faith the Lord Jesus Christ are born again of the Holy Spirit and thereby become children of God.

9. We believe in the bodily resurrection of the just and the unjust, the everlasting felicity of the saved and the everlasting conscious suffering of the lost.

* * *

Fundamentalism insists upon the plain intent of Scripture-speech. The members of this movement have no sympathy whatever for that weasel method of sucking the meaning out of words and then presenting the empty shells in an attempt to palm them off as giving the Christian faith a new and another interpretation. The absurdities to which such a spiritual-izing method may lead are fully revealed in the writings of Mary Baker Eddy and modernists in general. When one is permitted to discard established and scientific definitions and to create, at will, his own glossary, language fails to be longer a vehicle of thought, and inspiration itself may mean anything or nothing, according to the preference of its employer. Professor Machen of Princeton University has properly exposed this procedure, and in his volume, *Christianity and Liberalism,* has shown that, although modernism still calls itself Christianity, it has nothing in common with the faith that for two thousand years has worn that great and honorable name, and that as a religion it does not even belong to the same family with Christianity. With keen discernment he says: "In trying to remove from Christianity everything that could possibly be objected to in the name of science, in trying to bribe off the enemy by those concessions which the enemy most desires, the [modern] apologist has really abandoned what he started out to defend." It is because the true Fundamentalist utterly rejects that method that he remains and must forever remain a premillenarian. One of the leading opponents of modernism—an outstanding man in the divinity department of a great university—logically declares it to be foolish to profess faith in the literal Bible and deny its teachings concerning the personal, imminent and premillennial coming of Christ.

"FOREVER SETTLED IN HEAVEN"

There are men who would join us tomorrow if we omitted the seventh point from our doctrinal statement, and they marvel that we permit it to remain in our declaration, knowing its divisive effect. Our answer is: Fundamentalism insists upon the plain intent of Scripture-speech and knows no method by which it can logically receive the multiplied and harmonious teachings of the Book concerning one doctrine and reject them concerning another. The greater doctrines are not individual opinions that can be handled about at pleasure. In the judgment of the Fundamentalist they are "forever settled in heaven." "Holy men of God, who spake as they were borne along by the Holy Ghost," have told us the truth—God's truth—and truth is as unchangeable as imperishable. "Scripture cannot be broken." The "truth of the Lord endureth forever." . . . And it not only endures forever, but it remains forever the same—the same in words, the same in meaning, the same in spiritual intent. God's work is incapable of improvement. The sun is old, but the world needs no new or improved one!

Fundamentalism is forever the antithesis to modernist critical theology. It is made of another and an opposing school. Modernism submits all Scripture to the judgment of man. According to its method he may reject any portion of the Book as uninspired, unprofitable, and even undesirable, and accept another portion as from God because its sentences suit him, or its teachings determine every question upon which they have spoken with some degree of fullness, and its mandates are only disregarded by the unbelieving, the materialistic and the immoral. Fundamentalists hold that the world is illumined and the Church is instructed and even science itself is confirmed, when true, and condemned when false, by the clear teachings of the open Book, while Liberalism, as *The Nation* once said, "pretends to preach the higher criticism by interpreting the sacred writings as esoteric fables." In other words, the two have nothing in common save church membership, and all the world wonders that they do or can remain together; and the thinking world knows that but one tie holds them, and that is the billions of dollars invested.

Nine out of ten of those dollars, if not ninety-nine out of every hundred of them, spent to construct the great denominational universities, colleges, schools of second grade, theological seminaries, great denominational mission stations, the multiplied hospitals that bear denominational names, the immense publication societies and the expensive magazines, were given by Fundamentalists and filched by modernists. It took hundreds of years to collect this money and construct these institutions. It has taken only a quarter of a century for the liberal bandits to capture them, and the only fellowship that remains to bind modernists and Fundamentalists in one body, or a score of bodies, is the Irish fellowship of a free fight—Fundamentalists fighting to retain what they have founded, and modernists fighting to keep their hold on what they have filched. It is a spectacle to grieve angels and amuse devils; but we doubt not that even the devils know where justice lies, and the angels from heaven sympathize with the fight and trust that faithful men will carry on.

* * *

FUTURE OF FUNDAMENTALISM

The future of Fundamentalism is not with claims, but with conquests. Glorious as is our past, history provides only an adequate base upon which to build. Fundamentalists will never need to apologize for the part they have played in education; they have produced it; or for their relationship to colleges and universities and theological seminaries, and all forms of social service; they have created them! Even Walter Rauschenbusch, famed higher critic as he was, pertinently asked, "Has the Church not lifted woman to equality and companionship with man, secured the sanctity and stability of marriage, changed parental despotism to parental service, and eliminated unnatural vice, the abandonment of children, blood revenge, and the robbery of the shipwrecked from the customs of Christian nations? Has it not abolished slavery, mitigated war, covered all lands with a network of charities to uplift the poor and the fallen, fostered the institutions of education, aided the progress of civil liberty and social justice, and diffused a softening tenderness throughout human life? It has done all that, and vastly more. . . . " Rauschenbusch dared not say what history demanded of him, that each and every one of these conquests has been the fruit of Fundamentalism. But even that is not enough! Now that modernism has come in to filch from us these creations of our creed, we must either wrest them from bandit hands or begin and build again. In the last few years, in fact, since the modernist-highwaymen rose up to trouble the Church and snatch its dearest treasures, it has shown itself as virile as the promise of Christ, "The gates of hell shall not prevail against it," ever indicated. Today there are one hundred schools and colleges connected with our Fundamentalist Association, some of which have escaped the covetous clutches of modernism, but most of which have been brought into being as a protest against modernism itself. Their growth has been so phenomenal as to prove that the old tree is fruitful still, and that the finest fruit is to be found upon its newest branches, orthodox churches, Fundamentalist colleges, sound Bible training schools, evangelical publication societies, multiplied Bible conferences and stanch defenders of the faith in ever increasing numbers in each denomination. In fact, so fruitful is our movement that *The Christian Register,* the one clear mouthpiece of modernism, is not only alarmed, it is discouraged, and says, "Protestantism is in eclipse. Christianity enters a new dark age. The modernists who arose in the various denominations to fight Fundamentalism and to bring new freedom to the churches have all retired; their movement has collapsed; victory rests with the Fundamentalists." Harbor Allen, in a recent magazine article on "The War Against Evolution," makes a kindred concession as to the triumphs of Fundamentalism.

* * *

Who are my brethren? Baptists? Not necessarily, and, in thousands of instances, no! My brethren are those who believe in a personal God, in an inspired Book, and in a redeeming Christ.

Machen, J. Gresham. *Christianity and Liberalism*. Grand Rapids: Eerdmans, 1923. 1–3, 6–9, 54–68.

The purpose of this book is not to decide the religious issue of the present day, but merely to present the issue as sharply and clearly as possible, in order that the reader may be aided in deciding it for himself. Presenting an issue sharply is indeed by no means a popular business at the present time; there are many who prefer to fight their intellectual battles in what Dr. Francis L. Patton has aptly called a "condition of low visibility."

* * *

In the sphere of religion, in particular, the present time is a time of conflict; the great redemptive religion which has always been known as

Christianity is battling against a totally diverse type of religious belief, which is only the more destructive of the Christian faith because it makes use of traditional Christian terminology. This modern non-redemptive religion is called "modernism" or "liberalism." Both names are unsatisfactory, the latter, in particular, is question-begging. The movement designated as "liberalism" is regarded as "liberal" only by its friends; to its opponents it seems to involve a narrow ignoring of many relevant facts. And indeed the movement is so various in its manifestations that one may almost despair of finding any common name which will apply to all its forms. But manifold as are the forms in which the movement appears, the root of the movement is one; the many varieties of modern liberal religion are rooted in naturalism—that is, in the denial of any entrance of the creative power of God (as distinguished from the ordinary course of nature) in connection with the origin of Christianity. The word "naturalism" is here used in a sense somewhat different from its philosophical meaning. In this non-philosophical sense it describes with fair accuracy the real root of what is called, by what may turn out to be a degradation of an originally noble word, "liberal" religion.

The rise of this modern naturalistic liberalism has not come by chance, but has been occasioned by important changes which have recently taken place in the conditions of life. The past one hundred years have witnessed the beginning of a new era in human history, which may conceivably be regretted, but certainly cannot be ignored, by the most obstinate conservatism. The change is not something that lies beneath the surface and might be visible only to the discerning eye; on the contrary it forces itself upon the attention of the plain man at a hundred points. Modern inventions and the industrialism that has been built upon them have given us in many respects a new world to live in; we can no more remove ourselves from that world than we can escape from the atmosphere that we breathe.

But such changes in the material conditions of life do not stand alone; they have been produced by mighty changes in the human mind, as in their turn they themselves give rise to further spiritual changes. The industrial world of today has been produced not by blind forces of nature but by the conscious activity of the human spirit; it has been produced by the achievements of science. The outstanding feature of recent history is an enormous widening of human knowledge, which has gone hand in hand with such perfecting of the instrument of investigation that scarcely any limits can be assigned to future progress in the material realm.

The application of modern scientific methods is almost as broad as the universe in which we live. Though the most palpable achievements are in the sphere of physics and chemistry, the sphere of human life cannot be isolated from the rest, and with the other sciences there has appeared, for example, a modern science of history, which, with psychology and sociology and the like, claims, even if it does not deserve, full equality with its sister sciences. No department of knowledge can maintain its isolation from the modern lust of scientific conquest; treaties of inviolability, though hallowed by all the sanctions of age-long tradition, are being flung ruthlessly to the winds.

As a matter of fact, however, it may appear that the figure which has just been used is altogether misleading; it may appear that what the liberal theologian has retained after abandoning to the enemy one Christian doctrine after another is not Christianity at all, but a religion which is so entirely different from Christianity as to belong in a distinct category. It may appear further that the fears of the modern man as to Christianity were entirely ungrounded, and that in abandoning the embattled walls of the city of God he has fled in needless panic into the open plains of a vague natural religion only to fall an easy victim to the enemy who ever lies in ambush there.

Two lines of criticism, then, are possible with respect to the liberal attempt at reconciling science and Christianity. Modern liberalism may be criticized (1) on the ground that it is un-Christian and (2) on the ground that it is unscientific. We shall concern ourselves here chiefly with the former line of criticism; we shall be interested in showing that despite the liberal use of traditional phraseology modern liberalism not only is a different religion from Christianity but belongs in a totally different class of religions. But in showing that the liberal attempt at rescuing Christianity is false we are not showing that there is no way of rescuing Christianity at all; on the contrary, it may appear incidentally, even in the present little book, that it is not the Christianity of the New Testament which is in conflict with science, but the supposed Christianity of the modern liberal Church, and that the real city of God, and that city alone, has defenses which are capable of warding off the assaults of modern unbelief. However, our immediate concern is with the other side of the problem; our principal concern just now is to show that the liberal attempt at reconciling Christianity with modern science has really relinquished everything distinctive of Christianity, so that what remains is in essentials only that same indefinite type of religious aspiration which was in the world before

Christianity came upon the scene. In trying to remove from Christianity everything that could possibly be objected to in the name of science, in trying to bribe off the enemy by those concessions which the enemy most desires, the apologist has really abandoned what he started out to defend. Here as in many other departments of life it appears that the things that are sometimes thought to be hardest to defend are also the things that are most worth defending.

In maintaining that liberalism in the modern Church represents a return to an un-Christian and sub-Christian form of the religious life, we are particularly anxious not to be misunderstood. "Un-Christian" in such a connection is sometimes taken as a term of opprobrium. We do not mean it at all as such. Socrates was not a Christian, neither was Goethe; yet we share to the full the respect with which their names are regarded. They tower immeasurably above the common run of men; if he that is least in the Kingdom of Heaven is greater than they, he is certainly greater not by any inherent superiority, but by virtue of an undeserved privilege which ought to make him humble rather than contemptuous.

Such considerations, however, should not be allowed to obscure the vital importance of the question at issue. If a condition could be conceived in which all the preaching of the Church should be controlled by the liberalism which in many quarters has already become preponderant, then, we believe, Christianity would at last have perished from the earth and the gospel would have sounded forth for the last time. If so, it follows that the inquiry with which we are now concerned is immeasurably the most important of all those with which the church has to deal. Vastly more important than all questions with regard to methods of preaching is the root question as to what it is that shall be preached.

* * *

God and Man

It has been observed in the last chapter that Christianity is based on an account of something that happened in the first century of our era. But before that account can be received, certain presuppositions must be accepted. The Christian gospel consists in an account of how God saved man, and before that gospel can be understood something must be known (1) about God and (2) about man. The doctrine of God and the doctrine of man are the two great presuppositions of the gospel. With regard to these presuppositions, as with regard to the gospel itself, modern liberalism is diametrically opposed to Christianity.

* * *

Modern men have been so much impressed with this element in Jesus' teaching that they have sometimes been inclined to regard it as the very sum and substance of our religion. We are not interested, they say, in many things for which men formerly gave their lives; we are not interested in the theology of the creeds; we are not interested in the doctrines of sin and salvation; we are not interested in atonement through the blood of Christ: enough for us is the simple truth of the fatherhood of God and its corollary, the brotherhood of man. We may not be very orthodox in the theological sense, they continue, but of course you will recognize us as Christians because we accept Jesus' teaching as to the Father God.

It is very strange how intelligent persons can speak in this way. It is very strange how those who accept only the universal fatherhood of God as the sum and substance of religion can regard themselves as Christians or can appeal to Jesus of Nazareth. For the plain fact is that this modern doctrine of the universal fatherhood of God formed no part whatever of Jesus' teaching. Where is it that Jesus may be supposed to have taught the universal fatherhood of God? Certainly it is not in the parable of the Prodigal Son. For in the first place, the publicans and sinners whose acceptance by Jesus formed the occasion both of the Pharisees' objection and of Jesus' answer to them by means of the parable, were not any men anywhere, but were members of the chosen people and as such might be designated as sons of God. In the second place, a parable is certainly not to be pressed in its details. So here because the joy of the father in the parable is like the joy of God when a sinner receives salvation at Jesus' hand, it does not follow that the relation which God sustains to still unrepentant sinners is that of a Father to his children. Where else, then, can the universal fatherhood of God be found? Surely not in the Sermon on the Mount; for throughout the Sermon on the Mount those who can call God Father are distinguished in the most emphatic way from the great world of the Gentiles outside. One passage in the discourse has indeed been urged in support of the modern doctrine: "But I say unto you, love your enemies and pray for them that persecute you; that ye may be sons of your Father who is in heaven; for He maketh His sun to rise on evil and good and sendeth rain on just and unjust" (Matt. v. 44, 45). But the passage certainly will not bear the weight which is hung upon it. God is indeed represented here as caring for all men whether evil or good, but He is certainly not called the Father of all. Indeed it might almost be said that the point of the passage depends on the fact that He is not the Father of all. He cares even for those who are not His children but His enemies; so His children, Jesus' disciples, ought to imitate Him by loving even those who are not their brethren but their persecutors. The modern doctrine of the universal fatherhood of God is not to be found in the teaching of Jesus.

And it is not to be found in the New Testament. The whole New Testament and Jesus Himself do indeed represent God as standing in a relation to all men, whether Christians or not, which is analogous to that in which a father stands to his children. He is the Author of the being of all, and as such might well be called the Father of all. He cares for all, and for that reason also might be called the Father of all. Here and there the figure of fatherhood seems to be used to designate this broader relationship which God sustains to all men or even to all created beings. So in an isolated passage in Hebrews, God is spoken of as the "Father of spirits" (Heb. xii. 9). Here perhaps it is the relation of God, as creator, to the personal beings whom He has created which is in view. One of the clearest instances of the broader use of the figure of fatherhood is found in the speech of Paul at Athens, Acts xvii. 28: "For we are also His offspring." Here it is plainly the relation in which God stands to all men, whether Christians or not, which is in mind. But the words form part of an hexameter line and are taken from a pagan poet; they are not represented as part of the gospel, but merely as belonging to the common meeting-ground which Paul discovered in speaking to his pagan hearers. This passage is only typical of what appears, with respect to a universal fatherhood of God, in the New Testament as a whole. Something analogous to a universal fatherhood of God is taught in the New Testament. Here and there the terminology of fatherhood and sonship is even used to describe this general relationship. But such instances are extremely rare. Ordinarily the lofty term "Father" is used to describe a relationship of a far more intimate kind, the relationship in which God stands to the company of the redeemed.

The modern doctrine of the universal fatherhood of God, then, which is being celebrated as "the essence of Christianity," really belongs at best only to that vague natural religion which forms the presupposition which the Christian preacher can use when the gospel is to be proclaimed; and when it is regarded as a reassuring, all-sufficient thing, it comes into direct opposition to the New Testament. The gospel itself refers to something entirely different; the really distinctive New Testament teaching about the fatherhood of God concerns only those who have been brought into the household of faith.

There is nothing narrow about such teaching; for the door of the household of faith is open wide to all. That door is the "new and living way" which Jesus opened by His blood. And if we really love our fellow-men, we shall not go about the world, with the liberal preacher, trying to make men satisfied with the coldness of a vague natural religion. But by the preaching of the gospel we shall invite them into the warmth and joy of the house of God. Christianity offers men all that is offered by the modern liberal teaching about the universal fatherhood of God; but it is Christianity only because it offers also infinitely more.

But the liberal conception of God differs even more fundamentally from the Christian view than in the different circle of ideas connected with the terminology of fatherhood. The truth is that liberalism has lost sight of the very centre and core of the Christian teaching. In the Christian view of God as set forth in the Bible, there are many elements. But one attribute of God is absolutely fundamental in the Bible; one attribute is absolutely necessary in order to render intelligible all the rest. That attribute is the awful transcendence of God. From beginning to end the Bible is concerned to set forth the awful gulf that separates the creature from the Creator. It is true, indeed, that according to the Bible God is immanent in the world. Not a sparrow falls to the ground without Him. But he is immanent in the world not because He is identified with the world, but because He is the free Creator and Upholder of it. Between the creature and the Creator a great gulf is fixed.

In modern liberalism, on the other hand, this sharp distinction between God and the world is broken down, and the name "God" is applied to the mighty world process itself. We find ourselves in the midst of a mighty process, which manifests itself in the indefinitely small and in the indefinitely great—in the infinitesimal life which is revealed through the microscope and in the vast movements of the heavenly spheres. To this world-process, of which we ourselves form a part, we apply the dread name of "God." God, therefore, it is said in effect, is not a person distinct from ourselves; on the contrary our life is a part of His. Thus the Gospel story of the Incarnation, according to modern liberalism, is sometimes thought of as a symbol of the general truth that man at his best is one with God.

It is strange how such a representation can be regarded as anything new, for as a matter of fact, pantheism is a very ancient phenomenon. It has always been with us, to blight the religious life of man. And modern liberalism, even when it is not consistently pantheistic, is at any rate pantheizing. It tends everywhere to break down the separateness between God and the world, and the sharp personal distinction between God and man. Even the sin of man on this view ought logically to be regarded as part of the life of God. Very different is the living and holy God of the Bible and of Christian faith.

Christianity differs from liberalism, then, in the first place, in its conception of God. But it also differs in its conception of man.

Modern liberalism has lost all sense of the gulf that separates the creature from the Creator; its doctrine of man follows naturally from its doctrine of God. But it is not only the creature limitations of mankind which are denied. Even more important is another difference. According to the Bible, man is a sinner under the just condemnation of God; according to modern liberalism, there is really no such thing as sin. At the very root of the modern liberal movement is the loss of the consciousness of sin.

The consciousness of sin was formerly the starting-point of all preaching; but today it is gone. Characteristic of the modern age, above all else, is a supreme confidence in human goodness; the religious literature of the day is redolent of that confidence. Get beneath the rough exterior of men, we are told, and we shall discover enough self-sacrifice to found upon it the hope of society; the world's evil, it is said, can be overcome with the world's good; no help is needed from outside the world.

What has produced this satisfaction with human goodness? What has become of the consciousness of sin? The consciousness of sin has certainly been lost. But what has removed it from the hearts of men?

* * *

Only, let us not try to do without the Spirit of God. The fundamental fault of the modern Church is that she is busily engaged in an absolutely impossible task—she is busily engaged in calling the righteous to repentance. Modern preachers are trying to bring men into the Church without requiring them to relinquish their pride; they are trying to help men avoid the conviction of sin. The preacher gets up into the pulpit, opens the Bible, and addresses the congregation somewhat as follows: "You people are very good," he says; "you respond to every appeal that looks toward the welfare of the community. Now we have in the Bible—especially in the life of Jesus—something so good that we believe it is good enough even for you good people." Such is modern preaching. It is heard every Sunday in thousands of pulpits. But it is entirely futile. Even our Lord did not call the righteous to repentance, and probably we shall be no more successful than He.

Fosdick, Harry Emerson. "Shall the Fundamentalists Win?" *Christian Work* 102 (June 10, 1922): 716–22.

Already all of us must have heard about the people who call themselves the Fundamentalists. Their apparent intention is to drive out of the evangelical churches men and women of liberal opinions. I speak of them the more freely because there are no two denominations more affected by them than the Baptist and the Presbyterian. We should not identify the Fundamentalists with the conservatives. All Fundamentalists are conservatives, but not all conservatives are Fundamentalists. The best conservatives can often give lessons to the liberals in true liberality of spirit, but the Fundamentalist program is essentially illiberal and intolerant.

*   *   *

There is nothing new about the situation. It has happened again and again in history, as, for example, when the stationary earth suddenly began to move and the universe that had been centered in this planet was centered in the sun around which the planets whirled. Whenever such a situation has arisen, there has been only one way out—the new knowledge and the old faith had to be blended in a new combination. Now, the people in this generation who are trying to do this are the liberals, and the Fundamentalists are out on a campaign to shut against them the doors of the Christian fellowship. Shall they be allowed to succeed?

*   *   *

That we may be entirely candid and concrete and may not lose ourselves in any fog of generalities, let us this morning take two or three of these Fundamentalist items and see with reference to them what the situation is in the Christian churches.

*   *   *

We may well begin with the vexed and mooted question of the virgin birth of our Lord. I know people in the Christian churches, ministers, missionaries, laymen, devoted lovers of the Lord and servants of the Gospel, who, alike as they are in their personal devotion to the Master, hold quite different points of view about a matter like the virgin birth. Here, for example, is one point of view that the virgin birth is to be accepted as historical fact; it actually happened; there was no other way for a personality like the Master to come into this world except by a special biological miracle. That is one point of view, and many are the gracious and beautiful souls who hold it. But side by side with them in the evangelical churches is a group of equally loyal and reverent people who would say that the virgin birth is not to be accepted as an historic fact. To believe in virgin birth as an explanation of great personality is one of the familiar ways in which the ancient world was accustomed to account for unusual superiority. Many people suppose that only once in history do we run across a record of supernatural birth. Upon the contrary, stories of miraculous generation are among the commonest traditions of antiquity. Especially is this true about the founders of great religions. According to the records of their faiths, Buddha and Zoroaster and Lao-Tzu and Mahavira were all supernaturally born. Moses, Confucius and Mohammed are the only great founders of religions in history to whom miraculous birth is not attributed. That is to say, when a personality arose so high that men adored him, the ancient world attributed his superiority to some special divine influence in his generation, and they commonly phrased their faith in terms of miraculous birth. So Pythagoras was called virgin born, and Plato, and Augustus Caesar, and many more. Knowing this, there are within the evangelical churches large groups of people whose opinion about our Lord's coming would run as follows: those first disciples adored Jesus—as we do; when they thought about his coming they were sure that he came specially from God—as we are; this adoration and conviction they associated with God's special influence and intention in his birth—as we do; but they phrased it in terms of a biological miracle that our modern minds cannot use. So far from thinking that they have given up anything vital in the New Testament's attitude toward Jesus, these Christians remember that the two men who contributed most to the Church's thought of the divine meaning of the Christ were Paul and John, who never even distantly allude to the virgin birth.

Here in the Christian churches are these two groups of people and the question which the Fundamentalists raise is this—Shall one of them throw the other out? Has intolerance any contribution to make to this situation? Will it persuade anybody of anything? Is not the Christian Church large enough to hold within her hospitable fellowship people who differ on points like this and agree to differ until the fuller truth be manifested? The Fundamentalists say not. They say the liberals must go. Well, if the Fundamentalists should succeed, then out of the Christian Church would go some of the best Christian life and consecration of this generation—multitudes of men and women, devout and reverent Christians, who need the church and whom the church needs.

Consider another matter on which there is a sincere difference of opinion between evangelical Christians: the inspiration of the Bible. One point of view is that the original documents of the Scripture were inerrantly dictated by God to men. Whether we deal with the story of creation or the list of the dukes of Edom or the narratives of Solomon's reign or the Sermon on the Mount or the thirteenth chapter of First Corinthians, they all came in the same way, and they all came as no other book ever came. They were inerrantly dictated; everything there—scientific opinions, medical theories, historical judgments, as well as spiritual insight—is infallible. That is one idea of the Bible's inspiration. But side by side with those who hold it, lovers of the Book as much as they, are multitudes of people who never think about the Bible so. Indeed, that static and mechanical theory of inspiration seems to them a positive peril to the spiritual life. The Koran similarly has been regarded by Mohammedans as having been infallibly written in heaven before it came to earth. But the Koran enshrines the theological and ethical ideas of Arabia at the time when it was written. God an Oriental monarch, fatalistic submission to his will as man's chief duty, the use of force on unbelievers, polygamy, slavery—they are all in the Koran. When it was written, the Koran was ahead of the day but, petrified by an artificial idea of inspiration, it has become a millstone about the neck of Mohammedanism. When one turns from the Koran to the Bible, he finds this interesting situation. All of these ideas, which we dislike in the Koran, are somewhere in the Bible. Conceptions from which we now send missionaries to convert Mohammedans are to be found in the Bible. There one can find God thought of as an Oriental monarch; there too are patriarchal polygamy, and slave systems, and the use of force on unbelievers. Only in the Bible these elements are not final; they are always being superseded; revelation is progressive. The thought of God moves out from Oriental kingship to compassionate fatherhood; treatment of unbelievers moves out from the use of force to the appeals of love; polygamy gives way to monogamy; slavery, never explicitly condemned before the New Testament closes, is nevertheless being undermined by ideas that in the end, like dynamite, will blast its foundations to pieces. Repeatedly one runs on verses like this: "it was said to them of old time . . . but I say unto you"; "God, having of old time spoken unto the fathers in the prophets by divers portions and in divers manners, hath at the end of these days spoken unto us in his Son"; "The times of ignorance therefore God overlooked; but now he commandeth men that they should all everywhere repent"; and over the doorway of the New Testament into the Christian world stand the words of Jesus: "When he, the Spirit of truth, is come, he will guide you into all truth." That is to say, finality in the Koran is behind; finality in the Bible is ahead. We have not reached it. We cannot yet compass all of it. God is leading us out toward it. There are multitudes of Christians, then, who think, and rejoice as they think, of the Bible as the record of the progressive unfolding of the character of God to his people from early primitive days until the great unveiling in Christ; to them the Book is more inspired and more inspiring than ever it was before. To go back to a mechanical and static theory of inspiration would mean to them the loss of some of the most vital elements in their spiritual experience and in their appreciation of the Book.

Here in the Christian Church today are these two groups, and the question which the Fundamentalists have raised is this—Shall one of them drive the other out? Do we think the cause of Jesus Christ will be furthered by that? If He should walk through the ranks of his congregation this morning, can we imagine Him claiming as His own those who hold one idea of inspiration and sending from Him into outer darkness those who hold another? You cannot fit the Lord Christ into that Fundamentalist mold. The church would better judge His judgment. For in the Middle West the Fundamentalists have had their way in some communities and a Christian minister tells us the consequences. He says that the educated people are looking for their religion outside the churches.

Consider another matter upon which there is a serious and sincere difference of opinion between evangelical Christians: the second coming of our Lord. The second coming was the early Christian phrasing of hope. No one in the ancient world had ever thought, as we do, of development, progress, gradual change as God's way of working out His will in human life and institutions. They thought of human history as a series of ages succeeding one another with abrupt suddenness. The Graeco-Roman world gave the names of metals to the ages—gold, silver, bronze, iron. The Hebrews had their ages, too—the original Paradise in which man began, the cursed world in which man now lives, the blessed Messianic kingdom someday suddenly to appear on the clouds of heaven. It was the Hebrew way of expressing hope for the victory of God and righteousness. When the Christians came they took over that phrasing of expectancy and the New Testament is aglow with it. The preaching of the apostles thrills with the glad announcement, "Christ is coming!"

In the evangelical churches today there are differing views of this matter. One view is that Christ is literally coming, externally, on the clouds of heaven, to set up His kingdom here. I never heard that teaching in my youth at all. It has always had a new resurrection when desperate circumstances came and man's only hope seemed to lie in divine intervention. It is not strange, then, that during these chaotic, catastrophic years there has been a fresh rebirth of this old phrasing of expectancy. "Christ is coming!" seems to many Christians the central message of the Gospel. In the strength of it some of them are doing great service for the world. But, unhappily, many so overemphasize it that they outdo anything the ancient Hebrews or the ancient Christians ever did. They sit still and do nothing and expect the world to grow worse and worse until He comes.

Side by side with these to whom the second coming is a literal expectation, another group exists in the evangelical churches. They, too, say, "Christ is coming!" They say it with all their hearts; but they are not thinking of an external arrival on the clouds. They have assimilated as part of the divine revelation the exhilarating insight which these recent generations have given to us, that development is God's way of working out His will. They see that the most desirable elements in human life have come through the method of development. Man's music has developed from the rhythmic noise of beaten sticks until we have in melody and harmony possibilities once undreamed. Man's painting has developed from the crude outlines of the cavemen until in line and color we have achieved unforeseen results and possess latent beauties yet unfolded. Man's architecture has developed from the crude huts of primitive men until our cathedrals and business buildings reveal alike an incalculable advance and an unimaginable future. Development does seem to be the way in which God works. And these Christians, when they say that Christ is coming, mean that, slowly it may be, but surely, His will and principles will be worked out by God's grace in human life and institutions, until "He shall see of the travail of His soul and shall be satisfied."

These two groups exist in the Christian churches and the question raised by the Fundamentalists is—Shall one of them drive the other out? Will that get us anywhere? Multitudes of young men and women at this season of the year are graduating from our schools of learning, thousands of them Christians who may make us older ones ashamed by the sincerity of their devotion to God's will on earth. They are not thinking in ancient terms that leave ideas of progress out. They cannot think in those terms. There could be no greater tragedy than that the Fundamentalists should shut the door of the Christian fellowship against such.

I do not believe for one moment that the Fundamentalists are going to succeed. Nobody's intolerance can contribute anything to the solution of the situation which we have described. If, then, the Fundamentalists have no solution of the problem, where may we expect to find it? In two concluding comments let us consider our reply to that inquiry.

The first element that is necessary is a spirit of tolerance and Christian liberty. When will the world learn that intolerance solves no problems? . . . It was a wise liberal, the most adventurous man of his day—Paul the Apostle—who said, "Knowledge puffeth up, but love buildeth up."

* * *

The second element which is needed if we are to reach a happy solution of this problem is a clear insight into the main issues of modern Christianity and a sense of penitent shame that the Christian Church should be quarreling over little matters when the world is dying of great needs. If, during the war, when the nations were wrestling upon the very brink of hell and at times all seemed lost, you chanced to hear two men in an altercation about some minor matter of sectarian denominationalism, could you restrain your indignation? You said, "What can you do with folks like this who, in the face of colossal issues, play with the tiddledywinks and peccadillos of religion?" So, now, when from the terrific questions of this generation one is called away by the noise of this Fundamentalist controversy, he thinks it almost unforgivable that men should tithe mint and anise and cummin, and quarrel over them, when the world is perishing for the lack of the weightier matters of the law, justice, and mercy, and faith. These last weeks, in the minister's confessional, I have heard stories from the depths of human lives where men and women were wrestling with the elemental problems of misery and sin—stories that put upon a man's heart a burden of vicarious sorrow, even though he does but listen to them. Here was real human need crying out after the living God revealed in Christ. Consider all the multitudes of men who so need God, and then think of Christian churches making of themselves a cockpit of controversy when there is not a single thing at stake in the controversy on which depends the salvation of human souls. That is the trouble with this whole business. So much of it does not matter! And there is one thing that does matter—more than anything else in all the world—that men in their personal lives and in their social relationships should know Jesus Christ.

Just a week ago I received a letter from a friend in Asia Minor. He says that they are killing the Armenians yet; that the Turkish deportations still are going on; that lately they crowded Christian men, women and children into a conventicle of worship and burned them together in the house where they had prayed to their Father and to ours. During the war, when it was good propaganda to stir up our bitter hatred against the enemy, we heard of such atrocities, but not now! Two weeks ago Great Britain, shocked and stirred by what is going on in Armenia, did ask the government of the United States to join her in investigating the atrocities and trying to help. Our government said that it was not any of our business at all. The present world situation smells to heaven! And now, in the presence of colossal problems, which must be solved in Christ's name and for Christ's sake, the Fundamentalists propose to drive out from the Christian churches all the consecrated souls who do not agree with their theory of inspiration. What immeasurable folly!

Well, they are not going to do it; certainly not in this vicinity. I do not even know in this congregation whether anybody has been tempted to be a Fundamentalist. Never in this church have I caught one accent of intolerance. God keep us always so and ever increasing areas of the Christian fellowship; intellectually hospitable, open-minded, liberty-loving, fair, tolerant, not with the tolerance of indifference, as though we did not care about the faith, but because always our major emphasis is upon the weightier matters of the law.

* 3 *

Dispensational Premillennialism

EDITOR: *From roughly 1870 through the fundamentalist-modernist controversy of the 1920s, many evangelicals and fundamentalists adopted the end-times theology known as dispensational premillennialism. While some argue for more ancient roots for dispensationalism, in its modern form this type of prophecy belief was virtually invented by the nineteenth-century British evangelical John Nelson Darby. By the early twentieth century dispensationalism was becoming a major force within evangelicalism and was touted as a hallmark of fundamentalism by many popular preachers. Machen and most Presbyterian fundamentalists resisted dispensationalism, however, and in the 1940s when moderate fundamentalists sought to distance themselves from militant fundamentalism, dispensationalism was a major issue. The neoevangelicals, as these moderate fundamentalists of the 1940s and 1950s called themselves, thought that the militant fundamentalists put too much emphasis on dispensationalism.*

Almost all evangelicals today believe that Christ will literally return to earth someday, and most evangelicals are premillennialist, which means they believe that Christ will return before the inauguration of a millennial kingdom on Earth. Dispensationalism is a type of premillennialism, so it is possible to be a premillennialist without being a dispensationalist. By contrast, virtually all fundamentalists and many Pentecostal evangelicals are both premillennial and dispensational.

Below are three dispensational selections. The first is a remarkably clear exposition of dispensationalism by C. I. Scofield. The Scofield Reference Bible that he edited first appeared in 1909 from Oxford University Press and did more to popularize dispensationalism than any other development in the history of evangelicalism. The Scofield Bible is still the standard Bible used by many fundamentalists and some evangelicals.

In the early twentieth century, dispensationalists began to hold prophetic conferences. One of the first was held in Philadelphia in 1918. After the Scofield selection, readers will find the statement issued by the Philadelphia conference.

The third passage is more recent. It is an excerpt from Hal Lindsey's wildly popular 1970 book The Late Great Planet Earth, *which is one of the best selling books in the history of American publishing. Lindsey is a popular dispensational premillennialist author and speaker who popularized end-times prophecy, even with many nonevangelicals. By helping promote prophecy belief as something of an American folk religion, Lindsey's book prepared the way for the popular* Left Behind *novels, which were published between 1995 and 2003. The twelve novels in the series have sold more than sixty million copies.*

> Scofield, C. I. "The Seven Dispensations." In *Rightly Dividing the Word of Truth.* 1896.

The Scriptures divide time (by which is meant the entire period from the creation of Adam to the "new heaven and a new earth" of Rev. 21: 1) into seven unequal periods, usually called dispensations (Eph. 3:2), although these periods are also called ages (Eph. 2:7) and days, as in "day of the Lord."

These periods are marked off in Scripture by some change in God's method of dealing with mankind, or a portion of mankind, in respect of the two questions: of sin, and of man's responsibility. Each of the dispensations may be regarded as a new test of the natural man, and each ends in judgment, marking his utter failure in every dispensation. Five of these dispensations, or periods of time, have been fulfilled; we are living in the sixth, probably toward its close, and have before us the seventh, and last: the millennium.

1. Man innocent. This dispensation extends from the creation of Adam in Genesis 2:7 to the expulsion from Eden. Adam, created innocent and ignorant of good and evil, was placed in the garden of Eden with his wife, Eve, and put under responsibility to abstain from the fruit of the tree of the knowledge of good and evil. The dispensation of innocence resulted in the first failure of man, and in its far-reaching effects, the most disastrous. It closed in judgment: "So he drove out the man." See Gen. 1:26; Gen. 2:16,17; Gen. 3:6; Gen. 3:22-24.)

2. Man under conscience. By the fall, Adam and Eve acquired and transmitted to the race the knowledge of good and evil. This gave conscience a basis for right moral judgment, and hence the race came under this measure of responsibility-to do good and eschew evil. The result of the dispensation of conscience, from Eden to the flood (while there was no institution of government and of law), was that "all flesh had corrupted his way on the earth," that "the wickedness of man was great in the earth,

and that every imagination of the thoughts of his heart was only evil continually," and God closed the second testing of the natural man with judgment: the flood. See Gen. 3:7, 22; Gen. 6:5, 11-12; Gen. 7:11-12, 23.)

3. Man in authority over the earth. Out of the fearful judgment of the flood God saved eight persons, to whom, after the waters were assuaged, He gave the purified earth with ample power to govern it. This, Noah and his descendants were responsible to do. The dispensation of human government resulted, upon the plain of Shinar, in the impious attempt to become independent of God and closed in judgment: the confusion of tongues. (See Gen. 9: 1, 2; Gen. 11:1-4; Gen. 11:5-8.)

4. Man under promise. Out of the dispersed descendants of the builders of Babel, God called one man, Abram, with whom He enters into covenant. Some of the promises to Abram and his descendants were purely gracious and unconditional. These either have been or will yet be literally fulfilled. Other promises were conditional upon the faithfulness and obedience of the Israelites. Every one of these conditions was violated, and the dispensation of promise resulted in the failure of Israel and closed in the judgment of bondage in Egypt.

The book of Genesis, which opens with the sublime words, "In the beginning God created," closes with, "In a coffin in Egypt." (See Gen. 12:1-3; Gen. 13:14-17; Gen. 15:5; Gen. 26:3; Gen. 28:12-13; Exod. 1: 13-14.)

5. Man under law. Again the grace of God came to the help of helpless man and redeemed the chosen people out of the hand of the oppressor. In the wilderness of Sinai He proposed to them the covenant of law. Instead of humbly pleading for a continued relation of grace, they presumptuously answered: "All that the Lord hath spoken we will do." The history of Israel in the wilderness and in the land is one long record of flagrant, persistent violation of the law, and at last, after multiplied warnings, God closed the testing of man by law in judgment: first Israel, and then Judah, were driven out of the land into a dispersion which still continues. A feeble remnant returned under Ezra and Nehemiah, of which, in due time, Christ came: "Born of a woman—made under the law." Both Jews and Gentiles conspired to crucify Him. (See Exod. 19:1-8; 2 Kings 17:1-18; 2 Kings 25:1-11; Acts 2:22-23; Acts 7:51-52; Rom. 3:19-20; Rom. 10:5; Gal. 3:10.)

6. Man under grace. The sacrificial death of the Lord Jesus Christ introduced the dispensation of pure grace, which means undeserved favor, or God giving righteousness, instead of God requiring righteousness, as under law. Salvation, perfect and eternal, is now freely offered to Jew and Gentile upon the acknowledgment of sin, or repentance, with faith in Christ.

"Jesus answered and said unto them, This is the work of God, that ye believe on him whom he hath sent" (John 6:29). "Verily, verily, I say unto you, He that believeth on me hath everlasting life" (John 6:47). "Verily, verily, I say unto you, He that heareth my word, and believeth on him that sent me, hath everlasting life, and shall not come into condemnation; but is passed from death unto life" (John 5:24). "My sheep hear my voice, and I know them, and they follow me: and I give unto them eternal life; and they shall never perish" (John 10:27-28). "For by grace are ye saved through faith; and that not of yourselves: it is the gift of God: Not of works, lest any man should boast" (Eph. 2:8-9).

The predicted result of this testing of man under grace is judgment upon an unbelieving world and an apostate church. (See Luke 17:26-30; Luke 18:8; 2 Thess. 2:7-12; Rev. 3:15-16.)

The first event in the closing of this dispensation will be the descent of the Lord from heaven, when sleeping saints will be raised and, together with believers then living, caught up "to meet the Lord in the air: and so shall we ever be with the Lord" (I Thess. 4:16-17). Then follows the brief period called "the great tribulation." (See Jer. 30:5-7; Dan. 12:1; Zeph. 1:15-18; Matt. 24:21-22.)

After this the personal return of the Lord to the earth in power and great glory occurs, and the judgments which introduce the seventh, and last dispensation. (See Matt. 25:31-46 and Matt. 24:29-30.)

7. Man under the personal reign of Christ. After the purifying judgments which attend the personal return of Christ to the earth, He will reign over restored Israel and over the earth for one thousand years. This is the period commonly called the millennium. The seat of His power will be Jerusalem, and the saints, including the saved of the dispensation of grace, namely the church, will be associated with Him in His glory. (See Isa. 2:1-4; Isa. 11; Acts 15:14-17; Rev. 19:11-21; Rev. 20:1-6.)

But when Satan is "loosed a little season," he finds the natural heart as prone to evil as ever, and easily gathers the nations to battle against the Lord and His saints, and this last dispensation closes, like all the others, in judgment. The great white throne is set, the wicked dead are raised and finally judged, and then come the "new heaven and a new earth." Eternity is begun. (See Rev. 20:3,7-15; Rev. 21, 22.)

"Statement of Belief Adopted by the Philadelphia Prophetic Conference." In "Report of the Bible Conference Committee." *Light on Prophecy*. Philadelphia: 1918.

First: We believe that the Bible is the inerrant, one and final word of God; and therefore is our one authority.

Second: We believe in the Deity of our Lord Jesus Christ; that He is very God; and in His substitutionary death, as atonement for sin; in His bodily resurrection and ascension and certainty of His second appearance "without sin unto salvation."

Third: We believe that our Lord's prophetic Word is at this moment finding remarkable fulfillment; and that it does indicate the nearness of the close of this age and the coming of our Lord Jesus Christ.

Fourth: We believe that the completed Church will be translated to be forever with the Lord.

Fifth: We believe that there will be a gathering of Israel to her land in unbelief, and she will be afterward converted by the appearance of Christ on her behalf.

Sixth: We believe that all human schemes of reconstruction must be subsidiary to the coming of our Lord Jesus Christ, because all nations will be subjected to his rule.

Seventh: We believe that under the reign of Christ there will be a further great effusion of the Holy Spirit upon the flesh.

Eighth: We believe that the truths embodied in this statement are of the utmost importance in determining Christian character and action in reference to the pressing problem of the hour.

Resolves: If our Lord tarry, that a great world Bible Conference be held at Philadelphia, May 27th to June 1st, 1919.

Lindsey, Hal. *The Late Great Planet Earth*. Grand Rapids: Zondervan, 1970. Selected portions from 135–45, 157–68. Used by permission.

The Ultimate Trip

"One small step for a man—one giant leap for mankind." APOLLO 11 COMMANDER NEIL ARMSTRONG 20 JULY 1969

And the world caught its breath. Science fiction had prepared man for the incredible feats of the astronauts, but when the reality of the moon landing really hit, it was awesome.

On that historic Sunday in July we watched TV, laughing as Armstrong and Buzz Aldrin loped on the moon's surface. We walked out the front door and looked up at the Old Man and said, "It's really happening—there are a couple of guys walking around up there right now. Amazing."

Astounding as man's trip to the moon is, there is another trip which many men, women, and children will take some day which will leave the rest of the world gasping. Those who remain on earth at that time will use every invention of the human mind to explain the sudden disappearance of millions of people.

Reporters who wrote the historic story of Apollo 11 told how the astronauts collected rocks which may reveal the oldest secrets of the solar system. Those who are alive to tell the story of "Project Disappearance" will try in vain to describe the happening which will verify the oldest secrets of God's words.

What Will They Say?

"There I was, driving down the freeway and all of a sudden the place went crazy. . . . Cars going in all directions . . . and not one of them had a driver. I mean it was wild! I think we've got an invasion from outer space!"

"It was the last quarter of the championship game and the other side was ahead. Our boys had the ball. We made a touchdown and tied it up. The crowd went crazy. Only one minute to go and they fumbled—our quarterback recovered—he was about a yard from the goal when—zap—no more quarterback—completely gone, just like that!"

"It was puzzling—very puzzling. I was teaching my course in the Philosophy of Religion when all, of a sudden three of my students vanished. They simply vanished! They were quite argumentative—always trying to prove their point from the Bible. No great loss to the class. However, I do find this disappearance very difficult to explain."

"As an official spokesman for the United Nations I wish to inform all peace-loving people of the world that we are making every human effort to assist those nations whose leaders have disappeared. We have issued a general declaration of condemnation in the General Assembly concerning these heads of state. Their irresponsibility is shocking."

"My dear friends in the congregation. Bless you for coming to church today. I know that many of you have lost loved ones in this unusual disappearance of so many people. However, I believe that God's judgment has come upon them for their continued dissension and quarreling with the great advances of the church in our century. Now that the reactionaries are removed, we can progress toward our great and glorious goal of uniting all mankind into a brotherhood of reconciliation and understanding."

"You really want to know what I think? I think all that talk about the Rapture and going to meet Jesus Christ in the air wasn't crazy after all. I don't know about you, brother, but I'm going to find myself a Bible and read all those verses my wife underlined. I wouldn't listen to her while she was here, and now she's—I don't know where she is."

Rapture—What Rapture?

Christians have a tendency sometimes to toss out words which have no meaning to the non-Christian. Sometimes misunderstood terms provide the red flag an unbeliever needs to turn him from the simple truth of God's Word. "Rapture" may be one of those words. It is not found in the Bible, so there is no need to race for your concordance, if you have one. There are some Christians who do not use the word, but prefer "translation" instead.

The word "rapture" means to snatch away or take out. But whether we call this event: "the Rapture" or the "translation" makes no difference—the important thing is that it will happen.

It will happen!

Someday, a day that only God knows, Jesus Christ is coming to take away all those who believe in Him. He is coming to meet all true believers in the air. Without benefit of science, space suits, or interplanetary rockets, there will be those who will be transported into a glorious place more beautiful, more awesome, than we can possibly comprehend. Earth and all its thrills, excitement, and pleasures will be nothing in contrast to this great event.

It will be the living end. The ultimate trip.

* * *

EDITOR: *The events that Lindsey outlines below will take place during the Great Tribulation that dispensationalists believe will follow "the rapture." Notice that with the Christians gone from the earth, God's attention shifts back to the Jews. The world powers attempt to destroy Israel but are themselves destroyed instead. At the climactic moment in the Battle of*

Armageddon, Christ returns. All who have been raptured and all who have converted to Christ during the Tribulation will rule with Christ in a millennial, thousand-year reign on Earth.

World War III

The Classic Double-cross

When the Russians invade the Middle East with amphibious and mechanized land forces, they will make a "blitzkrieg" type of offensive through the area. As Daniel saw it centuries ago: " . . . and he [Russians] shall come into countries [of the Middle-East] and shall overflow and pass through. He will come into the glorious land [Israel]. And tens of thousands shall fall" (Daniel 11:40b, 41a).

Ezekiel describes the same invasion as follows: "Therefore, son of man, prophesy, and say to Gog [the Russian leader], Thus says the Lord GOD: On that day when my people Israel are dwelling securely, you will bestir yourself and come from your place out of the uttermost parts of the north [Daniel's king of the North], you and many peoples with you [i.e., the European iron curtain countries], all of them riding on horses, a great host, a mighty army; you will come up against my people Israel, like a cloud covering the land. In the latter days, I will bring you against my land . . . " (Ezekiel 3 8:14-16).

As previously quoted the Russians will make both an amphibious and land invasion of Israel. The current build-up of Russian ships in the Mediterranean serves as another significant sign of the possible nearness of Armageddon. They now have more ships in the Mediterranean than the United States, according to several recent news releases. The amphibious landings will facilitate a rapid encirclement of the middle section of "the land bridge."

The might of the Red Army is predicted. It will sweep over the Arab countries as well as Israel in a rapid assault over to Egypt to secure the entire land bridge. It is at this point that Russia double-crosses the United Arab Republic leader, Egypt. After sweeping over tens of thousands of people Daniel says of the Red army: "He shall stretch out his hand against the countries [Arab countries of the Middle East], and the land of Egypt shall not escape. He [Russian leader] shall become ruler of the treasures of gold and of silver, and all the precious things of Egypt; and the Libyans [African Arabs] and the Ethiopians [African blacks] shall follow in his train" (Daniel 11:42, 43).

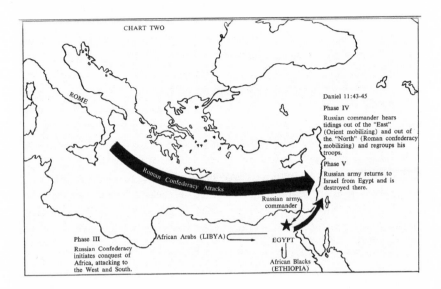

CHART TWO

ROME

Daniel 11:43-45

Phase IV

Russian commander hears tidings out of the "East" (Orient mobilizing) and out of the "North" (Roman confederacy mobilizing) and regroups his troops.

Phase V

Russian army returns to Israel from Egypt and is destroyed there.

Roman Confederacy Attacks

Russian army commander

Phase III

Russian Confederacy initiates conquest of Africa, attacking to the West and South.

African Arabs (LIBYA)

EGYPT

African Blacks (ETHIOPIA)

As we saw in Chapters 5 and 6, this prediction indicates that the Russian bloc will double-cross the Arabs, Egyptians, and Africans, and for a short while conquer the Middle East. At this time, with the main Russian force in Egypt, the commander will hear alarming news: "But rumors from the east [the Orient mobilizing] and from the north [the Western Europeans mobilizing] shall alarm and hasten him. And he shall go forth with great fury to destroy and utterly to sweep away many" (Daniel 11:44 Amplified).

As shown in Chart two (above), the Russian force will retrace its steps from Egypt to consolidate for a counter-attack in Israel. The Russians will be alarmed at the news of the Roman Dictator mobilizing forces around the world to put down this breach of peace. Apparently it will surprise the Russian leader who underestimated the revived Roman Empire's will to fight.

It is conjecture on this writer's part, but it appears that the Oriental powers, headed by Red China, will be permitted to mobilize its vast army by the Roman Dictator, thinking that they would be loyal to him against Russia. However, the Orientals will eventually double-cross him, and move a 200 million man army against the Antichrist, as we have seen in Chapter 7.

This Russian double-cross of the Arabs is predictable by any astute observer of the Middle East situation today. It is obvious that the Russians are playing games with the Arabs in order to accomplish the old Russian dream of year-round seaports and oil supplies. The Arab leaders think that they can accept Russian loans and supplies without strings, but there are steel cables of conditions behind every Russian ruble given in aid and they are used eventually to pull a country behind the iron curtain.

The Russian force will establish command headquarters on Mount Moriah or the Temple area in Jerusalem. Daniel pointed this out when he said: "And he shall pitch his palatial tents between the seas [Dead Sea and Mediterranean Sea] and the glorious holy mount Zion; yet he shall come to his end with none to help him" (Daniel 11:45 Amplified).

As the Russian commander confidently prepares to meet the forces of the revived Roman Empire in Palestine, he seeks to utterly destroy the Jewish people. This is the apparent meaning of verses 44 and 45. Perhaps no other great army of history has ever been so totally destroyed as this one will be.

The Russian Waterloo

Ezekiel sounded the fatal collapse of the Red Army centuries ago when inspired by the Spirit of the living God he said: "But on that day, when Gog shall come against the land of Israel, says the Lord GOD, my wrath will be roused. For in my jealousy and in my blazing wrath I declare, On that day there shall be a great shaking in the land of Israel; the fish of the sea, and the birds of the air, and the beasts of the field, and all creeping things that creep on the ground, and all the men that are upon the face of the earth, shall quake at my presence, and the mountains shall be thrown down, and the cliffs shall fall, and every wall shall tumble to the ground. I will summon every kind of terror against Gog, says the Lord GOD; every man's sword will be against his brother. With pestilence and bloodshed I will enter into judgment with him; and I will rain upon him and his hordes and the many peoples that are with him, torrential rains and hailstones, fire and brimstone" (Ezekiel 38:18-22).

" . . . then I will strike your bow from your left hand, and will make your arrows drop out of your right hand. You shall fall upon the mountains of Israel, you and all your hordes and the people that are with you; I will give you to birds of prey of every sort and to the wild beasts to be devoured. You shall fall in the open field; for I have spoken, says the Lord GOD" (Ezekiel 39:3-5).

The description of torrents of fire and brimstone raining down upon the Red Army, coupled with an unprecedented shaking of the land of Israel could well be describing the use of tactical nuclear weapons against them by the Romans. It explicitly says that this force would fall "in the open field," so apparently this position enables the use of nuclear weapons.

God consigns this whole barbarous army, which will seek to annihilate the Jewish race, to an utter and complete decimation. Ezekiel speaks of the Russians and " . . . all your hosts and the peoples who are with you . . . " being destroyed in Israel.

* * *

What About the United States?

The United States may be aligned with the Western forces headed by the ten-nation Revived Roman Empire of Europe. It is clear that the U.S. cannot be the leader of the West in the future. It is quite possible that Ezekiel was referring to the U.S. in part when he said: "I will send fire—upon those who dwell securely in the coastlands. . . . "

The word translated "coastlands" or "isle" in the Hebrew is *ai*. It was used by the ancients in the sense of "continents" today. It designated the great Gentile civilizations across the seas which were usually settled most densely along the coastlands. The idea here is that the Gentile nations on distant continents would all experience the impact of sudden torrents of fire raining down upon them. This can include prophetically the populated continents and islands of the Western hemisphere as well as the Far East. It pictures cataclysmic events which affect the whole inhabited earth.

The Greatest Battle of All Time

With the United Arab and African armies neutralized by the Russian invasion, and the consequent complete annihilation of the Russian forces and their homeland, we have only two great spheres of power left to fight the final climactic battle of Armageddon: the combined forces of the Western civilization united under the leadership of the Roman Dictator and the vast hordes of the Orient probably united under the Red Chinese war machine.

* * *

What and Where Is Armageddon?

Armageddon is a byword used through the centuries to depict the horrors of war. Dr. Seiss sums up its true significance as follows: "Harmageddon (Armageddon) means the Mount of Megiddo, which has also given its name to the great plain of Jezreel which belts across the middle of the

Holy Land, from the Mediterranean to the Jordan. The name is from a Hebrew root which means to cut off, to slay; and a place of slaughter has Megiddo ever been."

In Biblical history countless bloody battles were fought in this area. Napoleon is reported to have stood upon the hill of Megiddo and recalled this prophecy as he looked over the valley and said, " . . . all the armies of the world could maneuver for battle here." In the Old Testament book of Joel this valley was called the "valley of Jehoshaphat."

Today this valley's entrance has the port of Haifa at its Western end. This is one of the most accessible areas in Palestine for amphibious landing of troops. It also affords a great area for troop assembly, equipment, and organization. Some troops will doubtlessly be airlifted in as well, and this large valley is suited for that, too.

＊　＊　＊

World-wide Destruction

The conflict will not be limited to the Middle East. The apostle John warns that when these two great forces meet in battle the greatest shock wave ever to hit the earth will occur. Whether by natural force of an earthquake or by some super weapon isn't clear. John says that all the cities of the nations will be destroyed (Revelation 16:19).

Imagine, cities like London, Paris, Tokyo, New York, Los Angeles, Chicago—obliterated! John says that the Eastern force alone will wipe out a third of the earth's population (Revelation 9:15-18).

He also predicts that entire islands and mountains would be blown off the map. It seems to indicate an all-out attack of ballistic missiles upon the great metropolitan areas of the world.

＊　＊　＊

The Greatest Moment

As the battle of Armageddon reaches its awful climax and it appears that all life will be destroyed on earth—in this very moment Jesus Christ will return and save man from self-extinction. As history races toward this moment, are you afraid or looking with hope for deliverance? The answer should reveal to you your spiritual condition.

One way or another history continues in a certain acceleration toward the return of Christ. Are you ready?

* 4 *

Evangelicals and Evolution before Scopes

EDITOR: *In the 1920s the most visible public symbol of the fundamentalist-modernist controversy was evolution. This was odd for two reasons. First, as we saw in chapter 2, the fundamentalist-modernist controversy was theological, not scientific. Second, in the late nineteenth century the best evangelical theologians had responded to Darwin, not with animus and opposition, but with an effort to reconcile evolution with an orthodox understanding of scripture. While these evangelicals were attempting to harmonize science and religion, the so-called warfare model for understanding the relationship of Christianity and science had been promoted by secular thinkers such as John Draper and Andrew Dickson White. Ironically, by the 1920s, many fundamentalists had adopted the warfare model for themselves, as witnessed in the Scopes trial of 1925. Even as late as the publication of* The Fundamentals *(1910–1915), the effort to reconcile evangelical theology with evolution and the effort to refute it were present within early fundamentalism. The first two selections below, by Orr and Beach, are from* The Fundamentals. *They represent the two divergent evangelical approaches to evolution.*[1]

Orr, James. "Science and Christian Faith." In *The Fundamentals*. Edited by R. A. Torrey, A. C. Dixon, and others. 1910–15. Reprint, Grand Rapids: Baker, 1970.

In many quarters the belief is industriously circulated that the advance of "science," meaning by this chiefly the physical sciences—astronomy, geology, biology, and the like—has proved damaging, if not destructive, to the claims of the Bible, and the truth of Christianity. Science and Christianity are pitted against each other. Their interests are held to be antagonistic. Books are written, like Draper's *Conflict between Religion and Science*, White's *Warfare of Science with Theology in Christendom*, and Foster's

Finality of the Christian Religion, to show that this warfare between science and religion has ever been going on, and can never in the nature of things cease till theology is destroyed, and science holds sole sway in men's minds.

This was not the attitude of the older investigators of science. Most of these were devout Christian men. Naville, in his book, *Modern Physics,* has shown that the great discoverers in science in past times were nearly always devout men. This was true of Galileo, Kepler, Bacon, and Newton; it was true of men like Faraday, Brewster, Kelvin, and a host of others in more recent times.

* * *

If by a conflict of science and religion is meant that grievous mistakes have often been made, and unhappy misunderstandings have arisen, on one side and the other, in the course of the progress of science,—that new theories and discoveries, as in astronomy and geology, have been looked on with distrust by those who thought that the truth of the Bible was being affected by them,—that in some cases the dominant church sought to stifle the advance of truth by persecution,—this is not to be denied. It is an unhappy illustration of how the best of men can at times err in matters which they imperfectly understand, or where their prejudices and traditional ideas are affected. . . . It is well in any case that this alleged conflict of Christianity with science should be carefully probed, and that it should be seen where exactly the truth lies in regard to it.

I. Science and Law—Miracle

It is perhaps more in its general outlook on the world than in its specific results that science is alleged to be in conflict with the Bible and Christianity. The Bible is a record of revelation. Christianity is a supernatural system. Miracle, in the sense of a direct entrance of God in word and deed into human history for gracious ends, is of the essence of it. On the other hand, the advance of science has done much to deepen the impression of the universal reign of natural law. The effect has been to lead multitudes whose faith is not grounded in direct spiritual experience to look askance on the whole idea of the supernatural. God, it is assumed, has His own mode of working, and that is by means of secondary agencies operating in absolutely uniform ways; miracles, therefore, cannot be admitted. And, since miracles are found in Scripture,—since the entire Book rests on the idea of a supernatural economy of grace,—the whole must be dismissed as in conflict with the modern mind. Professor G. B. Foster goes so far as to declare that a man can hardly be intellectually honest who in these days professes to believe in the miracles of the Bible.

It is overstating the case to speak of this repugnance to miracle, and rejection of it in the Bible, as if it were really new. It is as old as rationalism itself. You find it in Spinoza, in Reimarus, in Strauss, in numberless others. DeWette and Vatke, among earlier Old Testament critics, manifested it as strongly as their followers do now, and made it a pivot of their criticism. It governed the attacks on Christianity made in the age of the deists. David Hume wrote an essay against miracles which he thought had settled the question forever. But, seriously considered, can this attack on the idea of miracle, derived from our experience of the uniformity of nature's laws, be defended? Does it not in itself involve a huge assumption, and run counter to experience and common sense? The question is one well worth asking.

First, what is a miracle? Various definitions might be given, but it will be enough to speak of it here as any effect in nature, or deviation from its ordinary course, due to the interposition of a supernatural cause. It is no necessary part, it should be observed, of the Biblical idea of miracle, that natural agencies should not be employed as far as they will go. If the drying of the Red Sea to let the Israelites pass over was due in part to a great wind that blew, this was none the less of God's ordering, and did not detract from the supernatural character of the event as a whole. It was still at God's command that the waters were parted, and that a way was made at that particular time and place for the people to go through. These are what theologians call "providential" miracles, in which, so far as one can see, natural agencies, under divine direction, suffice to produce the result. There is, however, another and more conspicuous class, the instantaneous cleansing of the leper, e.g., or the raising of the dead, in which natural agencies are obviously altogether transcended. It is this class about which the chief discussion goes on. They are miracles in the stricter sense of a complete transcendence of nature's laws.

What, in the next place, is meant by the uniformity of nature? There are, of course, laws of nature—no one disputes that. It is quite a mistake to suppose that the Bible, though not written in the twentieth century, knows nothing of a regular order and system of nature. The world is God's world; it is established by His decree; He has given to every creature its nature, its bounds, its limits; all things continue according to His ordinances (Psa. 119:91). Only, law in the Bible is never viewed as having an independent existence. It is always regarded as an expression of the power or wisdom of God. And this gives the right point of view for considering the relation of law to miracle. What, to begin with, do we mean by a "law" of nature? It is, as science will concede, only our registered observation of the order in which we find causes and events linked together in our experience. That they are so linked no one questions. If they were not, we should have no world in which we could live at all. But then, next, what do we mean by "uniformity" in this connection? We mean no more than this—that, given like causes, operating under like conditions, like effects will follow. Quite true; no one denies this either.

But then, as J. S. Mill, in his *Logic*, pointed out long ago, a miracle in the strict sense is not a denial of either of these truths. A miracle is not the assertion that, the same causes operating, a different result is produced. It is, on the contrary, the assertion that a new cause has intervened, and this a cause which the theists cannot deny to be a vera causa—the will and power of God. Just as, when I lift my arm, or throw a stone high in the air, I do not abolish the law of gravitation but counteract or overrule its purely natural action by the introduction of a new spiritual force; so, but in an infinitely higher way, is a miracle due to the interposition of the First Cause of all, God Himself. What the scientific man needs to prove to establish his objection to miracle is, not simply that natural causes operate uniformly, but that no other than natural causes exist; that natural causes exhaust all the causation in the universe. And that, we hold, he can never do.

It is obvious from what has now been said that the real question at issue in miracle is not natural law, but Theism. It is to be recognized at once that miracle can only profitably be discussed on the basis of a theistic view of the universe. It is not disputed that there are views of the universe which exclude miracle. The atheist cannot admit miracle, for he has no God to work miracles. The pantheist cannot admit miracle, for to him God and nature are one. The deist cannot admit miracle, for he has separated God and the universe so far that he can never bring them together again. The question is not, Is miracle possible on an atheistic, a materialistic, a pantheistic, view of the world, but, Is it possible on a theistic view—on the view of God as at once immanent in His world, and in infinite ways transcending it? I say nothing of intellectual "honesty," but I do marvel, as I have often said, at the assurance of any one who presumes to say that, for the highest and holiest ends in His personal relations with His creatures, God can work only within the limits which nature imposes;

that He cannot act without and above nature's order if it pleases Him to do so. Miracles stand or fall by their evidence, but the attempt to rule them out by any a priori dictum as to the uniformity of natural law must inevitably fail. The same applies to the denial of providence or of answers to prayer on the ground of the uniformity of natural law. Here no breach of nature's order is affirmed, but only a governance or direction of nature of which man's own use of natural laws, without breach of them, for special ends, affords daily examples.

II. Scripture and the Special Sciences

Approaching more nearly the alleged conflict of the Bible or Christianity with the special sciences, a first question of importance is, What is the general relation of the Bible to science? How does it claim to relate itself to the advances of natural knowledge? Here, it is to be feared, mistakes are often made on both sides—on the side of science in affirming contrariety of the Bible with scientific results where none really exists; on the side of believers in demanding that the Bible be taken as a textbook of the newest scientific discoveries, and trying by forced methods to read these into them. The truth on this point lies really on the surface. The Bible clearly does not profess to anticipate the scientific discoveries of the nineteenth and twentieth centuries. Its design is very different; namely, to reveal God and His will and His purposes of grace to men, and, as involved in this, His general relation to the creative world, its dependence in all its parts on Him, and His orderly government of it in Providence for His wise and good ends. Natural things are taken as they are given, and spoken of in simple, popular language, as we ourselves every day speak of them. The world it describes is the world men know and live in, and it is described as it appears, not as, in its recondite researches, science reveals its inner constitution to us. Wise expositors of the Scriptures, older and younger, have always recognized this, and have not attempted to force its language further. To take only one example, John Calvin, who wrote before the Copernican system of astronomy had obtained common acceptance, in his commentary on the first chapter of Genesis penned these wise words: "He who would learn astronomy and other recondite arts," he said, "let him go elsewhere. Moses wrote in a popular style things which, without instruction, all ordinary persons endued with common sense are able to understand. . . . He does not call us up to heaven, he only proposes things that lie open before our eyes." To this hour, with all the light of modern science around us, we speak of sun, moon and stars "rising" and "setting," and nobody misunderstands or affirms contradiction with science. There is no doubt another side to this, for it is just as true that in depicting natural things, the Bible, through the Spirit of revelation that animates it, seizes things in so just a light—still with reference to its own purposes—that the mind is prevented from being led astray from the great truths intended to be conveyed.

* * *

If the intention of the first chapter of Genesis was really to give us the "date" of the creation of the earth and heavens, the objection would be unanswerable. But things, as in the case of astronomy, are now better understood, and few are disquieted in reading their Bibles because it is made certain that the world is immensely older than the 6,000 years which the older chronology gave it. Geology is felt only to have expanded our ideas of the vastness and marvel of the Creator's operations through the aeons of time during which the world, with its teeming populations of fishes, birds, reptiles, mammals, was preparing for man's abode—when the mountains were being upheaved, the valleys being scooped out, and veins of precious metals being inlaid into the crust of the earth.

Does science, then, really, contradict Genesis I? Not surely if what has been above said of the essentially popular character of the allusions to natural things in the Bible be remembered. Here certainly is no detailed description of the process of the formation of the earth in terms anticipative of modern science—terms which would have been unintelligible to the original readers—but a sublime picture, true to the order of nature, as it is to the broad facts even of geological succession. If it tells how God called heaven and earth into being, separated light from darkness, sea from land, clothed the world with vegetation, gave sun and moon their appointed rule of day and night, made fowl to fly, and sea-monsters to plow the deep, created the cattle and beasts of the field, and finally made man, male and female, in His own image, and established him as ruler over all God's creation, this orderly rise of created forms, man crowning the whole, these deep ideas of the narrative, setting the world at the very beginning in its right relation to God, and laying the foundations of an enduring philosophy of religion, are truths which science does nothing to subvert, but in myriad ways confirms. The "six days" may remain as a difficulty to some, but, if this is not part of the symbolic setting of the picture—a great divine "week" of work—one may well ask, as was done by

Augustine long before geology was thought of, what kind of "days" these were which rolled their course before the sun, with its twenty-four hours of diurnal measurement, was appointed to that end? There is no violence done to the narrative in substituting in thought "aeonic" days—vast cosmic periods—for "days" on our narrower, sun-measured scale. Then the last trace of apparent "conflict" disappears.

III. Evolution and Man

In recent years the point in which "conflict" between Scripture and science is most frequently urged is the apparent contrariety of the theory of evolution to the Bible story of the direct creation of the animals and man. This might be met, and often is, as happened in the previous cases, by denying the reality of any evolutionary process in nature. Here also, however, while it must be conceded that evolution is not yet proved, there seems a growing appreciation of the strength of the evidence for the fact of some form of evolutionary origin of species—that is, of some genetic connection of higher with lower forms. Together with this, at the same time, there is manifest an increasing disposition to limit the scope of evolution, and to modify the theory in very essential points—those very points in which an apparent conflict with Scripture arose.

Much of the difficulty on this subject has arisen from the unwarrantable confusion or identification of evolution with Darwinism. Darwinism is a theory of the process of evolution, and both on account of the skill with which it was presented, and of the singular eminence of its propounder, obtained for a time a very remarkable prestige. In these later days, as may be seen by consulting a book like R. Otto's *Naturalism and Religion*, published in *The Crown Library*, that prestige has greatly declined. A newer evolution has arisen which breaks with Darwin on the three points most essential to his theory: 1. The fortuitous character of the variations on which "natural selection" works. Variations are now felt to be along definite lines, and to be guided to definite ends. 2. The insufficiency of "natural selection" (on which Darwin almost wholly relied) to accomplish the tasks Darwin assigned to it. 3. The slow and insensible rate of the changes by which new species were supposed to be produced. Instead of this the newer tendency is to seek the origin of new species in rapid and sudden changes, the causes of which lie within the organism—in "mutations," as they are coming to be called—so that the process may be as brief as formerly it was supposed to belong. "Evolution," in short, is coming to be recognized as but a new name for "creation," only that the creative power now works from within, instead of, as in the old conception, in an external, plastic fashion. It is, however, creation none the less.

In truth, no conception of evolution can be formed, compatible with all the facts of science, which does not take account, at least at certain great critical points, of the entrance of new factors into the process we call creation. 1. One such point is the transition from inorganic to organic existence—the entrance of the new power of life. It is hopeless to seek to account for life by purely mechanical and chemical agencies, and science has well-nigh given up the attempt. 2. A second point is in the transition from purely organic development to consciousness. A sensation is a mental fact different in kind from any merely organic change, and inexplicable by it. Here, accordingly, is a new rise, revealing previously unknown spiritual powers. 3. The third point is in the transition to rationality, personality, and moral life in man. This, as man's capacity for self-conscious, self-directed, progressive life evinces, is something different from the purely animal consciousness, and marks the beginning of a new kingdom. Here, again, the Bible and science are felt to be in harmony. Man is the last of God's created works—the crown and explanation of the whole—and he is made in God's image. To account for him, a special act of the Creator, constituting him what he is, must be presupposed. This creative act does not relate to the soul only, for higher spiritual powers could not be put into a merely animal brain. There must be a rise on the physical side as well, corresponding with the mental advance. In body, as in spirit, man comes from his Creator's hand.

If this new evolutionary conception is accepted, most of the difficulties which beset the Darwinian theory fall away. (1) For one thing, man need no longer be thought of as a slow development from the animal stage—an ascent through brutishness and savagery from an ape-like form. His origin may be as sudden as Genesis represents. (2) The need for assuming an enormous antiquity of man to allow for the slow development is no longer felt. And (3), the need of assuming man's original condition to have been one of brutal passion and subjection to natural impulse disappears. Man may have come from his Creator's hand in as morally pure a state, and as capable of sinless development, as Genesis and Paul affirm. This also is the most worthy view to take of man's origin. It is a view borne out by the absence of all reliable evidence of those ape-like intermediate forms which, on the other hypothesis, must have intervened between the animal-progenitors and the finished human being. It is a view not contradicted by the alleged evidences of man's very great antiquity—100,000, 200,000, or 500,000 years—frequently relied on; for most of these and the extravagant measurements of time connected with them, are precarious in the extreme. The writer's book, *God's Image in Man and Its Defacement*, may be consulted on these points.

The conclusion from the whole is, that, up to the present hour, science and the Biblical views of God, man, and the world, do not stand in any real relation of conflict. Each book of God's writing reflects light upon the pages of the other, but neither contradicts the other's essential testimony. Science itself seems now disposed to take a less materialistic view of the origin and nature of things than it did a decade or two ago, and to interpret the creation more in the light of the spiritual. The experience of the Christian believer, with the work of missions in heathen lands, furnishes a testimony that cannot be disregarded to the reality of this spiritual world, and of the regenerating, transforming forces proceeding from it. To God be all the glory!

Beach, Henry H. "The Decadence of Darwinism." In *The Fundamentals*. Edited by R. A. Torrey, A. C. Dixon, and others. 1910–15. Reprint, Grand Rapids: Baker, 1970.

This paper is not a discussion of variations lying within the boundaries of heredity; nor do we remember that the Hebrew and Greek Scriptures reveal anything on that subject; nor do we think that it can be rationally discussed until species and genus are defined.

Failure to condition spontaneous generation by sterilized hay tea, and a chronic inability to discover the missing link, have shaken the popularity of Darwinism. Will it recover? Or is it falling into a fixed condition of innocuous desuetude?

As a purely academic question, who cares whether a protoplastic cell, or an amoeba, or an ascidian larva, was his primordial progenitor? It does not grip us. It is doubtful whether any purely academic question ever grips anybody. But the issue between Darwinism and mankind is not a purely academic question.

Half his life Charles Darwin was afraid of the reproaches of Christians. It was something like the fear felt by another Charles, of the reproaches of the Huguenots were he to consent to the assassination of Coligny. He refers to it in the "Introduction" to the *Descent of Man*: "During many years I collected notes on the origin and descent of man, without any intention of publishing on the subject, but rather with the determination not to publish; as I thought that I should thus add to the prejudices against my views."

At the end of the book he says: "I am aware that the conclusions arrived at in this work will be denominated by some as highly irreligious; but he who denounces them is bound to show why it is more irreligious to explain the origin of man as a distinct species by descent from some lowly form, through the laws of variation and natural selection, than to explain the birth of the individual through the laws of ordinary reproduction."

He confessed his fear by protesting his innocence: "I have done nothing—only explained a choice between two theories of bringing man into the world." This way of putting it is characteristic. He often refers to traversing the doctrine of successive creations, as the sum of his offending. The prestidigitator calls special attention to one hand while he works the trick with the other. His apprehensions were not altogether groundless.

Professor Haeckel was braver, or more rash, when he styled the *Descent of Man* as "anti-Genesis"; with equal truth and moderation he might have added, anti-John, anti-Hebrews and anti-Christ. The point to pierce the business and bosoms of men is a denial of the integrity and reliability of the Word of God. We cannot depend on the Bible to show us "how to go to heaven" if it misleads us as to "how the heavens go" regarding the origin, nature, descent and destiny of brutes and men. Darwinists have been digging at the foundations of society and souls; and their powers of endurance are a matter of some moment.

We venture to differentiate life and if we go too far are sure to be corrected:

1. Vegetable life is the sum of the forces which pervade the organism, causes it to grow and preserves it from decay.
2. Brute life is the sum of the forces which pervade the organism, causes it to grow, preserves it from decay, is conscious and thinks.
3. Human life is the sum of the forces which pervade the organism, causes it to grow, preserves it from decay, is conscious, thinks and is religious.

It is logical to assume, until disproved, that these three kinds of life touch each other, but never merge. They associate as intimately as air and light, but are as far from passing from plants to brutes and from brutes to men as from not-being to being. "By faith we understand the ages to be set in order by the saying of God, in regard to the things seen not having come out of the things manifest" (Heb. 11:3).

He who would overthrow Biblical Christianity expects to take the initiative. He recognizes that there is always a Presumption in favor of an existing institution; and has always been swift to open the battle.

Professor Huxley, in his article on evolution, in the ninth edition of the *Britannica*, has ably brought together the arguments for Darwinism; and we will follow his order.

Growth

Given a nucleated cell, and Darwinists have watched the process of generation from its beginning to birth, "with the best optical instruments," there have been two theories. The first theory is that nothing new is produced in the living world; the germs from which all organisms have developed have contained in miniature, and passed on down through successive generations, all the essential organs of adults. To get anything out of anything it must first be in it. This is archaic. The second theory is that evolution is progressive; it results from something innate in things, dynamic and pantheistic. This is up to date.

All that the Darwinists, "with the best optical instruments", have actually seen is growth; but they have inferred a whole pantheon. Natural selection is the supreme demiurge; sexual selection and variation are subordinates. A billion years ago there was a God, but He immediately disappeared. It was necessary to have Him then, to bridge the gulf between nothing and something. Having discovered growth, they called it evolution, thinking perhaps the name might prove useful, but we trust not to be blamed for preferring growth, for "evolution" is something of a harlequin, having turned a complete somersault within a hundred years, while growth is universally acknowledged to be a character of vegetable, animal, and human life.

In addition to finding natural growth, Professor Huxley claims the discovery of a "tendency to assume a definite living form." This of course is ridiculous. The sun rises with sufficient regularity to become a striking phenomenon, and we have discovered a tendency towards sunrises. Speculation is invoked, but speculation died with the great god Pan when Jesus was born. Scientific observations are dumb, except to say that all God's creatures are fearfully and wonderfully made.

Likenesses

It is settled that low adult forms and embryos of higher order are strikingly alike. An embryonic reptile passes through the transformations of a fish, and a man in the germ cannot be distinguished from any other mammal. Here the Darwinist drops his glass and jumps at the conclusion that all creations, even vegetables, are consanguined brothers. His microscope has failed him and he has forgotten the ardent astronomer who saw strange quadrupeds in the moon, until he discovered the mouse nest in the telescope. The apparently similar cells are different. The outcome proves it. One is a butterfly and the other is a whale. Indeed, Oscar Hertwig now claims to have found the differences of the denouement in the cells themselves. But it does not matter. The Darwinist has mistaken likeness for proof of parentage; as a matter of fact it never proves it. Parentage is more likely to prove likeness. In either case the origin must first be established and then the likeness may illustrate it.

* * *

But we submit a broader generalization. The whole universe bears a family resemblance. It is the warm touch of the Maker, and His universal style. Light is truth, and darkness is error. Holiness is purity, and sin is dirt. Physical birth and growth, decay and death, typify spiritual birth and growth, decay and death.

* * *

Selections

Sexual selection, as the name implies, is concerned with pairing and reproduction; but the Darwinian end in view, like that of natural selection, is evolution. But sexual selection fails to discriminate, and turns out degeneration. Feral and unregenerate sexual selection is more lust than love. From hares to elephants wild things are blinded by jealousy and crazed by heat. Like the Jukes' family, they drop their young by the highway. We domesticate brutes and plants and, with great care and skill, breed them for improved points; but we soon tire and then dogs become pariahs, cats turn vagabonds, potatoes grow small, and horses are not worth catching and breaking. Cultivated apples never repeat their parent trees, but nine hundred and ninety-nine times out of a thousand sink far below them.

The "loves of the plants," as Darwin's whimsical grandfather called them, are disreputable, and even, to this civilized day, human beings need to be restrained by law to prevent them from contracting unhealthful alliances. When the string breaks the kite falls.

* * *

To sum up the case for natural selection:

(1) It is poor morals. A theory of nature must be ideal to be true. Natural selection is a scheme for the survival of the passionate and the violent, the destruction of the weak and defenseless. To be true, black must be white, and wrong must be right, and God an Ivan the terrible.

(2) Its assumptions are false. It is false that unlimited attenuation of the steps of the process, and unlimited time for the accomplishment of it, assure us that it might have been possible. "Attenuation" and "time" would have been but conditions, not causes. They could prove nothing.

It is false that in the struggle for existence the "fittest" survive. The "fittest" is an ambiguous word. With natural selection it means the strongest and best armed. They do not survive; they degenerate and expire. They who bear arms challenge attack. This providence may be penal or corrective.

It is false that man is derived from a brute and a brute from a vegetable. One of the forces of human life makes for a recognition of God and a consciousness of sin against Him. This was not unfolded from anthropoid apes, for it is not in them. Brutes are distinguished from plants by self-consciousness, and this was not developed from plants, for it is not in them.

(3) Natural selection is self-contradictory and impossible. Fifty years ago, Alfred Russel Wallace devised the scheme and wrote Charles Darwin about it. Mr. Darwin published the plan. He afterwards refers to Mr. Wallace as having "an innate genius for solving difficulties" (Descent," p. 344). Two years ago, Mr. Wallace, in an address at the Darwin anniversary, before the Royal Institution in London, referring to Professor Haeckel said: "These unavailing efforts seem to lead us to the irresistible conclusion that beyond and above all terrestrial agencies, there is some great source of energy and guidance, which in unknown ways pervades every form of organized life, and which we ourselves are the ultimate and foreordained outcome."

Thus an author of the theory, himself, admits the contradiction of claiming a "selection" and denying a selector.

* * *

The teaching of Darwinism, as an approved science, to the children and youth of the schools of the world is the most deplorable feature of the whole wretched propaganda. It would be difficult to fix the responsibility of it. Darwin himself hesitated. Virchow tried, nobly, to protect the primary schools of Germany. The burden of his lecture at Munich is throughout a caution against evading the distinction between the problematical and the proven; they are not on the same evidential level. "He would teach," he said, "evolution, if it were only proven; it is, as yet, in the hypothetical stage; the audience ought to be warned that the speculative is only the possible, not actual truth; that it belongs to the region of belief, and not to that of demonstration. As long as a problem continues in the speculative stage, it would be mischievous to teach it in our schools. We ought not to represent our conjecture as a certainty, nor our hypothesis as a doctrine." Haeckel, always rash, advocated it. As they struggled, somebody lighted the fire. It was like the burning of the temple at Jerusalem. Titus had issued an order to spare it, but a Roman soldier threw a blazing torch into a small window and the whole structure was in flames. It was like the revenge of the Pied Piper of Hamlin Town. It was "Rachel weeping for her children, and she would not be comforted, because they were not."

* * *

EDITOR: *The next selection is the speech William Jennings Bryan prepared for the Scopes trial of 1925 where John Thomas Scopes was found guilty of teaching evolution in violation of Tennessee law. Scopes was fined. In the famous play and film* Inherit the Wind, *an addled Brady, the Bryan character, attempts to give the speech in the courtroom after the judge has adjourned the trial. With no one paying any attention to his rantings, Brady becomes increasingly exasperated then falls over dead in the courtroom. Like much of the play and film, this scene is fictional. Bryan never gave his speech during the trial. Rather, he delivered the speech at various locations in the days following and then died one week after the trial.*

Note Bryan's reasons for opposing the teaching of evolution in schools. Biblical literalism makes up only part of his argument. When questioned by defense attorney Clarence Darrow during the trial, the real trial, Bryan admitted to believing that the days of Genesis may not be literal twenty-four-hour days. Like many fundamentalists in the 1920s, he interpreted Genesis in such a way that the age of the earth was not an issue. Rather, Bryan seemed most concerned about the potential for evolution to undercut the moral basis for human behavior.

Bryan, William Jennings. "Closing Statement of William Jennings Bryan at the Trial of John Scopes." Given in Dayton, Tennessee, 1925.

May it please the Court, and gentlemen of the jury:

Demosthenes, the greatest of ancient orators, in his "oration on the crown," the most famous of his speeches, began by supplicating the favor of all the gods and goddesses of Greece. If, in a case which involved only his own fame and fate, he felt justified in petitioning the heathen gods of his country, surely we, who deal with the momentous issues involved in this case, may well pray to the Ruler of the universe for wisdom to guide us in the performance of our several parts in this historic trial.

* * *

Let us now separate the issues from the misrepresentations, intentional or unintentional, that have obscured both the letter and the purpose of the law. This is not an interference with freedom of conscience. A teacher can think as he pleases and worship God as he likes, or refuse to worship God at all. He can believe in the Bible or discard it; he can accept Christ or reject Him. This law places no obligations or restraints upon him. And so with freedom of speech, he can, so long as he acts as an individual, say anything he likes on any subject. This law does not violate any rights guaranteed by any Constitution to any individual. It deals with the defendant, not as an individual, but as an employee, official or public servant, paid by the State, and therefore under instructions from the State.

The right of the State to control the public schools is affirmed in the recent decision in the Oregon case, which declares that the State can direct what shall be taught and also forbid the teaching of anything "manifestly inimical to the public welfare." The above decision goes even further and declares that the parent not only has the right to guard the religious welfare of the child but is in duty bound to guard it. That decision fits this case exactly. The State had a right to pass this law and the law represents the determination of the parents to guard the religious welfare of their children.

It need hardly be added that this law did not have its origin in bigotry. It is not trying to force any form of religion on anybody. The majority is not trying to establish a religion or to teach it—it is trying to protect itself from the effort of an insolent minority to force irreligion upon the children under the guise of teaching science. What right has a little irresponsible oligarchy of self styled "intellectuals" to demand control of the schools of the United States; in which twenty-five millions of children are being educated at an annual expense of nearly two billions of dollars?

Christians must, in every State of the Union build their own colleges in which to teach Christianity; it is duly simple justice that atheists, agnostics and unbelievers should build their own colleges if they want to teach their own religious views or attack the religious views of others.

The statute is brief and free from ambiguity. It prohibits the teaching, in the public schools, of "any theory that denies the story of divine creation as taught in the Bible," and teaches, instead, that man descended from a lower order of animals. The first sentence sets forth the purpose of those who passed the law. They forbid the teaching of any evolutionary theory that disputes the Bible record of man's creation and, [to] make sure that there shall be no misunderstanding, they place their own interpretation on their language and specifically forbid the teaching of any theory that makes man a descendant of any lower form of life.

* * *

Religion is not hostile to learning; Christianity has been the greatest patron learning has ever had. But Christians know that "the fear of the Lord is the beginning of wisdom" now just as it has been in the past, and they therefore oppose the teaching of guesses that encourage godlessness among the students.

* * *

Christianity welcomes truth from whatever source it comes and is not afraid that any real truth from any source can interfere with the divine truth that comes by inspiration from God Himself. It is not scientific truth to which Christians object, for true science is classified knowledge, and nothing therefore can be scientific unless it is true.

Evolution is not truth; it is merely a hypothesis—it is millions of guesses strung together. It had not been proven in the days of Darwin—he expressed astonishment that with two or three million species it had been impossible to trace any species to any other species—it had not been proven in the days of Huxley, and it has not been proven up to today. It is less than four years ago that Professor Bateson came all the way from London to Canada to tell the American scientists that every effort to trace one species to another had failed—every one. He said he still had faith in evolution but had doubts about the origin of species. But of what value is evolution if it cannot explain the origin of species? While many scientists accept evolution as if it were a fact, they all admit, when questioned, that no explanation has been found as to how one species developed into another.

Darwin suggested two laws, sexual selection and natural selection. Sexual selection has been laughed out of the classroom and natural selection is being abandoned, and no new explanation is satisfactory even to scientists. Some of the more rash advocates of evolution are wont to say that evolution is as firmly established as the law of gravitation or the Copernican theory. The absurdity of such a claim is apparent when we remember that any one can prove the law of gravitation by throwing a weight into the air and that any one can prove the roundness of the earth by going around it, while no one can prove evolution to be true in any way whatever.

* * *

Most of the people who believe in evolution do not know what evolution means. One of the science books taught in the Dayton High School has a chapter on the "The Evolution of Machinery." This is a very common misuse of the term. People speak of the evolution of the telephone, the automobile and the musical instrument. But these are merely illustrations of man's power to deal intelligently with inanimate matter; there is no growth from within in the development of machinery.

Equally improper is the [use] of the word "evolution" to describe the growth of a plant from a seed, the growth of a chicken from an egg, or the development of any form of animal life from a single cell. All these give us a circle, not a change from one species to another.

Evolution—the evolution in this case, and the only evolution that is a matter of controversy anywhere—is the evolution taught by defendant, set forth in the books now prohibited by the new State law, and illustrated in the diagram printed on page 194 of Hunter's *Civic Biology*. The author estimates the number of species in the animal kingdom at 518,900. These are divided into eighteen classes and each class is indicated on the diagram by a circle, proportionate in size to the number of species in each class and attached by a stem to the trunk of the tree. It begins with protozoa and ends with the mammals. Passing over the classes with which the average man is unfamiliar, let me call your attention to a few of the larger and better-known groups. The insects are numbered at three hundred and sixty thousand, over two-thirds of the total number of species in the animal world. The fishes are numbered at thirteen thousand, the amphibians at fourteen hundred, the reptiles at thirty-five hundred, and the birds at thirteen thousand, while thirty-five hundred mammals are crowded together in a little circle that is barely higher than the bird circle. No circle is reserved for man alone. He is, according to the diagram, shut up in the little circle entitled "mammals," with 3,499 other species of mammals. Does it not seem a little unfair not to distinguish between that and lower forms of life? What shall we say of the intelligence, not to say religion, of those who are so particular to distinguish between fishes and reptiles and birds but put a man with an immortal soul in the same circle with the wolf, the hyena and the skunk? What must be the impression made upon children by such a degradation of man?

In the preface of this book the author explains that it is for children and adds that "the boy or girl of average ability upon admission to the secondary school is not a thinking individual." Whatever may be said in favor of teaching evolution to adults it surely is not proper to teach it to children who are not yet able to think.

The evolutionist does not undertake to tell us how protozoa, moved by interior and resident forces, sent life up through all the various species, and cannot prove that there was actually any such compelling power at all. And yet the school children are asked to accept their guesses and build a philosophy of life upon them. If it were not so serious a matter, one might be tempted to speculate upon the various degrees of relationship that, according to evolutionists exist between man and other forms of life. It might require some very nice calculation to determine at what degree of relationship the killing of a relative ceases to be murder and the eating of one's kin ceases to be cannibalism.

But it is not a laughing matter when one considers that evolution not only offers no suggestions as to a Creator but tends to put the creative act so far away as to cast doubt upon creation itself. And, while it is shaking faith in God as a beginning, it is also creating doubt as to a heaven at the end of life. Evolutionists do not feel that it is incumbent upon them to show how life began or at what point in their long drawn out scheme of changing species man became endowed with hope and promise of immortal life. God may be a matter of indifference to the evolutionists, and a life beyond may have no charm for them, but the mass of mankind will continue to worship their Creator and continue to find comfort in the promise of their Saviour that he has gone to prepare a place for them.

Christ has made of death a narrow, star-lit strip between the companionship of yesterday and the reunion of tomorrow; evolution strikes out the stars and deepens the gloom that enshrouds the tomb.

If the results of evolution were unimportant, one might require less proof in support of the hypothesis; but, before accepting a new philosophy of life built upon a materialistic foundation, we have reason to demand something more than guesses: "we may well suppose" is not a sufficient substitute for "thus saith the Lord."

* * *

Our first indictment against evolution is that it disputes the truth of the Bible account of man's creation and shakes faith in the Bible as the word of God. This indictment we prove by comparing the processes described as evolutionary with the text of Genesis. It not only contradicts the Mosaic record as to the beginning of human life, but it disputes the Bible doctrine of reproduction according to kind—the greatest scientific principle known.

Our second indictment is that the evolutionary hypothesis, carried to its logical conclusion, disputes every vital truth of the Bible. Its tendency, natural, if not inevitable, is to lead those who really accept it, first to agnosticism and then to atheism. Evolutionists attack the truth of the Bible, not openly at first, but by using weasel-words like "poetical," "symbolical" and "allegorical" to suck the meaning out of the inspired record of man's creation.

We call as our first witness Charles Darwin. He began life a Christian. On Page 39, Vol. I, of the *Life and Letters of Charles Darwin*, by his son, Francis Darwin, he says, speaking of the period from 1828 to 1831: "I did not then in the least doubt the strict and literal truth of every word in the Bible." On Page 412 of Vol. II of the same publication, he says: "When I was collecting facts for the *Origin* my belief in what is called a personal God was as firm as that of Dr. Pusey himself." It may be a surprise to your Honor and to you, gentlemen of the jury, as it was to me, to learn that Darwin spent three years at Cambridge studying for the ministry.

This was Darwin as a young man, before he came under the influence of the doctrine that man came from a lower order of animals. The change wrought in his religious views will be found in a letter written to a German youth in 1879 and printed on Page 277 of Vol. I of the *Life and Letters* above referred to. The letter begins, "I am much engaged, an old man, and but of health, and I cannot spare time to answer your questions fully—nor indeed can they be answered. Science has nothing to do with Christ, except in so far as the habit of scientific research makes a man cautious in admitting evidence." For myself, I do not believe that there ever has been any revelation. As for a future life, every man must judge for himself between conflicting vague probabilities."

Note that "science has nothing to do with Christ, except in so far as the habit of scientific research makes a man cautious in admitting evidence." Stated plainly, that simply means that "the habit of scientific research" makes one cautious in accepting the only evidence that we have of Christ's existence, mission, teachings, crucifixion and resurrection, namely the evidence found in the Bible. To make this interpretation of his words the only possible one, he adds "for myself, I do not believe that there ever has been any revelation," in rejecting the Bible as a revelation from God, he rejects the Bible's conception of God, and he rejects also the supernatural Christ of whom the Bible, and the Bible alone, tells. And, it will be observed, he refuses to express any opinion as to a future life.

* * *

Here is the explanation: [Darwin] drags man down to the brute level, and then, judging man by brute standards, he questions whether man's mind can be trusted to deal with "God and immortality"!

How can any teacher tell his students that evolution does not tend to destroy his religious faith? How can an honest teacher conceal from his students the effect of evolution upon Darwin himself? And is it not stranger still that preachers who advocate evolution never speak of Darwin's loss of faith, due to his belief in evolution? The parents of Tennessee have reason enough to fear the effect of evolution upon the minds of their children. Belief in evolution cannot bring to those who hold such a belief any compensation for the loss of faith in God, trust in the Bible, and belief in the supernatural character of Christ. It is belief in evolution that has caused so many scientists and so many Christians to reject the miracles of the Bible, and then give up, one after another, every vital truth of Christianity. They finally cease to pray and sunder the tie that binds them to their Heavenly Father.

* * *

But I have some more evidence of the effect of evolution upon the life of those who accept it and try to harmonize their thought with it.

James H. Leuba, a professor of psychology at Bryn Mawr College, Pennsylvania, published a few years ago a book entitled *Belief in God and Immortality*. In this book he relates how he secured the opinions of scientists as to the existence of a personal God and a personal immortality. He used a volume entitled *American Men of Science*, which he says included the names of "practically every American who may properly be called a scientist." There were fifty-five hundred names in the book. He selected one thousand names as representative of the fifty-five hundred and addressed them personally. Most of them, he said, were teachers in schools of higher learning. The names were kept confidential. Upon the answers received, he asserts that over half of them doubt or deny the existence of a personal God and a personal immortality, and he asserts that unbelief increases in proportion to prominence, the percentage of unbelief being greatest among the most prominent. Among biologists, believers in a personal God numbered less than 31 per cent, while believers in a personal immortality numbered only 37 per cent.

He also questioned the students in nine colleges of high rank and from 1,000 answers received, 97 per cent of which were from students between 18 and 20, he found that unbelief increased from 18 per cent in the freshman class up to 40 to 45 per cent among the men who graduated. On Page 280 of this book we read: "The students' statistics show that young people enter college possessed of the beliefs still accepted, more or less perfunctorily, in the average home of the land, and gradually abandon the cardinal Christian beliefs." This change from belief to unbelief he attributes to the influence of the persons "of high culture under whom they studied."

The people of Tennessee have been patient enough; they acted none too soon. How can they expect to protect society, and even the Church, from the deadening influence of agnosticism and atheism if they permit the teachers employed by taxation to poison the minds of the youth with this destructive doctrine? And remember that the law has not heretofore required the writing of the word "poison" on poisonous doctrines. The bodies of our people are so valuable that druggists and physicians must be careful to properly label all poisons. Why not be as careful to protect the spiritual life of our people from the poisons that kill the soul?

There is a test that is sometimes used to ascertain whether one suspected of mental infirmity is really insane. He is put into a tank of water and told to dip the tank dry while a stream of water flows into the tank. If he has not sense enough to turn off the water, he is adjudged insane.

Can parents justify themselves if, knowing the effect of belief in evolution, they permit irreligious teachers to inject skepticism and infidelity in the minds of their children?

Do bad doctrines corrupt the morals of students? We have a case in point, Mr. Darrow, one of the most distinguished criminal lawyers in our land, was engaged about a year ago in defending two rich men's sons who were on trial for as dastardly a murder as was ever committed. The older one, "Babe" Leopold, was a brilliant student, 19 years old. He was an evolutionist and an atheist. He was also a follower of Nietzsche, whose books he had devoured and whose philosophy he had adopted. Mr. Darrow made a plea for him, based upon the influence that Nietzsche's philosophy had exerted upon the boy's mind. Here are the extracts from his speech:

* * *

"If this boy is to blame for this, where did he get it? Is there any blame attached because somebody took Nietzsche's philosophy seriously and fashioned his life upon it? And there is no question in this case but what that is true. Then who is to blame? The university would be more to blame than he is; the scholars of the world would be more to blame than he is. The publishers of the words . . . are more to blame than he is. Your Honor, it is hardly fair to hang a 19-year-old boy for the philosophy that was taught him at the university. It does not meet my ideas of justice and fairness to visit upon his head the philosophy that has been taught by university men for twenty-five years."

* * *

This is a damnable philosophy, and yet it is the flower that blooms on the stalk of evolution. Mr. Darrow thinks the universities are in duty bound to feed out this poisonous stuff to their students, and when the students become stupefied by it and commit murder neither they nor the universities are to blame. I am sure, your Honor, and gentlemen of the jury, that you agree with me when I protest against the adoption of any such a philosophy in the State of Tennessee. A criminal is not relieved from responsibility merely because he found Nietzsche's philosophy in a library which ought not to contain it. Neither is the university guiltless if it permits such corrupting nourishment to be fed to the souls that are entrusted to its care. But go a step further: Would the State be blameless if it permitted the universities under its control to be turned into training schools for

murderers? When you get back to the root of this question, you will find
that the Legislature not only had a right to protect the students from the
evolutionary hypothesis, but was in duty bound to do so.

* * *

Our third indictment against evolution is that it diverts attention from
pressing problems of great importance to trifling speculations. While one
evolutionist is trying to imagine what happened in the dim past, another
is trying to pry open the door of the distant future. One recently grew
eloquent over ancient worms and another predicted that 75,000 years
hence every one will be bald and toothless. Both those who endeavor to
clothe our remote ancestors with hair and those who endeavor to remove
the hair from the heads of our remote descendants ignore the present,
with its imperative demands.

The science of "How to Live" is the most important of all the sciences;
but it is necessary to know how to live. Christians desire that their children shall be taught all the sciences, but they do not want them to lose
sight of the Rock of Ages while they study the age of the rocks; neither
do they desire them to become so absorbed in measuring the distance between the stars that they will forget Him who holds the stars in His hand.

While not more than 2 per cent of our population are college gradu-
ates, these, because of enlarged powers, need a "heavenly vision" even
more than those less learned, both for their own restraint and to assure
society that their enlarged powers will be used for the benefit of society
and not against the public welfare.

Evolution is deadening the spiritual life of a multitude of students.
Christians do not desire less education, but they desire that religion shall
be entwined with learning so that our boys and girls will return from
college with their hearts aflame with love of God and love of fellowmen,
and prepared to lead in the altruistic work that the world so sorely needs.
The cry in the business world, in the industrial world, in the professional
world, in the political world—even in the religious world—is for consecrated talents—for ability plus a passion for service.

Our fourth indictment against the evolutionary hypothesis is that, by
paralyzing the hope of reform, it discourages those who labor for the
improvement of man's condition. Every upward-looking man or woman
seeks to lift the level upon which mankind stands, and they trust that they
will see beneficent changes during the brief span of their own lives. Evolution chills their enthusiasm by substituting eons for years. It obscures

all beginnings in the mists of endless ages. It is represented as a cold and heartless process, beginning with time and ending in eternity, and acting so slowly that even the rocks cannot preserve a record of the imaginary changes through which it is credited with having carried an original germ of life that appeared some time from somewhere. Its only program for man is scientific breeding, a system under which a few supposedly superior intellects, self-appointed, would direct the mating and the movements of the mass of mankind—an impossible system. Evolution, disputing the miracle, and ignoring the spiritual in life, has no place for the regeneration of the individual. It recognizes no cry of repentance and scoffs at the doctrine that one can be born again.

* * *

Our fifth indictment of the evolutionary hypothesis is that, if taken seriously and made the basis of a philosophy of life, it would eliminate love and carry man back to a struggle of tooth and claw. The Christians who have allowed themselves to be deceived into believing that evolution is a beneficient, or even a rational process have been associating with those who either do not understand its implications or dare not avow their knowledge of these implications.

* * *

Can any Christian remain indifferent? Science needs religion, to direct its energies and to inspire with lofty purpose those who employ the forces that are unloosed by science. Evolution is at war with religion because religion is supernatural; it is therefore the relentless foe of Christianity, which is a revealed religion.

Let us, then, hear the conclusion of the whole matter. Science is a magnificent material force, but it is not a teacher of morals. It can perfect machinery, but it adds no moral restraints to protect society from the misuse of the machine. It can also build gigantic intellectual ships, but it constructs no moral rudders or the control of storm-tossed human vessels. It not only fails to supply the spiritual element needed, but some of its unproven hypotheses rob the ship of its compass and thus endanger its cargo.

* * *

The world needs a savior more than it ever did before and there is only one "Name under Heaven given among men whereby we must be saved."

It is this Name that evolution degrades, for, carried to its logical conclusion, it robs Christ of the glory of a virgin birth, of the majesty of His deity and mission, and of the triumph of His resurrection. It also disputes the doctrine of the atonement.

* * *

Again force and love meet face to face, and the question, "What shall I do with Jesus?" must be answered. A bloody, brutal doctrine—evolution—demands, as the rabble did 1,900 years ago, that He be crucified. That cannot be the answer of this jury, representing a Christian state and sworn to uphold the laws of Tennessee. Your answer will be heard throughout the world; it is eagerly awaited by a praying multitude. If the law is nullified, there will be rejoicing wherever God is repudiated, the Saviour scoffed at and the Bible ridiculed. Every unbeliever of every kind and degree will be happy. If, on the other hand, the law is upheld and the religion of the school children protected, millions of Christians will call you blessed and, with hearts full of gratitude to God, will sing again that grand old song of triumph:

> Faith of our fathers, living still,
> In spite of dungeon, fire and sword;
> O, how our hearts beat high with joy,
> Whene'er we hear that glorious word;
> Faith of our fathers—holy faith–
> We will be true to thee till death!

5

Evangelicals and Science
after Scopes

EDITOR: *In the three decades after the Scopes trial, the strategy of fundamentalists began to shift from antievolution to pro-Creation Science. This was especially so after the Supreme Court struck down all antievolution laws in the 1967 case* Epperson v. Arkansas. *During the decades leading up to that case, John Whitcomb Jr. and Henry Morris developed the theory that came to be known as Creation Science as an alternative to Darwinian evolution. Creation Science is part of "flood geology," which was first developed by a Seventh-day Adventist pop scientist named George McGready Price (1870–1963). Creation Science proponents teach that the Old Testament event known as Noah's flood is responsible for the earth's geologic strata, giving the appearance that the earth is ancient when in fact the earth is less than ten thousand years old and was created pretty much as we see it today. The selection below is from Morris, who received his Ph.D. in hydraulics from the University of Minnesota in 1950 and then taught at his alma mater, Rice University, the University of Louisiana-Lafayette, and Virginia Tech during his long academic career. Morris and his associate Whitcomb built on Price's flood geology, developing modern Creation Science. While Creation Science proponents have continued to develop their theories in increasingly sophisticated ways, the broad outlines of the Creation Science critique of evolution are as outlined below by Morris.*

Morris, Henry M. "The Meaning of Evolution." In *Evolution and the Modern Christian*. Phillipsburg: Presbyterian and Reformed Publishing Company, 1967. 11–20. Used by permission.

"Why should Christians be concerned with evolution? Assuming that God is really the one who began it all, what difference does it make whether He created the world instantaneously or allowed everything to develop gradually over long ages? Isn't it more important for the Christian to be involved in present-day issues and to concentrate on living a fruitful Christian life than it is to worry and argue about the distant past?" These objections and others like them are frequently heard in modern Christian circles, especially among high school and college young people. On the surface they seem to make good sense. Surely one's present activity and future destiny are much more important than his primeval origin. Or so it would seem.

But when one begins to study the question, not just on the surface but beneath the surface as well, he soon realizes that this problem of origins is not a secondary issue at all but rather one of profound importance. One's beliefs concerning origins will inevitably condition his beliefs concerning intrinsic meanings and ultimate destinies. The modern intellectual and social climate has been in large measure the product of a century or more of evolutionary philosophy. The various modern issues confronting young people—problems of war and peace, racial conflicts, the so-called "new" morality, nationalism versus world federalism, communism, and others—are all closely related to the old conflict between creationism and evolutionism.

Importance of Evolution

A recent manifesto (H. J. Muller: "Is Biological Evolution a Principle of Nature that Has Been Well Established by Science?" . . . circulated by world-renowned geneticist, H. J. Muller, and signed by 177 American biologists), asserts unequivocally that the organic evolution of all living things, man included, from primitive life forms and even ultimately from non-living materials, is a fact of science as well established as the fact that the earth is round! The widely-accepted Biological Sciences Curriculum Study high school biology textbooks, financed by the National Science Foundation, have organized their entire treatment of biological science around the assumed evolutionary framework of life history. In fact, al-most all the books and articles on biology published by secular publishers for at least the past two generations have been written from evolutionary presuppositions.

The obvious fact that most biologists are committed to the evolution-ary philosophy is, of course, a major factor in the reluctance of young Christians and of educated people generally to take a stand in favor of Biblical creationism. In this modern scientific age, one just does not op-pose science! Furthermore, this commitment to evolution is not confined to biologists. Most astronomers, for example, assume that the universe is continually evolving, and much of their work is directed to an understanding of "stellar evolution." The geologist utilizes evolution as the main tool in his interpretation of the earth's physical history. Even physicists and chemists often think in terms of a primeval evolution of the chemical elements and molecules from basic particles.

But if the concept of evolution is widespread in the physical and biological sciences, it is even more influential in the social sciences and the humanities, and it is these fields of study that most directly impinge on man's daily thoughts and activities. Sociology, psychology, economics, literature, the fine arts—these and others of the "liberal arts" have direct bearing on our everyday concerns and decisions, our morals and recreations.

It is thus highly significant that these "social sciences," as well as the "humanities," are now nearly always taught in an evolutionary framework. It is generally assumed nowadays that the Biblical record of origins is "prescientific," at best only allegorical and certainly not literal and historical. The Biblical teachings of man's responsibility to his Creator, the fact of sin and the fall of man, and the necessity of redemption and regeneration, have all been set aside in favor of the concepts of evolutionary progress, of universal struggle and natural selection, of man's genetic kinship with the animals, of a "this-life-only" approach to social problems, and of humanistic, rather than theistic, criteria for decision- making in every area of life.

Nor is this evolutionary emphasis confined to the secular realm. The theology of most religious denominations has long since been adapted to the perspective of evolution, especially among religious "liberals." The concept of theistic evolution (or, what amounts to almost the same thing, "progressive creation") is widely accepted, according to which evolution is God's "method of creation." The Genesis record is not considered to be actual history, but rather a "cosmogonic myth," or perhaps an "allegory" or "poem." In fact, the entire Bible is taken simply as one religious book among others, the record of the religious and cultural evolution of the Hebrews and early Christians. It is said to contain much of lasting moral and religious value but also much which is unacceptable in the enlightened world of the twentieth century. The "liberal" Christian, therefore, is concerned much more with the continuing evolution of the social order (e.g., the labor movement, civil rights, welfare legislation, etc.) than he is with the defense and propagation of the gospel.

The evolution virus has infected even the sphere of evangelical Christianity. Especially is this true among the "new evangelicals," who have been diligently laboring for the past quarter of a century to render Biblical Christianity more palatable to modern tastes. Many once strongly fundamental schools, seminaries, publications, and even mission boards have in the past decade or so accepted evolution in greater or lesser degree and have sought to accommodate the Biblical record to this assumption.

But of special significance is the fact that the various movements and philosophies of the present day which have been in formal opposition to Biblical Christianity have all based their claims for validity on the supposed historical fact of evolutionary struggle and progress. This is especially true for the systems of Communism and Nazism, for the amoral psychologies of behaviorism and Freudianism, and for the religious philosophies of existentialism and the "death of God."

For these, among many other, reasons, it ought to be obvious that no serious Christian can properly ignore the evolution question. It is not some sort of peripheral issue of little relevance to the demands of the Christian life, but rather it has profound effect, whether he realizes it or not, in every area of his life. It is not too much to say that the evolutionary philosophy, consistently accepted and applied, squarely contradicts Biblical Christianity in every essential feature. It is therefore extremely important that Christians, especially young people, be well informed on the evidences for and against evolution, as well as its significance in light of the Biblical revelation.

The Evidential Basis

One would suppose that a theory of such universal acceptance and influence must be supported by innumerable and incontrovertible evidences. This, indeed, is what its proponents claim.

However, when we seek to examine these evidences in detail, we begin to encounter problems. Professor Muller in the manifesto mentioned previously says concerning these evidences for evolution: "It would be impossible in a few hours to make clear the significance and the weight of this great mass of extraordinary and intricate findings, to persons not already possessed of a considerable biological background. In fact, even they could hardly grasp them in full without long and deep study, preferably extending over years."

If this judgment is true, then, of course, ordinary laymen, without the advantages of years of graduate work and deep study in the biological sciences, could not hope to evaluate the significance of the proffered evidences for evolution. Consequently we are supposed to leave decisions of this sort up to the experts. If Dr. Muller and his colleagues say evolution is true, then it must be true. They say so; it is presumptuous of us to raise questions! If this means that the Bible is false, that the God-idea is dead, that Communism is the next stage of evolutionary history, and that men are merely animals who have learned to understand and control their own future evolution, then so be it. The authorities have decreed what we are to believe and that is that!

Fortunately, however, biological textbooks commonly do at least enumerate and briefly discuss the various lines of evidence that supposedly prove evolution to be a fact. Thus, even though we have been forewarned that we are not qualified to weigh the merits of these evidences, we can at least ascertain what they are. The listings vary somewhat from one book to another but the following constitute at least the main lines of evidence.

(1) Evidence from Classification. The fact that it is possible to arrange the various kinds of plants and animals into categories of species, genera, families, orders, etc., is supposed to suggest that there are genetic relationships between them.

(2) Evidence from Comparative Anatomy. Similarities in skeletal structure, such as between apes and men or horses and elephants, are assumed to imply evolutionary kinship.

(3) Evidence from Embryology. Similarities in embryos of different kinds of animals and the supposed "evolutionary" growth of the embryo into the adult animal are taken as evidence that the animals are related and that they have passed through an analogous evolutionary development into their present forms during the geologic past.

(4) Evidence from Biochemistry. The fact that all living organisms are composed of certain basic chemical substances (amino acids, proteins, deoxyribose nucleic acid, etc.) is supposed to prove that all living organisms have a common ancestry.

(5) Evidence from Physiology. Certain similarities in physiological factors, especially blood precipitates, and of behavior characteristics are offered as further evidences of genetic kinships.

(6) Evidence from Geographical Distribution. The tendency of certain kinds of plants and animals to vary in character with geographic location, and especially to assume distinct characteristics when

isolated from similar populations in other regions, is presumed to suggest evolution.

(7) Evidence from Vestigial Organs. Certain supposedly useless structures and organs (e.g., the appendix in man) are believed to represent "vestiges" of characters which were once useful and functional in a previous evolutionary stage.

(8) Evidence from Breeding Experiments. The many new varieties of plants and animals that have been developed by hybridization and other breeding techniques are taken as indicative of the evolutionary potential implicit in living organisms, which presumably has been realized over the geologic ages through the mechanism of "natural selection," just as "artificial selection" has been used by man to develop new varieties.

(9) Evidence from Mutations. The observed fact that entirely new varieties or species suddenly appear in a particular organism (or "population" of organisms) is offered as the best present-day visual proof of evolution; these new characteristics are called "mutations" and it is said that, if these turn out to be favorable, they will be preserved by natural selection and thus contribute to the long-term evolutionary process.

(10) Evidence from Paleontology. The fossil record of former living things, as preserved in the sedimentary rocks of the earth's crust, is offered as an actual documented history of organic evolution, with the degree of complexity of the fossils supposedly increasing with the passage of geologic time, thus marking the gradual development of the present organic world from primitive and simple beginnings about a billion years ago.

With these ten major lines of evidence, taken from ten important fields of science, it does seem at first that the evidence for evolution is indeed very strong.

However, upon closer examination, it is evident that these are all circumstantial, rather than demonstrative, evidences. It is therefore possible that some other explanation can account for them as well as, or better than, the theory of evolution.

Thus the first five evidences listed above are merely evidences of similarities of one kind or another. Such similarities can surely be understood in terms of creation by a common Creator, even better than in terms of evolutionary kinships.

The next four evidences call attention to the fact that certain biological changes can and do take place. But again, this obvious fact can be explained equally well in terms of the special creation of all the basic "kinds" of organisms, with provision in their respective genetic structures for such variations as might be required in the future for adaptation to different environments.

It is only the last of the evidences, that from paleontology, that purports to present actual historical proof of evolution on a large scale. But even this evidence, which is by far the most important of all the supposed evidences for evolution, is also really only circumstantial in nature. The fact that two different assemblages of organisms may have lived during two different epochs of geologic history does not by any means prove that one group evolved into the other group.

Thus none of the ten evidences necessarily prove evolution. And when we examine the respective evidences still more closely, as we shall do in later chapters, we shall find that there are almost insuperable difficulties with the evolutionary explanation of each of the different evidences. They can all be understood much better in terms of special creation than in terms of evolution.

The belligerent commitment to the evolutionary philosophy on the part of so many intellectuals today is, therefore, not due to the idea that there is no other satisfying explanation of the biological world but rather due to the fact that they prefer to believe in evolution! The only alternative to an evolutionary origin for the universe and its life is that of creation. And since creation is assumed to be outside the sphere of scientific study, evolution is chosen as the only alternative.

As a matter of fact, the entire question of origins (whether by creation or evolution) is really outside the domain of science, not being susceptible to scientific experimentation and analysis. Knowledge of origins must come from outside of science—it is, therefore, not really a scientific question at all. This will be discussed more fully later. Suffice it to say for the present that only the Creator—God Himself—can tell us what is the truth about the origin of all things. And this He has done, in the Bible, if we are willing simply to believe what He has told us.

EDITOR: *Following on the heels of Creation Science, developing from the 1980s to the present, is the movement known as Intelligent Design (ID). A small cadre of scientists, engineers, and philosophers have argued that there are biological organisms that are irreducibly complex—that is, they serve no function until fully assembled and therefore cannot have evolved. The analogy is that of a mousetrap. A mousetrap could not have evolved through natural selection because it can serve no function until fully assembled. The base of a mousetrap would not acquire a spring in order to be more functionally efficient because the base of the mousetrap has no function until all the other components are assembled. So it is, ID theorists argue, with many molecular entities. Evolution depends on a lower but still useful form of life evolving toward a higher form. This is impossible when the lower form, say the base of the mousetrap, serves no biological function at all. Rather than showing evidence of having evolved bit by bit over time, such molecular structures seem to indicate that they appeared intact, ready to function. This is evidence of design, also called "the design inference."*

Some ID proponents do not argue against evolution per se but against evolution as an adequate theory for explaining all of life. Moreover, while most ID proponents are Christians, they claim that ID is a science and therefore makes no claims about a designer. Rather, ID claims merely that some life forms show evidence of having been designed. Theories about who or what designed them are beyond the realm of science. Below are two texts from William Dembski, the most famous and controversial ID theorist. With Ph.D.s in both mathematics and philosophy, Dembski has used probability theory to argue for design in nature. He has published numerous books, usually with reputable publishers, and even more articles. He maintains an active website that carries a wealth of ID materials. These two selections have been chosen because they are intended for general readers, not scientists, and are therefore quite accessible.

William A. Dembski. "Why President Bush Got It Right about Intelligent Design." August 4, 2005. http://www.designinference.com. Used by permission.

President Bush is to be commended for his courage, wisdom, and foresight in publicly supporting the teaching of intelligent design alongside evolution.

Courage—because intelligent design is for now a minority position in science that faces fierce criticism from many in the scientific mainstream (criticism that he himself will now have to face).

Wisdom—because he understands that ideas are best taught not by giving them a monopoly (which is how evolutionary theory is currently presented in all high school biology textbooks) but by being played off against well-supported competing ideas.

Foresight—because he sees that intelligent design holds a winning hand in the scientific debate over biological origins.

Intelligent design is a winner in the public debate over biological origins not only because it has the backing of powerful ideas, arguments, and evidence but also because it does not turn this debate into a Bible-science controversy. Intelligent design, unlike creationism, is a science in its own right and can stand on its own feet.

Christians need to view this as a strength rather than as a weakness of intelligent design. There is a long tradition in Christian theology that sees God's revelation as coming through "two books": the Book of Nature, which is God's general revelation to all people; and the Book of Scripture, which is God's special revelation to the redeemed.

Accordingly, intelligent design should be understood as the evidence that God has placed in nature to show that the physical world is the product of intelligence and not simply the result of mindless material forces. This evidence is available to all apart from the special revelation of God in salvation history as recounted in Scripture.

Creationism, by contrast, takes a particular interpretation of Genesis (namely, it interprets the days of creation as six consecutive twenty-four-hour days occurring roughly 6,000 years ago) and then tries to harmonize science with this interpretation.

Now, it's true that creationism was largely the position of the Church from the Church Fathers through the Reformers (though there were exceptions, such as Origen and Augustine). Yet, during that time, church teaching also held that the earth was stationary. Psalm 93 states that the earth is established forever and cannot be moved. A literal interpretation of Psalm 93 seems to require geocentrism. And yet every creationist I know accepts the Copernican Revolution.

Although acceptance of intelligent design has now gone international and includes scholars of many different religious faiths and philosophical worldviews, among Christian proponents of intelligent design, the majority hold to a non-literal interpretation of Genesis 1. I'm one of them.

In our view, the evidence of cosmology and geology strongly confirms a universe that is not thousands but rather billions of years old. Granted, this raises problems of theodicy: how, for instance, does one explain death, disease, and suffering among animals prior to the emergence of humans, whose sin, according to Romans 5, appears responsible for these evils. Yet, in our view, such problems are answerable whereas the scientific evidence for an old Earth and old universe seems unanswerable.

Precisely because intelligent design does not turn the study of biological origins into a Bible-science controversy, intelligent design is a position around which Christians of all stripes can unite. And, indeed, there are creationists who also call themselves design theorists (e.g., Paul Nelson).

To be sure, creationists who support intelligent design think it does not go far enough in elucidating the Christian understanding of creation. And they are right!

Intelligent design is a modest position theologically and philosophically. It attributes the complexity and diversity of life to intelligence, but does not identify that intelligence with the God of any religious faith or philosophical system. The task for the Christian who accepts intelligent design is therefore to formulate a theology of nature and creation that makes sense of intelligent design in light of one's Christian faith.

Even so, there is an immediate payoff to intelligent design: it destroys the atheistic legacy of Darwinian evolution. Intelligent design makes it impossible to be an intellectually fulfilled atheist. This gives intelligent design incredible traction as a tool for apologetics, opening up the God-question to individuals who think that science has buried God.

The evidence for design in biology is now overwhelming. In the last thirty years, advances in molecular biology and the information sciences have revealed that the most basic form of life, the cell, is an automated city complete with miniature motors and engines, digital data storage, signal transduction circuitry, monorails that move packages from one location to another, and information processing at a level that human technology has not begun to approximate.

Even the simplest cell is a nano-engineered marvel. Indeed, biologists now need to be engineers to understand life at the subcellular level. Contrast this with Darwin and his contemporaries, who saw the cell as extremely simple—basically, they saw the cell as a blob of Jell-O enclosed by a membrane. No wonder Darwin never addressed the origin of life in his published writings. For him, the origin of life was not a problem. Rather, how life diversified once it got here was for him the problem. That's why he wrote *On the Origin of Species* rather than *On the Origin of Life*.

The theory of intelligent design confronts biology with an immediacy of design that many scientists, committed as many of them are to a materialist worldview, are reluctant to accept. But for true scientists, this reluctance must be justified by evidence and not by an allergic reaction to design that is the result of cultural conditioning.

Twenty years ago, Oxford biologist Richard Dawkins asserted that "the evidence of evolution reveals a universe without design." A lot has happened since then, with the evidence of biology now revealing a universe chock-full of design. President Bush is therefore completely on target in wanting intelligent design taught in the public school science curriculum.

William Dembski. "Open Letter to George Will (Long Overdue)." 25 August 2005. http://www.designinference.com. Used by permission.

[In July, George Will, a columnist I enjoy and find insightful on so many topics, weighed in on ID. I've been meaning to respond to his remarks on ID for some time now.]

Dear Mr. Will:

In the July 4th, 2005 issue of *Newsweek,* you offered the following criticism of intelligent design (ID):

> Today's proponents of "intelligent design" theory are doing nothing novel when they say the complexity of nature is more plausibly explained by postulating a designing mind (a.k.a. God) than by natural adaptation and selection. . . . The problem with intelligent-design theory is not that it is false but that it is not falsifiable: Not being susceptible to contradicting evidence, it is not a testable hypothesis. Hence it is not a scientific but a creedal (tenet) matter of faith, unsuited to a public school's science curriculum.

As for intelligent design bringing nothing new to the discussion of complexity in nature, this claim is difficult to sustain. Darwin, in his *Origin of Species,* wrote, "If it could be demonstrated that any complex organ existed which could not possibly have been formed by numerous, successive, slight modifications, my theory would absolutely break down." ID, in arguing for design on the basis of complexity, takes up Darwin's gauntlet. But it does so by looking to novel results from molecular biology and novel methods for assessing the complexity and design characteristics of such systems.

My own book with Cambridge University Press (1998) titled *The Design Inference* is a case in point. Ask yourself why Cambridge would publish this book if indeed there was nothing new in it. Or consider, why would scholars such as William Wimsatt or Jon Jarrett, neither of whom are ID advocates, offer the following duskjacket endorsements (endorsements for which they have endured considerable heat from Darwinists):

> Dembski has written a sparklingly original book. Not since David Hume's *Dialogues Concerning Natural Religion* has someone taken such a close look at the design argument, but it is done now in a much broader post-Darwinian context. Now we proceed with modern characterizations of probability and complexity, and the results bear fundamentally on

notions of randomness and on strategies for dealing with the explanation of radically improbable events. We almost forget that design arguments are implicit in criminal arguments "beyond a reasonable doubt," plagiarism, phylogenetic inference, cryptography, and a host of other modern contexts. Dembski's analysis of randomness is the most sophisticated to be found in the literature, and his discussions are an important contribution to the theory of explanation, and a timely discussion of a neglected and unanticipatedly important topic.

—William Wimsatt, University of Chicago

In my view, Dembski has given us a brilliant study of the precise connections linking chance, probability, and design. A lucidly written work of striking insight and originality, *The Design Inference* provides significant progress concerning notoriously difficult questions. I expect this to be one of those rare books that genuinely transforms its subject.

—Jon P. Jarrett, University of Illinois at Chicago

Your deeper concern is that intelligent design is not science because it is not testable. If ID were not testable, you would have a point. But the fact is that ID is eminently testable, a fact that is easy to see.

To test ID, it is enough to show how systems that ID claims lie beyond the reach of Darwinian and other evolutionary mechanisms are in fact attainable via such mechanisms. For instance, ID proponents have offered arguments for why non-teleological evolutionary mechanisms should be unable to produce systems like the bacterial flagellum (see chapter 5 of my book *No Free Lunch* [Rowman & Littlefield, 2002] and Michael Behe's essay in my co-edited collection titled *Debating Design* [Cambridge, 2004]). Moreover, critics of ID have tacitly assumed this burden of proof—see Ken Miller's book *Finding Darwin's God* (Harper, 1999) or Ian Musgrave's failed attempt to provide a plausible evolutionary story for the bacterial flagellum in *Why Intelligent Design Fails* (Rutgers, 2004).

Intelligent design and evolutionary theory are either both testable or both untestable. Parity of reasoning requires that the testability of one entails the testability of the other. Evolutionary theory claims that certain material mechanisms are able to propel the evolutionary process, gradually transforming organisms with one set of characteristics into another (for instance, transforming bacteria without a flagellum into bacteria with one). Intelligent design, by contrast, claims that intelligence needs to supplement material mechanisms if they are to bring about organisms with certain complex features. Accordingly, testing the adequacy or inadequacy of evolutionary mechanisms constitutes a joint test of both evolutionary theory and intelligent design.

Unhappy with thus allowing ID on the playing field of science, evolutionary theorist now typically try the following gambit: Intelligent design, they say, constitutes an argument from ignorance or god-of-the-gaps, in which gaps in the evolutionary story are plugged by invoking intelligence. But if intelligent design by definition constitutes such a god-of-the-gaps, then evolutionary theory in turn becomes untestable, for in that case no failures in evolutionary explanation or positive evidence for ID could ever overturn evolutionary theory.

I cited earlier Darwin's well-known statement, "If it could be demonstrated that any complex organ existed which could not possibly have been formed by numerous, successive, slight modifications, my theory would absolutely break down." Immediately after this statement Darwin added, "But I can find out no such case." Darwin so much as admits here that his theory is immune to disconfirmation. Indeed, how could any contravening evidence ever be found if the burden of proof on the evolution critic is to rule out all conceivable evolutionary pathways— pathways that are left completely unspecified.

In consequence, Darwin's own criterion for defeating his theory is impossible to meet and effectively shields his theory from disconfirmation. Unless ID is admitted onto the scientific playing field, mechanistic theories of evolution win the day in the absence of evidence, making them a priori, untestable principles rather than inferences from scientific evidence.

Bottom line: For a claim to ascertainably true it must be possible for it to be ascertainably false. The fate of ID and evolutionary theory, whether as science or non-science, are thus inextricably bound. No surprise therefore that Darwin's *Origin of Species* requires ID as a foil throughout.

Sincerely,
Bill Dembski

EDITOR: *The warfare model for science and religion understandably gets most of the press coverage because such aspects of the recent culture wars are so interesting. There are many evangelicals who operate in much quieter ways to foster understanding of the sciences and even harmonization between evolution and evangelical Christianity. The American Scientific Affiliation was founded in 1941. The organization's stated purpose is "to investigate any area relating Christian faith and science" and "to make known the results of such investigations for comment and criticism by the Christian community and by the scientific community."[1] Below is the ASA platform of faith.*

> American Scientific Affiliation. "What does the ASA believe?" 1941. http://
> www.asa3.org/ASA/aboutASA.html. Used by permission.

As an organization, the ASA does not take a position when there is honest disagreement between Christians on an issue. We are committed to providing an open forum where controversies can be discussed without fear of unjust condemnation. Legitimate differences of opinion among Christians who have studied both the Bible and science are freely expressed within the Affiliation in a context of Christian love and concern for truth.

Our platform of faith has four important planks:

1. We accept the divine inspiration, trustworthiness and authority of the Bible in matters of faith and conduct.

2. We confess the Triune God affirmed in the Nicene and Apostles' creeds which we accept as brief, faithful statements of Christian doctrine based upon Scripture.

3. We believe that in creating and preserving the universe God has endowed it with contingent order and intelligibility, the basis of scientific investigation.

4. We recognize our responsibility, as stewards of God's creation, to use science and technology for the good of humanity and the whole world.

These four statements of faith spell out the distinctive character of the ASA, and we uphold them in every activity and publication of the Affiliation.

EDITOR: *The last selection of this chapter is by John Wilson, editor of* Books and Culture: A Christian Review. *As can be gleaned from his article, Wilson is a moderate evangelical seeking to broker some semblance of understanding between evangelicals and secular scientists who adopt the warfare model for understanding the relationship of religion and science. Wilson is particularly interested in the way that two different sets of evangelical scientists—theistic evolutionists and ID theorists—seem at times to adopt the warfare model, engaging in exchanges that vilify each other. It is interesting that the first selection in this chapter, the one written by James Orr, also sought to find common ground between evangelical Christianity and modern science. In*

the late nineteenth and early twentieth centuries the best evangelical thinkers sought such common ground, but most of the twentieth century was typi-
fied by a Scopes-type warfare mentality. Wilson and many other moderate
evangelicals hope to return to the common-ground model in the twenty-first
century, eschewing the warfare model that is adopted by many evangelicals,
virtually all fundamentalists, and most secular scientists.

Wilson, John. "Unintelligent Debate: It's Time To Cool the Rhetoric in the
Intelligent Design Dispute." *Christianity Today* (September 1, 2004). Used
by permission.

A couple years ago at a Christian publishing convention, I was talking
trends with an astute industry veteran. We happened to be standing near
a table on which several books relating to evolution and Intelligent Design (ID) were arrayed. "Well," my friend said with a dismissive backhand
wave, "at least that seems to be just about played out."

My friend was guilty of wishful thinking. Like many Christian intellectuals, he was weary of the evolution debate, which had seemed not so
long ago to have settled down to a low murmur. Then Phillip Johnson and
his crowd of ID troublemakers came along, challenging the Darwinian establishment head-on (couldn't they have been less confrontational about
it?), and then there was a flurry of school cases (mostly in Bible Belt regions), and before you knew what hit you it was starting all over again,
like an embarrassing family episode brought to light.

At the moment, at least, there are no signs that the debate is cooling
down—on the contrary. And there is a good deal to celebrate in that.
In particular, the ID movement has performed an invaluable service in
highlighting the way in which much Darwinian thinking rests on philosophical assumptions that have no scientific warrant. At the same time,
the aggressive ID attacks on Christian scientists who have not rejected
evolutionary theory lock, stock, and barrel—"accommodationists," as they
are called in ID literature, where they are treated rather like collabora-
tionists with the Nazis during World War II—have pushed theistic evolutionists to formulate their own views more cogently. And of course the
attention garnered by the ID movement has also provoked a vigorous
range of responses from hardcore Darwinians that are often inadvertently
revealing—especially of the extraordinary arrogance that still infests the
field—but which also at times score telling points against ID weaknesses.

In short, there is real engagement (see for example the just-published
volume, *Debating Design*, from Cambridge University Press, edited by

William Dembski and Michael Ruse). And yet for all that, the state of the debate is deeply unsatisfactory, often obscuring more than it clarifies. Certainly the fiercely anti-Christian wing of the Darwinian establishment—headed by Richard Dawkins, who has just been named Britain's #1 public intellectual in a widely publicized poll conducted by *Prospect* magazine—bears the greatest responsibility for this murkiness. (It was Dawkins who notoriously wrote in his bestseller *The Blind Watchmaker*: "It is absolutely safe to say that if you meet somebody who claims not to believe in evolution, that person is ignorant, stupid or insane—or wicked, but I'd rather not consider that." There is a good deal of this ritual strutting in the Darwinist camp.)

But Christian participants in the evolution debate are guilty as well. What is needed most right now is a step back from the fray, a reorienting. What follows are some suggestions for that next stage.

What We All Share

Let's begin with the admirably concise opening question from the old Baltimore Catechism, on which generations of Catholics were nurtured: "Who made me?" The answer minced no words: "God made me." Protestants and indeed all Christians, whether or not they practice formal catechesis, will readily agree. God made us; God made our world; God made the unimaginably vast universe in which our world is but a speck. Implicit in the question and its answer is the strange compound of smallness and greatness that is the essence of our human nature. As creatures we will never grasp the fullness of Creation, but as creatures made in the Creator's image we are designed to learn, to seek to understand, even (as Tolkien put it) to be "sub-creators." And as we think explicitly about Creation, we must keep in mind that tension between our limitations and our high calling. Let either end slacken and we are sure to go awry.

This suggests priorities. As Christians we all acknowledge that God made us. But we may differ—we will differ—in our understanding of how that making unfolded. Some of those differences may be significant (though we must remember our limitations, the fallibility of our knowledge, even as we forcefully argue our case). They may have far-reaching implications. And yet they must be seen as subordinate to the affirmation that unites us, the recognition of the source of our being.

Seen in this light, one of the most unsatisfactory aspects of the evolution debate is the acrimony between ID proponents and theistic evolutionists (some of whom, notably Howard Van Till, don't like that term; let their objection be duly noted). Both sides, it should be obvious, see "intelligent design" at work in the universe. Van Till's "robust formative economy principle" is a case in point: The creation is endowed with the capacity to evolve. Moreover, Van Till and some others in his camp—like the ID thinkers—emphasize God's ongoing action in the world. (Their God doesn't simply build in complexity at the moment before the Big Bang and then take himself off, like the Absentee Landlord of the Deists.)

To note these affinities is not to trivialize the differences between the two factions (in which there are further internal differences: neither side is monolithic). Let them pursue their differences with passion and rigor. But it is time for the ID crowd to stop suggesting that their "accommodationist" rivals are largely driven by fear and careerism and other craven motives rather than by intellectual conviction. ("The path of least resistance," Phillip Johnson writes in *The Right Question* in a typically patronizing analysis of biology professors at Christian colleges, "is to pretend that there is no conflict between evolutionary naturalism and Christian theism.") It is time for the IDers to stop suggesting that theistic evolutionism is functionally equivalent to Dawkins's rabid naturalism. It is time, on the other side, for the theistic evolutionists to stop treating the ID movement as either a conspiracy or a joke—or simply ignoring ID as beneath contempt. And it's time for them to mount more sustained critiques of naturalistic dogmas.

The mutual slanders exchanged in this ongoing debate are especially harmful as they are absorbed and further dumbed down by a larger audience of Christians who want to know what side they should take. Again, there is no need to apologize for sharp disagreement. But the disagreements should clarify, not obscure, what is really at stake.

The Need for Intellectual Honesty

Neither Intelligent Design nor theistic evolutionism, alas, is the most influential position among the evangelical rank and file, where Young Earth creationism still holds sway. Hence another unsatisfactory aspect of the current debate is the strategic refusal of the ID movement to engage in constructive criticism of the Young Earth view.

But haven't I just been calling for mutual recognition among Christians of their unity in affirming God as Creator, and for mutual respect?

Yes, and there's no contradiction here. What is needed from the ID movement is principled disagreement. Whereas whole books published by various ID figures have been devoted to meticulously unpacking some of the errors perpetuated in the Darwinist literature (see for example the work of Jonathan Wells), they are virtually silent about the egregious intellectual errors that abound in Young Earth literature. By contrast, Hugh Ross, who has some affinities both with ID and with the theistic evolutionists, has been more forthright; his work could serve as a model in this respect.

The decision of the ID movement not to engage critically with the Young Earth view is one aspect of ID's much-discussed "Wedge" strategy: ID is presenting a united front against the enemy, naturalism—and indeed, a handful of Young Earth figures have been involved in ID projects. Here the strategy comes at a great cost. Many Christians are raised to believe that they are faced with a stark choice: Either they accept the most literal Young Earth account of Creation or they abandon their faith. The ID movement includes a number of penetrating thinkers who could show that these are not the only alternatives—while maintaining respect for fellow Christians who believe otherwise. And now is the perfect time for them to do so, as ID has begun to gain credibility in some of the circles where Young Earth creationism is the default position.

In some cases, however, the reluctance on the ID side may not be attributable solely to the Wedge strategy. There were indications in Johnson's recent book, *The Right Questions*, that he is sympathetic to a Young Earth reading of Genesis. For instance, he suggests that the great age of the early patriarchs may—may, he emphasizes—be accounted for "on the assumption that the basic 'constants' of physics may have changed over time." Johnson writes that, while he makes "no dogmatic claims," he does "predict that scientists who are genuinely trying to find a set of physical constants that would permit greatly extended human lifespans will be able to do so in good faith." It's hard to know how seriously to take this proposal, no doubt calculated to administer a salutary shock to the Enlightened and set their tongues a-wagging. In any case, others will have to explain what form such a "research project" might actually take.

In the same passage from which I have just quoted, Johnson observes that "the accuracy of any prediction can be determined only in the light of what actually transpires." It's a good reminder especially today in a media environment where this basic principle is routinely violated. And it may remind some readers of the astonishing rhetoric coming from the

Darwinian establishment, where it is asserted categorically that ID "simply isn't science" and moreover can never be science. Evidently there is no need to wait and see what actually transpires.

But this is also a reminder of another unsatisfactory aspect on the Christian side of the evolution debate: the boastful triumphalism of much ID rhetoric. If ID is going to foster the pursuit of first-rate scientific work "on a philosophically liberated basis," it would be more becoming to do some of the work first and boast later.

Fleshing out the design, how much of the "evolution debate" is really about science, anyway? Consider the evolutionary roots of vertebrate immunity, the subject of the cover package in the July 8 issue of *Nature*. (This British-based journal and its American equivalent, *Science*, are the two leading English-language science journals, meaning the two most influential, period.) The cover photo is a close-up of lampreys, looking cheerfully hideous as usual. A brief article (a summary of sorts for those who won't make their way through the full-dress research paper also in the issue) explains that the lamprey and its cousin, the hagfish, are anomalies: They are jawless vertebrates, presumed to be the remnants of a much larger such group "deep in vertebrate family history." They are of interest to immunologists because they have seemed to lack one part of the two-part immune system characteristic of vertebrates, the "adaptive system." The article summarizes new research suggesting that the lamprey has an alternative adaptive immune system.

Let me interrupt for a moment to suggest that your attention may already be wandering—indeed you may have already skipped ahead. Vertebrate immunity? Lampreys? Antigen receptors and lymphocytes? No offense, but you aren't really interested in this technical stuff.

But that's the stuff of science. Built into this research are many assumptions based on the latest generation of evolutionary theory, ranging from fundamental governing assumptions to those more specific to this branch of study. So, for example, on a basic level, there's the assumption of common ancestry (hard to deny, it seems to me, though most of the ID people disagree, as does the formidable philosopher Alvin Plantinga) and an evolutionary conception of the family history of vertebrates.

How would an ID immunologist interact with this material? What assumptions would he accept? Which ones would he reject? What sort of work might he be doing alongside or in contrast to the research reported here? Those are the kinds of questions that need to be answered in the next stage, if ID is going to do science. "Design" needs to be fleshed out.

At the same time, the big questions that the ID movement has taken on are indispensable. As it happens, the author of the brief article in *Nature*, Martin F. Flajnik, who is in the department of microbiology and immunology at the University of Maryland, issues a provocation in the title of his piece: "Another Manifestation of GOD." Having explained how the vertebrate adaptive immune system typically operates, generating "a huge repertoire of antigen receptors" to marshal the body's defenses, Flajnik comments: "Immunologists irreverently refer to this process as GOD (generation of diversity)."

So Flajnik tweaks a certain slackness in many Christian claims to see God's hand evident in his world. And don't we have to plead guilty as charged, at least on occasion? We all have suffered through some of the same slide shows (now converted to PowerPoint) in churchy gatherings over the years: magnificent mountain peaks, waterfalls, leafy glades, gamboling lambs and pink-cheeked babies, with voiceovers from the Psalms. I like babies and waterfalls as much as the next man, but don't these kitschy versions of God's manifest presence in his creation—however well intended—subtly suggest that we can domesticate him? Next time, include a shot of the lamprey, and maybe a diagram of its adaptive immune system.

God's designs will always elude our expectations, blow away our tidy, settled theories. And yet this uncontainable force is personal, cares for us, and has arranged his creation so that we know everything we absolutely need to know, even as our hunger to understand will never be quieted.

* 6 *

Evangelicals and Politics before 1980

EDITOR: *In the nineteenth century, evangelical Protestants were active in several major social reform movements—antislavery, women's rights, education, prison reform, and temperance. According to the interpretation of some scholars, the early twentieth century saw a decline in this reform impulse. As the battles between theological liberals and conservatives heated up, many on the conservative side decided that reform was part of the liberal agenda while conservatives should concentrate on personal salvation. This was especially so for many dispensational premillennialists who believed Christ was returning soon. Evangelist D. L. Moody spoke for many when he described his ministry as a lifeboat into which he hoped to rescue individuals from a shipwrecked world.*

While this interpretation is open to challenge, historians agree that even if there were a decline in social reform among evangelicals and fundamentalists in the early twentieth century, one great issue stood as the major exception to such political quietism—prohibition. The prohibition movement was hardly the concern of fundamentalists alone. Liberal Social Gospelers and even secular progressives believed that legally prohibiting the manufacture and sale of alcoholic beverages would be a major step toward decreasing crime, poverty, abuse of women and children, and social degradation generally. The first selection in this chapter comes from the most famous evangelist of the early twentieth century, Billy Sunday, who appears on the cover of this book. The former major league baseball player turned evangelist spent a good deal of his time attacking Protestant liberals and even more time attempting to win souls to Christ. In between, he was also one of America's leading, and loudest, voices favoring prohibition. This is but a small excerpt from a 12,000- word sermon in which he catalogued a multitude of statistics and anecdotes demonstrating the harmful effects of drink. Very little of what he had to say was about personal sin. Rather, like other reformers who supported prohibition, he was most concerned about the harm alcohol abuse brought to society. While there is no date attached to this sermon, Sunday seems to have preached it, perhaps multiple times, between 1909 and 1912 as the prohibition movement was gaining momentum. The movement culminated in the 1918 passing of the Eighteenth Amendment, which went into effect in 1920, barring the manufacture and sale of alcoholic beverages in the United States until the amendment's repeal in 1933.

Sunday, Billy. "Booze." Sermon, c. 1910. http://www.biblebelievers.com.

I am a temperance Republican down to my toes. Who is the man that fights the whisky business in the South? It is the Democrats! They have driven the business from Kansas, they have driven it from Georgia, and Maine and Mississippi and North Carolina and North Dakota and Oklahoma and Tennessee and West Virginia. And they have driven it out of 1,756 counties. And it is the rock-ribbed Democratic South that is fighting the saloon. They started this fight that is sweeping like fire over the United States. You might as well try and dam Niagara Falls with toothpicks as to stop the reform wave sweeping our land. The Democratic party of Florida has put a temperance plank in its platform and the Republican party of every state would nail that plank in their platform if they thought it would carry the election. It is simply a matter of decency and manhood, irrespective of politics. It is prosperity against poverty, sobriety against drunkenness, honesty against thieving, heaven against hell. Don't you want to see men sober? Brutal, staggering men transformed into respectable citizens? "No," said a saloonkeeper, "to hell with men. We are interested in our business, we have no interest in humanity."

* * *

The Parent of Crimes

The saloon is the sum of all villanies. It is worse than war or pestilence. It is the crime of crimes. It is the parent of crimes and the mother of sins. It is the appalling source of misery and crime in the land. And to license such an incarnate fiend of hell is the dirtiest, low-down, damnable business on top of this old earth. There is nothing to be compared to it.

The legislature of Illinois appropriated $6,000,000 in 1908 to take care of the insane people in the state, and the whisky business produces seventy-five per cent of the insane. That is what you go down in your pockets . . . to help support. Do away with the saloons and you will close these institutions. The saloons make them necessary, and they make the poverty and fill the jails and the penitentiaries. Who has to pay the bills? The landlord who doesn't get the rent because the money goes for whisky; the butcher and the grocer and the charitable person who takes pity on the children of drunkards, and the taxpayer who supports the insane asylums and other institutions, [and] the whisky business keeps full of human wrecks.

Do away with the cursed business and you will not have to put up to support them. Who gets the money? The saloonkeepers and the brewers, and the distillers, while the whisky fills the land with misery, and poverty, and wretchedness, and disease, and death, and damnation, and it is being authorized by the will of the sovereign people.

You say that "people will drink anyway." Not by my vote. You say, "Men will murder their wives anyway." Not by my vote. "They will steal anyway." Not by my vote. You are the sovereign people, and what are you going to do about it?

Let me assemble before your minds the bodies of the drunken dead, who crawl away "into the jaws of death, into the mouth of hell," and then out of the valley of the shadow of the drink. Let me call the appertaining motherhood, and wifehood, and childhood, and let their tears rain down upon their purple faces. Do you think that would stop the curse of the liquor traffic? No! No!

In these days when the question of saloon or no saloon is at the fore in almost every community, one hears a good deal about what is called "personal liberty." These are fine, large, mouth-filling words, and they certainly do sound first rate; but when you get right down and analyze them in the light of common old horse-sense, you will discover that in their application to the present controversy they mean just about this: "Personal liberty" is for the man who, if he has the inclination and the price, can stand up at a bar and fill his hide so full of red liquor that he is transformed for the time being into an irresponsible, dangerous, evil-smelling brute. But "personal liberty" is not for his patient, long-suffering wife, who has to endure with what fortitude she may his blows and curses; nor is it for his children, who, if they escape his insane rage, are yet robbed of every known joy and privilege of childhood, and too often grow up neglected, uncared for and vicious as the result of their surroundings and the example before them. "Personal liberty" is not for the sober, industrious citizen who from the proceeds of honest toil and orderly living, has to pay, willingly or not, the tax bills which pile up as a direct result of drunkenness, disorder and poverty, the items of which are written in the records of every police court and poorhouse in the land; nor is "personal liberty" for the good woman who goes abroad in the town only at the risk of being shot down by some drink-crazed creature. This rant about "personal liberty" as an argument has no leg to stand upon.

The Economic Side

Now, in 1913 the corn crop was 2,373,000,000 bushels, and it was valued at $1,660,000,000. Secretary Wilson says that the breweries use less than two per cent; I will say that they use two per cent. That would make 47,000,000 bushels, and at seventy cents a bushel that would be about $33,000,000. How many people are there in the United States? Ninety millions. Very well, then, that is thirty-six cents per capita. Then we sold out to the whisky business for thirty-six cents apiece—the price of a dozen eggs or a pound of butter. We are the cheapest gang this side of hell if we will do that kind of business.

Now listen! Last year the income of the United States government, and the cities and towns and counties, from the whisky business was $350,000,000. That is putting it liberally. You say that's a lot of money. Well, last year the workingmen spent $2,000,000,000 for drink, and it cost $1,200,000,000 to care for the judicial machinery. In other words, the whisky business cost us last year $3,400,000,000. I will subtract from that the dirty $350,000,000 which we got, and it leaves $3,050,000,000 in favor of knocking the whisky business out on purely a money basis. And listen, we spend $6,000,000,000 a year for our paupers and criminals insane, orphans, feeble-minded, etc., and eighty-two per cent of our criminals are whisky-made, and seventy-five per cent of the paupers are whisky-made. The average factory hand earns $450 a year, and it costs us $1,200 a year to support each of our whisky criminals. There are 326,000 enrolled criminals in the United States and 80,000 in jails and penitentiaries. Three-fourths were sent there because of drink, and then they have the audacity to say the saloon is needed for money revenue. Never was there a baser he. "But," says the whisky fellow, "we would lose trade"; I heard my friend ex-Governor Hanly [sic], of Indiana, use the following illustrations:

"Oh, but," they say, "Governor, there is another danger to the local option, because it means a loss of market to the farmer. We are consumers of large quantities of grain in the manufacture of our products. If you drive us out of business you strike down that market and it will create a money panic in this country, such as you have never seen, if you do that." I might answer it by saying that less than two per cent of the grain produced in this country is used for that purpose, but I pass that by. I want to debate the merit of the statement itself, and I think I can demonstrate in ten minutes to any thoughtful man, to any farmer, that the brewer who furnishes him a market for a bushel of corn is not his benefactor, or the benefactor of any man, from an economic standpoint. Let us see. A farmer brings to the brewer a bushel of corn. He finds a market for it. He gets fifty cents and goes his way, with the statement of the brewer ringing in his ears, that the brewer is the benefactor. But you haven't got all the factors in the problem, Mr. Brewer, and you cannot get a correct solution of a problem without all the factors in the problem. You take the farmer's bushel of corn, brewer or distiller, and you brew and distill from it four and one-half gallons of spirits. I don't know how much he dilutes them before he puts them on the market. Only the brewer, the distiller and God know. The man who drinks it doesn't, but if he doesn't dilute it at all, he puts on the market four and a half gallons of intoxicating liquor, thirty-six pints. I am not going to trace the thirty-six pints. It will take too long. But I want to trace three of them and I will give you no imaginary stories plucked from the brain of an excited orator. I will take instances from the judicial pages of the Supreme Court and the Circuit Court judges' reports in Indiana and in Illinois to make my case.

Several years ago in the city of Chicago a young man of good parents, good character, one Sunday crossed the street and entered a saloon, open against the law. He found there boon companions. There were laughter, song and jest and much drinking. After awhile, drunk, insanely drunk, his money gone, he was kicked into the street. He found his way across to his mother's home. He importuned her for money to buy more drink. She refused him. He seized from the sideboard a revolver and ran out into the street and with the expressed determination of entering the saloon and getting more drink, money or no money. His fond mother followed him into the street. She put her hand upon [him] in a loving restraint. He struck it from him in anger, and then his sister came and added her entreaty in vain. And then a neighbor, whom he knew, trusted and respected, came and put his hand on him in gentleness and friendly kindness, but in an insanity of drunken rage he raised the revolver and shot his friend dead in his blood upon the street. There was a trial; he was found guilty of murder. He was sentenced to life imprisonment, and when the little mother heard the verdict—a frail little bit of a woman— she threw up her hands and fell in a swoon. In three hours she was dead.

EDITOR: *Sunday followed with two more similar stories.*

* * *

Personal Liberty

Personal liberty is not personal license. I dare not exercise personal liberty if it infringes on the liberty of others. Our forefathers did not fight and die for personal license but for personal liberty bounded by laws. Personal liberty is the liberty of a murderer, a burglar, a seducer, or a wolf that wants to remain in a sheep fold, or the weasel in a hen roost. You have no right to vote for an institution that is going to drag your sons and daughters to hell.

If you were the only persons in this city you would have a perfect right to drive your horse down the street at breakneck speed; you would have a right to make a race track out of the streets for your auto; you could build a slaughter house in the public square; you could build a glue factory in the public square. But when the population increases from one to 600,000 you can't do it. You say, "Why can't I run my auto? I own it. Why can't I run my horse? I own it. Why can't I build the slaughter house? I own the lot." Yes, but there are 600,000 people here now and other people have rights.

So law stands between you and personal liberty, you miserable dog. You can't build a slaughter house in your front yard, because the law says you can't. As long as I am standing here on this platform I have personal liberty. I can swing my arms at will. But the minute any one else steps on the platform my personal liberty ceases. It stops just one inch from the other fellow's nose.

When you come staggering home, cussing right and left and spewing and spitting, your wife suffers, your children suffer. Don't think that you are the only one that suffers. A man that goes to the penitentiary makes his wife and children suffer just as much as he does. You're placing a shame on your wife and children. If you're a dirty, low-down, filthy, drunken, whisky-soaked bum you'll affect all with whom you come in contact. If you're a God-fearing man you will influence all with whom you come in contact. You can't live by yourself with my business?

* * *

The liver is the largest organ of the body. It takes all of the blood in the body and purifies it and takes out the poisons and passes them on to the gall and from there they go to the intestines and act as oil does on machinery. When a man drinks the liver becomes covered with hob nails, and then refuses to do the work, and the poisons stay in the blood. Then the victim begins to turn yellow. He has the jaundice. The kidneys take what is left and purify that. The booze that a man drinks turns them hard.

That's what booze is doing for you. Isn't it time you went red hot after the enemy? I'm trying to help you. I'm trying to put a carpet on your floor, pull the pillows out of the window, give you and your children and wife good clothes. I'm trying to get you to save your money instead of buying a machine for the saloonkeeper while you have to foot it.

By the grace of God I have strength enough to pass the open saloon, but some of you can't, so I owe it to you to help you.

I've stood for more sneers and scoffs and insults and had my life threatened from one end of the land to the other by this God-forsaken gang of thugs and cutthroats because I have come out uncompromisingly against them. I've taken more dirty, vile insults from this low-down bunch than from any one on earth, but there is no one that will reach down lower, or reach higher up or wider, to help you out of the pits of drunkenness than I.

Ockenga, Harold J. "The Christian Answer to Communism." Sermon given
at the Rose Bowl Rally in Pasadena, Calif. In *America's Hour of Decision*.
Wheaton: Van Kampen Press, 1951. 149–57.

MAY I SAY that there is a burden on my heart? I do not understand how anyone in a day like this can be without a burden, as he reads the reports in the papers and knows something of what is occurring throughout the world. These days communism, atheistic communism, is marching to the attack. Let me repeat that: atheistic communism is marching to the attack.

The spiritual struggle now going on in the world has never been equaled. There has never been a time when Theism (and atheism) were in such a life-and-death struggle throughout the world as they are today. Now, there are many people in America and the theistic countries which in turn deny God in practice and also in experience, but, in a general sense, in a theoretical sense, there is definitely a belief in God as the very basis of Western culture. And today these two view-points are locked in a life-and-death struggle as never before. It is light or darkness, it is God or Satan, it is the belief in God or the denial of the existence of God! And in the midst of that, in our day, we stand in the crucible.

War has broken throughout the world. Now this war in Korea is war—real, terrible, awful war—but it is not the great third world war. And yet that third world war may come at any time. Today we can look out and see the possibility in the offing as it is impending over the whole world. I needn't tell you that. Practically every magazine of our day is declaring that in its major articles of the moment. We look out at the break-out of a great world struggle in Korea. Yesterday, it was China. Tomorrow, it may be in Germany, in Iran, or in Japan, or in some other section of the world. It's all part and parcel of one great struggle. That which is now happening in Korea is the same kind of thing which happened back in Manchuria under the Japanese, in Ethiopia under the Italians, in Austria and Sudetenland under the Germans—and if it were not stopped now, in a few years it would have been absolutely too late. If the puppet governments can be stopped now and compelled to retreat, there can be a respite for the whole world, for a brief period at least, and it is that issue which is being tested by the communists today. The determination of the United States of America to stand as the great bulwark against this incoming tide of communism is something which ought to hearten us all. Our forces today are in Berlin and in Korea, on one side of the world and on the other side of the world. If either of these bastions goes now, we are put on the defensive in that fall.

We ought as Christian people, we ought as American citizens, we ought as those who are looking for peace and for some kind of hope in the world, firmly to support a government that is willing to stand firmly in such an hour against that incoming tide of atheistic communism and all that comes in its wake.

We must remember that at this moment all of civilization is in the crucible. It hangs in the balance. It is in a crisis, and the crisis means that a man can—as he hovers between life or death—either get better or sink down into the pit, as it were, into death itself. And so civilization hangs at this moment in that great crisis, and nobody knows when "the great sneak attack" may come. Remember what many people have forgotten (and I quote to you now from Lenin, but I want to introduce it by a word from Stalin). On April 9, 1947, when Harold Stassen was talking to Stalin in the Kremlin, Mr. Stalin said: "We, the Soviet people, are disciples of Lenin. Lenin is our teacher." Now, if that is true, and spoken as lately as that, what did Lenin teach? Let me quote you just one little verse from Lenin. Lenin said in his collective works, in Volume 17, page 398: "As long as communism and capitalism exist in the same world we cannot have peace. A funeral requiem will be sung in or over the Soviet republic or over world capitalism. There is no respite in a war. There is no middle course. Either the Soviet government will triumph over the civilized nations of the earth or reactionary capitalism will triumph. There is no middle ground."

Those words same from Lenin, the teacher of the Soviets. Lenin also: "Resist and strike the bourgeois wherever it is necessary but strike them only in the chest, when you are sure of victory." Now when the communists are sure of victory, then, according to communist morality, which is a relativistic morality based upon whatever is for the advancement of the communist cause, it is perfectly permissible for them to work for peace ostensibly in the United Nations and then to launch a sneak attack such as Pearl Harbor, with atom bombs and with all manner of germicidal warfare in the cities and harbors of our nation so as to knock us out in one single blow. That's the teaching of Lenin.

There are those in the United States, and we could quote them tonight, who have been talking about a preventive war; about prophylactic war; about the United States driving into the Kremlin now, instead of waiting until the sneak attack. That cannot be done, however, on the basis of the principles of Western civilization and Western culture, because of our basis of Christian principles. To talk about that thing and publicize it in our magazines is simply to put ammunition in the hands of communists, which in turn will be believed by them and they will think that is what we are going to do, and will have the courage to do that thing, and do it first to us. We deplore that kind of business.

Now, what is the Christian answer in a day like this? May I very briefly say to you tonight that there are three things which we ought to keep in mind as an answer. I suggest to you that the first answer to communism in the world is *righteousness*; without righteousness there will be no answer to communism. The second is *reason*, and the third is *resistance* in a way of war.

We can turn to such a man as W. T. Stace of Princeton, or John Baillie of Edinburgh, or to Butterfield of Cambridge who is the successor of Lord

Acton, the great modern historian, and each one of these men declares to us today that three things are the foundation of Western culture. The first is the belief in God as Creator, as Governor, or Providential ruler of this universe. They don't give us the thought of Redeemer, but they give us the thought of God. Secondly that there is a moral structure to the universe. Thirdly, that we as individuals are of infinite value before God and therefore we are responsible to that eternal, moral law before God. Now, those three convictions expressed in community life are the basis of Western culture. We cannot deny them, we cannot act against them, we cannot contradict them, if we are going to continue to be a civilization such as our tradition of the past.

But what is happening? In America today we are flaunting God's law individually. Look at the gambling record of thirteen billion dollars a year siphoned off our economy. The crime record of fifteen billion dollars a year, the drunkenness and the consuming of liquor, and the immorality, and the juvenile delinquency, and the divorce and the injustice, and the idolatry, and all these things contrary to God's Book and to God's Law. And as God brought Israel and Judah low in judgment because of the fact that they violated His laws and set up idolatry and injustice and immorality, I say unto you tonight, you can't flaunt God's law individually and then act upon it internationally. You can't think that internationally God is going to defend you and that God is going to support you, as the sovereign God of a moral universe, if the same nation individually violates His law and flaunts it in His face. When Moses and the people came out of Egypt and later went into Canaan land, remember that the Israelites came against greater foes and they defeated them all. And when Moses wrote about this thing in Deuteronomy, we read: "How should one chase a thousand, and two put ten thousand to flight except their Rock had sold them, and the Lord had shut them up?" May God grant that we shall never be sold by the sovereign God of a moral universe because we have repudiated Him and exercised the folly of inconsistency in a moral universe, and thus have gone down into God's judgment.

It is perfectly possible tonight, perfectly possible, that God should judge us and use the two hundred and fifty divisions of the Soviet people to whip us and scourge us and drive us to our knees before Him in repentance. That is a principal which God uses in history. Remember this principle: "That servant which knew his Lord's will and prepared not himself, neither did according to his will, shall be beaten with many stripes. But he that knew not, and did commit things worthy of stripes, shall be beaten with few stripes." The communists have not the Word of God. The communists have not the churches of God. The communists have no light of God in this day. We have had it. The Bible is in our court rooms. On our coins is written: "In God we trust." It is in the churches of our land on every corner, and on the radio, blanketing the whole of our nation, and, if, in the light of this thing, we turn against God, I say unto you, that God can scourge us and drive us to our knees by the whip of an unbelieving and; heathen nation. You remember that, in Chronicles, the Chronicler said that the war would be God's, that God raised up and stirred up the spirit of Pul, king of Assyria and of Tilgathpileser, king of Assyria, and He carried them away, even the Reubenites and the Gadites and the half-tribe of Manasseh into captivity. He conquered His own people. He drove His own people out with a scourge of chastisement and of punishment because of their evil. And beloved, it can happen to us just as it happened to the Israelites again and, again of old. And God is warning us in this hour that that alternative stands before us.

Now, I declare to you that the only answer to that need is for a nation that was founded upon the belief in God and a moral universe of law expressed in its constitution, placing it above the President, above the Legislature, above the officers of the government, to return to belief in God, to repentance of sins, and, in returning, to acceptance of Almighty God as sovereign and His law as the way of living for our nation in this day.

* * *

We've got to believe in God, in His sovereignty as the God of justice, of hope, of mercy, of truth, of love—not a sobby, sentimental God made by our own imaginations. But the God of the Bible, the God of mystery, the God of logical structure who makes you able to understand what I am saying to you tonight because we live in a logical world patterned after the projection of a divine mind reaching into men's lives at this present time. Believe in God. Then we believe in the gospel: that there must be a way for a sinful, wicked man, for a degenerate, broken culture to be reclaimed, to be redeemed, to be regenerated, to be restored, to be reconciled unto God and once again to live in redemptive activity before men. And we believe that that comes through the cross of the Lord Jesus Christ, who came to reveal God to us and to reconcile us to God.

And then we must believe in the gospel's power for the community. We must believe, my friends, in the fact that these things can be expressed in social action; they can be expressed in government and in education, and in business, and in the home life, and in all phases of our lives. We must come with that unwavering faith in Almighty God to our tasks of the day. Every child today should learn those words of Lincoln, "With firmness in the right, as God gives us to see the right, let us strive on to finish the work we are in" and the time comes when we must do away with this vacillation, with its treasonable activity of appeasement, with these activities and these practices of giving in constantly to those who have no faith in God, or righteousness, or in the advancement of God's cause. We must be firm, I say, and then, if necessary, take out of the Bible the very teaching of God's revelation: that God ordains the sword for defense and for the protection of righteousness and, if necessary, for the advancement of righteousness in the world.

* * *

And the son of God will never be with the wicked, profligate, corrupt, weakened people because they have chosen sin and rebelled against Him. And so tonight in a preliminary way I call this nation back to God. I call this nation to repentance, to get upon its knees before God. I call it to faith in the Son of God, which faith has been the source of moral fiber and righteousness of our nation. I call it back because, as I say, it is the only reasonable way and ground of moral action and progress and defense and righteousness in the earth. And if our nation turns now, in fulfillment of the divine promise given unto us there is hope that the sovereign God will turn enemies one against another! China against Russia, if you please; Yugoslavia and Russia, or others against another; and we can have respite and peace and progress and plenty and purity and we can go forward to evangelize and preach and to bring the gospel of God throughout the earth.

And I thank God with all my soul that He has raised up this man to whom people have come tonight to listen, that we might once again hear from a prophetic voice, in a strategic way, the message of the Word of God in order to turn us to our knees in repentance and faith.

EDITOR: *Carl F. H. Henry was the leading theologian of the neoevangelical movement that began in the mid-twentieth century. The key difference between fundamentalism and neoevangelicalism was that the neoevangelicals wanted to drop the militant and separatist aspects of fundamentalism and reengage American culture in a constructive way. The selection below is from a little book Henry wrote in 1947. The book was a call for Christian reengagement with culture and became a key component in the development of the neoevangelical movement.*

Henry, Carl F. H. *The Uneasy Conscience of Modern Fundamentalism*. Grand Rapids: Eerdmans, 1947. 36–38, 44–45, 76–81, 84–89. Used by permission.

For the first protracted period in its history, evangelical Christianity stands divorced from the great social reform movements.

* * *

Fundamentalism today denies that Christian ethics is in any sense to be identified with the humanistic moralism of modern reformers. Yet it is specifically the humanism of the day that is most vocal and vigorous in the attack on admitted social ills. As a consequence, Protestant evangelicalism without a world program has largely relegated itself to a secondary, or even more subordinate, role of challenge to the prevailing cultural mood.

One of the ironies of this predicament is that some important benefits have accrued to evangelicals from the very agencies they oppose. A Fundamentalist chaplain recently remarked, for example, that the opportunity to proclaim the evangelical Gospel freely to servicemen had been safeguarded for him by the influence of the Federal Council of Churches with the national government. He did not mean that the Federal Council had interceded by any means for the historic evangelical message as differentiated from religious modernism, but rather that the whole chaplaincy plan from its inception was closely watched by the Council whereas the evangelicals more or less fell in with it.

Protestantism's embarrassing divorce is apparent. Whereas in previous eras of Occidental history no spiritual force so challenged the human scene as did Christianity with its superlife in the area of conduct, its supernatural world view in the area of philosophy, and its superhope in the area of societal remaking, the challenge of modern Fundamentalism to the present world mind is almost nonexistent on the great social issues. Through the Christian centuries, assuredly, the evangelical challenge came always in a specifically redemptive framework. But in modern times the challenge is hardly felt at all. For Fundamentalism in the main fails to make relevant to the great moral problems in twentieth-century global living the implications of its redemptive message.

* * *

Today, Protestant Fundamentalism although heir-apparent to the super-naturalist gospel of the Biblical and Reformation minds, is a stranger, in its predominant spirit, to the vigorous social interest of its ideological forebears. Modern Fundamentalism does not explicitly sketch the social implications of its message for the non-Christian world; it does not challenge the injustices of the totalitarianisms, the secularisms of modern education, the evils of racial hatred, the wrongs of current labor-management relations, the inadequate bases of international dealings. It has ceased to challenge Caesar and Rome, as though in futile resignation and submission to the triumphant Renaissance mood. The apostolic Gospel stands divorced from a passion to right the world. The Christian social imperative is today in the hands of those who understand it in sub-Christian terms.

But evangelicalism is disturbed proportionately as it senses this contradiction of its own history. Fundamentalism is agitating today with two great convictions, the affirmation of which is necessary if Fundamentalism is to express the genius of the Christian tradition: (1) That Christianity opposes any and every evil, personal and social, and must never be represented as in any way tolerant of such evil; (2) That Christianity opposes to such evil, as the only sufficient formula for its resolution, the redemptive work of Jesus Christ and the regenerative work of the Holy Spirit. It rejects the charge that the Fundamentalist ideology logically involves an indifference to social evils, and presses the contention that the non-evangelical ideology involves an essential inability to right the world order. It is discerning anew that an assault on global evils is not only consistent with, but rather is demanded by, its proper world-life view

* * *

"The Evangelical Formula of Protest"

The future kingdom in evangelical thought, it has already been insisted, does not displace an interim world program. That contemporary program in evangelicalism is (1) predicated upon an all-inclusive redemptive context for its assault upon global ills; (2) involves total opposition to all moral evils, whether societal or personal; (3) offers not only a higher ethical standard than any other system of thought, but provides also in Christ a dynamic to lift humanity to its highest level of moral achievement.

But the spearhead of the current attack on moral evils is not directed, as we have observed, by evangelical forces. Rather, the non-evangelical humanistic movements are heading up the agitation for a new and better world. The social program is, by and large, projected constructively today by non-evangelical groups.

Yet the non-evangelical camp has been plunged into considerable confusion, at the moment, by the collapse of its vision for an utopian world. The convictions of non-evangelicals are on the move; liberals are moving upward toward neo-supernaturalism or downward toward humanism, and some humanists are moving downward toward pessimism, while some others are impatiently marking time.

This creates the most favorable opportunity evangelicalism has had since its embarrassing divorce from a world social program, to recapture its rightful leadership in pressing for a new world order. Any conviction of foredoomed failure does not automatically cancel the missionary obligation. The futility of trying to win all does not mean that it is futile to try to win some areas of influence and life. An evangelical world program has its timeliest opportunity at the present hour.

But a difficult problem is projected by the fact that evangelicals are found in fellowships which often seek elimination of social evils in a context which is not specifically redemptive, and often hostile to supernatural redemptionism. Since the evangelicals are convinced that a non-redemptive attack on any problem is sentenced to failure, what would be a consistent attitude in such circumstances? This is not an easy question to answer, and the writer does not pretend to offer more than preliminary reflection with regard to it. But it is a problem which confronted the apostolic church, and with the desupernaturalization of western culture it again looms large. The best evangelical thought may well occupy itself with the query in the immediate present. The spirit of the evangelical seminaries and colleges may largely determine the interpretation of social need which crystallizes during this post-war crisis period among Fundamentalist leaders. No framework is really relevant today unless it has an answer to the problem of sin and death in every area of human activity. Confronted by this problem, the evangelical mind will have to work out a satisfactory solution proportionate to its conviction of evangelical relevance.

The statement of a few pertinent considerations, however preliminary, may contribute to the ultimate solution, whether by action or reaction. Surely Christianity ought not to oppose any needed social reform. It ought, indeed, to be in the forefront of reformative attack. And it ought, if it has a historical consciousness, to press its attack on a redemption foundation, convinced that every other foundation for betterment, because of inherent weaknesses, cannot sustain itself.

While the evangelical will resist the non-evangelical formulas for solution, he assuredly ought not on that account to desist from battle against world evils. Just because his ideology is unalterably opposed to such evils, the evangelical should be counted upon not only to "go along" with all worthy reform movements, but to give them a proper leadership. He must give unlimited expression to his condemnation of all social evils, coupled with an insistence that a self-sustaining solution can be found only on a redemptive foundation. More vigorously than the humanists and religious modernists press their battle, the evangelical ought to be counted upon in the war against aggressive conflict, political naturalism, racial intolerance, the liquor traffic, labor-management inequities, and every wrong. And as vigorously as the evangelical presses his battle, he ought to be counted upon to point to the redemption that is in Christ Jesus as the only adequate solution. This appears to the writer to be the true evangelical methodology; to fill this form with content, in its application, is the difficult task which remains undone.

Evangelical action is not complicated within movements or organisms composed entirely of historic Christian theists, who, therefore, are united not only on the need for a social program, but also on the context within which such world renewal is a possibility. And yet only a minimal effort has been made in such circles, to articulate the Christian message in its social challenge. There are here and there conservative denominational groups, like the Reformed movements and the great Southern Baptist Convention, which have maintained or are beginning to reflect a vigorous social interest. But to capture for the church all of the social zeal through redemptive categories, would involve even here a considerable change.

*   *   *

There are Fundamentalists who will insist immediately that no evangelical has a right to unite with non-evangelicals in any reform. It is not the task of this volume to evaluate the possibility or impossibility of evangelical loyalty to Christ within large modern denominations, each differing somewhat in organization and condition. Assuredly, no demand for loyalty can be recognized by the evangelical as higher than that by Christ Jesus, and each evangelical must settle, to the satisfaction of his own conscience, whether such loyalty is best served, or is impeded by loyalty within his denomination. But unrestricted loyalty to Christ cannot be interpreted as consistent with a tacit condonement of great world evils.

Apart from denominational problems, it remains true that the evangelical, in the very proportion that the culture in which he lives is not actually Christian, must unite with non-evangelicals for social -betterment if it is to be achieved at all, simply because the evangelical forces do not predominate. To say that evangelicalism should not voice its convictions in a non-evangelical environment is simply to rob evangelicalism of its missionary vision.

It will be impossible for the evangelical to cooperate for social betterment with any group only when that group clearly rules out a redemptive reference as a live option for the achievement of good ends. If evangelicals in such groups are not accorded the democratic parliamentary right of minority action, there remains no recourse but that of independent action. Action there must be if evangelicalism is to recapture the spirit of its evangel. In non-evangelical groups, the evangelical must have opportunity to witness to the redemptive power of Jesus. Because of his convictions, he ought never to vote for something lower than his position except with an accompanying protest. This is a far truer road of expression for his convictions than to decline to support an attack on admitted evils—because the latter course tacitly withdraws his opposition to that which the Redeemer would unhesitatingly condemn. In point of fact, those movements for a "pure evangelicalism," which have come out of larger denominational groups, have not infrequently done so with a sacrifice of social vision and a concentration on redemptive rescue of individuals from an environment conceded to be increasingly hostile. The point here is not that they needed to become socially indifferent as a consequence of a rupture with denominationalism, but rather that such movements so frequently sacrifice an evangelical ecumenicity, and replace a world view with a fragmentary isolationism that "breaks through" its adverse environment with atomistic missionary effort, at home and abroad, with whatever heroic and genuine sacrifices.

It cannot be held then that the social indifference of evangelicals is attributable to organic denominational associations with liberalism. For Fundamentalist churches in no liberal association whatever are often as socially inactive as others. Curiously, some Fundamentalist churches in liberal associations have had more ecumenical awareness by far than many churches in purely evangelical environments.

And yet it remains true that evangelical convictions need a united voice; the force of the redemptive message will not break with apostolic power upon the modern scene unless the American Council of Churches and the National Association of Evangelicals meet at some modern Antioch, and Peter and Paul are face to face in a spirit of mutual love and compassion. If, as is often remarked, the Federal Council of Churches is the voice of Protestant liberalism in America, Protestant evangelicalism too needs a single voice. When such a unity comes, the present competitive spirit of evangelical groups shall be overruled to the glory of God, and the furtherance of the Gospel witness. If this does not come, groups most responsible will inevitably wither.

"The Dawn of a New Reformation"

The need for a vital evangelicalism is proportionate to the world need. The days are as hectic as Nero's Rome, and they demand attention as immediate as Luke's Macedonia.

The cries of suffering humanity today, are many. No evangelicalism which ignores the totality of man's condition dares respond in the name of Christianity. Though the modern crisis is not basically political, economic or social—fundamentally it is religious—yet evangelicalism must be armed to declare the implications of its proposed religious solution for the politico-economic and sociological context for modern life.

However marred, the world vessel of clay is not without some of the influence of the Master Molder. God has not left Himself entirely without witness in the global calamity; He discloses Himself in the tragedies as well as the triumphs of history. He works in history as well as above history. There is a universal confrontation of men and women by the divine Spirit, invading all cultures and all individual lives. There is a constructive work of God in history, even where the redemptive Gospel does not do a recreating work. The evangelical missionary message cannot be measured for success by the number of converts only. The Christian message has a salting effect upon the earth. It aims at a recreated society; where it is resisted, it often encourages the displacement of a low ideology by one relatively higher. Democratic humanitarianism furnishes a better context for human existence than political naturalism, except as it degenerates to the latter.

Modern evangelicalism need not substitute as its primary aim the building of "relatively higher civilizations." To do that is to fall into the error of yesterday's liberalism. Its supreme aim is the proclamation of re-deeming grace to sinful humanity; there is no need for Fundamentalism to embrace liberalism's defunct social gospel. The divine order involves a supernatural principle, a creative force that enters society from outside its natural sources of uplift, and regenerates humanity. In that divine reversal of the self-defeating sinfulness of man is the only real answer to our prob-lems—of whatever political, economic, or sociological nature. Is there po-litical unrest? Seek first, not a Republican victory, or a labor victory, but the kingdom of God and His righteousness. Then there will be added—not necessarily a Republican or labor victory, but—political rest. Is there economic unrest? Seek first, not an increase of labor wages coupled with shorter hours, with its probable dog-eat-dog resultant of increased com-modity cost, but the divine righteousness; this latter norm will involve fairness for both labor and management. But there will be added not only the solution of the problems of the economic man, but also those of the spiritual man. There is no satisfying rest for modern civilization if it is found in a context of spiritual unrest. This is but another way of declar-ing that the Gospel of redemption is the most pertinent message for our modern weariness, and that many of our other so-called solutions are quite impertinent, to say the least.

But that does not mean that we cannot cooperate in securing relatively higher goods, when this is the loftiest commitment we can evoke from humanity, providing we do so with appropriate warning of the inadequacy and instability of such solutions. The supernatural regenerative grace of God, proffered to the regenerate, does not prevent His natural grace to all men, regenerate and unregenerate alike. Because He brings rivers of living water to the redeemed, He does not on that account withhold the rain from the unjust and just alike. The realm of special grace does not preclude the realm of common grace. Just so, without minimizing the re-demptive message, the church ministers by its message to those who stop short of commitment, as well as to regenerate believers.

The implications of this for evangelicalism seem clear. The battle against evil in all its forms must be pressed unsparingly; we must pursue the enemy, in politics, in economics, in science, in ethics—everywhere, in every field, we must pursue relentlessly. But when we have singled out the enemy—when we have disentangled him from those whose com-pany he has kept and whom he has misled—we must meet the foe head-on, girt in the Gospel armor. Others may resist him with inadequate weapons; they do not understand aright the nature of the foe, nor the requirements for victory. We join with them in battle, seeking all the while more clearly to delineate the enemy, and more precisely to state the redemptive formula.

EDITOR: *During the period between Scopes and the 1980s, Billy Graham emerged as America's most visible evangelical. He became the leading popular spokesperson for the nonseparatist, nonmilitant neoevangelical movement that broke with militant fundamentalism in the 1940s. He was a close confident and friend of presidents Dwight D. Eisenhower, Lyndon B. Johnson, and Richard Nixon. His association with Nixon became an embarrassment when the Watergate scandal broke in the early 1970s. The interview below was published eight months before Nixon became the only president in American history to resign his office in disgrace. Note not only what Graham reveals about his relationship with presidents personally but also his views of the role of an evangelical in politics. It is worth mentioning that Graham would never again allow himself to get too close to a president, and he steered clear of Christian Right politics in the 1980s and 1990s.*

Graham, Billy. "Watergate." *Christianity Today* (January 4, 1974): 9–18.

Question: What was your reaction when you received the invitation to speak at the White House?

Answer: I was in Switzerland attending an administrative committee meeting of the International Congress on World Evangelization when Mrs. Nixon called. She asked if I would come and hold a Christmas service on December 16. Naturally, I realized the delicacy of such a visit in the present "Watergate" climate. However, I recognized also the responsibility of such a service and the opportunity to present the Gospel of Christ within a Christmas context to a distinguished audience. I have said for many years that I will go anywhere to preach the Gospel, whether to the Vatican, the Kremlin, or the White House, if there are no strings on what I am to say. I have never had to submit the manuscript to the White House or get anybody's approval. I have never informed any President of what I was going to say ahead of time. They all have known that when I come I intend to preach the Gospel. If Senator McGovern had been elected President and had invited me to preach, I would gladly have gone. I am first and foremost a servant of Jesus Christ. My first, allegiance is not to America but to "the Kingdom of God."

Q. How do you answer those who say this implies a kind of benediction on everything that happens at the White House?

A. That view is ridiculous. Twenty years ago we called such thinking "McCarthyism"—guilt by association. This was the accusation of the Pharisees against Jesus, that he spent time with "publicans and sinners." Through the years I have stated publicly that I do not agree with all that any administration does. I certainly did not agree with everything that President Johnson did, and I was at the White House as often under Johnson as under Nixon. I preached before Johnson more than I have preached before Nixon and had longer and more frequent conversations with him. But I did not agree with everything Johnson did. I publicly stated so on several occasions. On one of those occasions, I think he was irritated with me, but he soon got over it. Since then, I have tried to make it a point, which I am sure is obscured and blurred, that I go to the White House to preach the Gospel and that my preaching visits have absolutely nothing to do with the current political situation. It is quite obvious that I do not agree with everything the Nixon administration does.

Q. Do you think Watergate and its related events were illegal and unethical?

A. Absolutely. I can make no excuses for Watergate. The actual break-in was a criminal act, and some of the things that surround Watergate, too, were not only unethical but criminal. I condemn it and I deplore it. It has hurt America.

Q. Some of our evangelical friends wonder why you don't go into the White House like a Nathan and censure the President publicly in these services. What's your response?

A. Let's remember that I am not a "Nathan." David was the leader of "the people of God," and it was a totally different situation than today's secularistic America. A better comparison would be with ancient Rome and Paul's relationship with Caesar. Also, when a pastor has in his congregation a mayor or a governor who may be in some difficulty, he doesn't point this man out publicly from the pulpit. He tries to encourage and help him and to lead him. Perhaps in private he will advise him on the moral and spiritual implications of the situation, but I don't think the average clergyman in the pulpit would take advantage of such a situation and point to this man and say publicly, "You ought to do thus and so."

Let's also remember that in America a person is presumed innocent until proven guilty. As far as I know, the President has not been formally charged with a crime. Mistakes and blunders have been made. Some of them involved moral and ethical questions, but at this point if I have anything to say to the President it will be in private.

* * *

Q. What kind of a man is Nixon, really? Most people think that he is a loner and isolated, that people don't see the real Nixon.

* * *

A. I have to speak about the Nixon I knew before he became President. To me, he was always a warm and gracious person with a great sense of humor. He was always thoughtful. Sometimes I have been with him when he was preoccupied, but I never had the impression that he was cold or diffident. Of course, other people know him better than I do and have known him in a different way. For example, some people have accused him of using profanity, but the strongest word I have heard from him is "hell," and that only on a few occasions. But you know, people act differently around clergymen than they do other friends. I have always admired Nixon's close family life. I admire his love for his mother, his wife, and their daughters. I admire his tremendous passion for "peace," which I think came partly from his Quaker background. I also admire his personal discipline. I've known few men that live such a disciplined life. He once told me that the reason he gave up golf was that there were too many books to read, and too many interesting conversations to hold. He said, "I may never be elected President but I'm going to continue preparing myself."

That brings up another interesting point. During 1967 and early 1968 he really did not want to run for President. He almost decided not to. He was actually afraid that what is happening now would happen to him. I think his running for President came partially as a result of ambition but mostly as a result of sheer patriotism. He really felt he could make a contribution not only to America but to the world, especially foreign affairs. He seemed to feel the mid-seventies would be very dangerous for America and the world.

* * *

Q. How do you think that the seemingly good, upright men of the Nixon administration went wrong?

A. First I would like to clarify one other thing. I noticed one or two religious press articles that tried to tie evangelicals in with the men that had been accused in the Watergate affair. As far as I know there were no evangelicals involved with the possible exception of one.

I think these men have what I would call a "magnificent obsession" to change the country and the world. A year before Mr. Nixon decided to run for President, he listed to me point by point what he thought ought to be done. One thing was to end the cold war. He also wanted to balance the budget. Another goal was to control crime, which was growing rampant at about that time. And another one was ending the Viet Nam war. This was his number-one concern, and I think he really thought he could end Viet Nam much quicker than he did end it. (It was interesting to me—by way of parenthesis—to watch the show on the late President Kennedy the other night in Europe. His speeches were hawkish. I mean, if Nixon were saying the things Kennedy said ten years ago, we would condemn him. We forget how fast things change. We have become dovish and isolationist, in many of our viewpoints.)

These Nixon aides thought his re-election was the most important thing in the world. They thought that future peace depended on him. I think most of them were very sincere, but they began to rationalize that the "end" justified the "means," even if it meant taking liberties with law and the truth. They had seen the law broken by people who had other "causes." They had heard people call for all kinds of civil disobedience. They felt that their "cause" was just as great as peace in Viet Nam and civil rights. In fact, they felt peace in Viet Nam could only be achieved by the re-election of Mr. Nixon. Many of these men were very young. In fact, the President had the youngest staff in the history of the White House. In addition, I think the President himself was so occupied with "détente" with the Soviet Union and China and giving so much time and thought to it that he gave little thought to his re-election campaign. I think he was so sure of his election that he just left it to other people, and I think that this was part of the problem.

Q. Do you think that the absence of an absolute standard of right and wrong contributed to wrongdoing?

A. Yes, I do. We've been told by popular theologians for some years that morals are determined by the situation, and now we are reaping the bitter fruits of that teaching. Some of the men involved in Watergate practiced that kind of ethics. If God is, then what God says must be "absolute"— man must have moral boundaries. He cannot devise his own morals to fit his own situation. The Bible tells us that with what judgment we judge we shall be judged. So we must avoid hypocritical and self-righteous glee at the evil that has been done. The Bible also teaches us, "Lie not one to another." There is no blinking at the fact that Watergate has become a symbol of political corruption and evil. But let us hope that by God's grace we may turn the corner. Let's hope we realize that there is one crisis more urgent than the energy crisis and that this is the crisis in integrity and in Christian love and in forgiveness.

Q. Do you think that the McGovern campaign did as many "dirty tricks" as the Nixon campaign?

A. I don't know whether they did as many or not, but you still have the same "absolute" involved, even if they did only one, don't you? The principle would be the same whether it was one or a hundred tricks. Also, don't forget that corporations gave money to both parties, and both parties have historically been guilty of unethical practices that do violence to the sincere Judeo-Christian conscience. No political party has any corner on ethics.

Q. Do you think that President Nixon will resign or be impeached?

A. I do not know. I think that if no other bomb explodes he might well survive. He still has time to recover a great deal of lost credibility in his remaining three years. If another bomb explodes he is in serious trouble.

Q. Do you think that evangelical Christianity is now America's civil religion? Is there an alliance between government and evangelicalism?

A. I don't think that at all, any more than there was an alliance between President Franklin Roosevelt and the old Federal Council of Churches. I don't recall Roosevelt ever seeing evangelical leaders. During his administration, evangelicalism was at a very low ebb. It was the heyday of modernism and liberalism. Perhaps he did have evangelicals to the White House, but I don't recall it. In the Truman administration, I don't recall evangelicals trooping in and out of the White House either. Dr. Edward Pruden was his pastor at the First Baptist Church here in the city, and he was a wonderful man. Under the Eisenhower administration it was largely Dr. Edward L. R. Elson who had the influence, though I was at the White House a few times myself and knew Eisenhower quite well. Evangelicalism has become so strong in the country in recent years and has gained such momentum that now "we" are targets of criticism at every level because we are, as someone has said, "where the action is." By we, I don't mean Billy Graham. I mean the evangelical movement as a whole. Today almost all denominations are divided between the evangelicals on the one hand and the liberals on the other.

I think another point ought to be made: having a conservative theology does not necessarily mean a person is a sociological or political conservative. I consider myself a liberal on many social subjects, but in the eyes of most informed Christians I am a theological evangelical. I gladly take my stand with them. However, some of the criticism hurled at evangelical theology lands on me, and I suppose when I make a mistake it hurts the evangelical cause. I sometimes put my foot in my mouth. I've made many statements I wish I could recall. I am an erring, fallible disciple of our Lord Jesus Christ and subject to all the temptations, human frailties, and errors of other disciples of the Lord.

One of the leaders of the evangelical revival has been *Christianity Today*, along with other para-church organizations that have come to the front in recent years. I think these things have given an intellectual respectability to evangelicalism that did not exist in the country twelve years ago.

Getting back to civil religion, I don't recall a single President, including President Nixon, talking about Jesus Christ publicly. Nearly all Presidents in their public statements have talked about God. Our civil religion in America has always been a sort of unitarianism. This was true of Kennedy, of Eisenhower, and Presidents all the way back. I don't think America has ever been an all-out Christian nation, such as Great Britain, where you have an official relationship between church and state. The *London Telegraph* last September made an interesting point along this line. They said, "Why should we ask Billy Graham about Watergate any more than we ask the Archbishop of Canterbury about our scandals?" And they said the Archbishop of Canterbury is tied in far more closely with the government than Billy Graham is in Washington. That's quite a valid point. In countries where there is a state-church relationship, people don't necessarily hold the church or church leaders responsible for all the political decisions. I've never quite understood why I am considered in some way responsible for or part of any administration, whether under President Johnson or Nixon. I just happened to be friends with both of them long before they became prominent in public life. We should guard against guilt by association. As I said before, twenty years ago we called it McCarthyism. Since you are someone's friend you are supposed to be guilty of the same things he's guilty of.

*   *   *

Q. You continually preach that a change of heart in the individual is the answer to our problems. The criticism we keep getting is that regeneration in so many people does not seem to be having the effect we claim it will have, and that we are not seeing the fruit of the Spirit among believing Christians in America. Our compassion is so minimal for people who are downtrodden and wanting for one reason or another . . .

A. I think evangelicals have been far too much on the defensive at this point. Many of the great social movements of our generation have had their roots in regeneration and in evangelical theology. They asked Martin Luther King, when he was receiving the Nobel Peace Prize, where he got his motivation, and he said, "From my father's preaching." Well, his father is a real evangelical preacher. However, I think that beginning about the middle of the 1920s, in reaction to modernism evangelicals went too far in defending the redemptive Gospel to the exclusion of the great social content of Scripture. The parable of the Good Samaritan is a dramatic case in point. We have a social responsibility, and I could identify with most of the recent Chicago Declaration of Evangelical Social Concern. I think we have to identify with the changing of structures in society and try to do our part.

Q. What is your reaction to Nixon's disclosure of his charitable giving for the past few years?

A. I must say I was surprised at the small amount he reported giving to charities in relation to his total income, but there may be some other explanation in that his finances and contributions were left to other people. I believe that every Christian should give 10 per cent of his income to his church or charity, and above that if the Lord so prospers him.

* * *

Q. Dr. Graham, most people tend to turn to the Church more in times of trouble. Does it concern you that during this crisis the opposite seems to be true of Mr. Nixon, that he has attended hardly any religious services in the past year and sought hardly any spiritual counsel?

A. I would like to see any President who is a professing Christian go to church every Sunday, and attend the prayer meetings at the White House— and show up once in a while for the Senate and House prayer breakfasts. It is my prayer that all the events that have happened during the past few months will tend to deepen the religious convictions of the President. The agonies of the Civil War caused Lincoln to turn to God in a greater dependence than ever before. This tends to be true of most Presidents in periods of crisis.

7

Evangelicals and Politics since 1980

EDITOR: *In 1980, with Ronald Reagan running as the Republican candidate for president, an organization called the Moral Majority that had been founded in 1979 became a significant and highly visible force in politics. This was the beginning of a movement that was at first called the New Religious Right, in contrast to the old anti-Communist right, and would later become simply the Christian Right. Largely as a result of the Christian Right's efforts during the final two decades of the twentieth century, evangelicals became the most reliable constituency in the Republican Party. In short, the Christian Right is to the Republican Party what big labor was to the Democrats in the 1950s and 1960s. The selection below is the agenda of the early Christian Right as articulated by fundamentalist pastor Jerry Falwell. Ironically, as a separatist Fundamentalist, Falwell had opposed political activism earlier in his career. He even preached a well-known sermon condemning the political activity of liberal preachers involved in the civil rights movement during the 1960s. With the rise of the abortion issue, government regulation of private schools, gay rights, the teaching of evolution in public schools, and so forth, Falwell changed his mind about political activism. He came to symbolize the politicization of many formerly separatist fundamentalists. As noted in chapter two, he and other fundamentalists left their separatism behind but carried their militancy into the political realm, thus becoming fundamentalistic evangelicals.*

Falwell, Jerry. "Future-word: An Agenda for the Eighties." In *The Fundamentalist Phenomena*. Edited by Jerry Falwell with Ed Dobson and Ed Hinson. Garden City: Doubleday, 1981. 186–220. Used by permission.

These are the greatest days of the twentieth century. We have the opportunity to formulate a new beginning for America in this decade. For the first time in my lifetime we have the opportunity to see spiritual revival and political renewal in the United States. We now have a platform to express the concerns of the majority of moral Americans who still love those things for which this country stands. We have the opportunity to rebuild America to the greatness it once had as a leader among leaders in the world.

The 1980s are certainly a decade of destiny for America. The rising tide of secularism threatens to obliterate the Judeo-Christian influence on American society. In the realm of religion, liberal clergy have seduced the average American away from the Bible and the kind of simple faith on which this country was built. We need to call America back to God, back to the Bible, and back to moral sanity.

Positive Christianity recognizes that reformation of the institutional structure of the Church is futile without the spiritual revitalization of people's lives. It is the people whose lives have been dynamically changed by their personal relationship to Christ who are the real strength of the Church. It is no "mere pietism" that will dynamically energize the evangelical church into social action. In our attempt to rally a diversity of morally conservative Americans together in Moral Majority, we were convinced that millions of people were fed up with the fruits of liberalism, both in politics and in religion. I am well aware that it is unpopular in some circles to equate the two. But I say that they must be viewed as cousins of the same family because both rest upon the same foundational presupposition of the inherent goodness of mankind. The ultimate product of theological Liberalism is a vague kind of religious humanism that is devoid of any true Gospel content.

* * *

MORAL ISSUES

Imperative of Morality

As a pastor, I kept waiting for someone to come to the forefront of the American religious scene to lead the way out of the wilderness. Like thousands of other preachers, I kept waiting, but no real leader appeared. Finally I realized that we had to act ourselves. Something had to be done now. The government was encroaching upon the sovereignty of both the Church and the family. The Supreme Court had legalized abortion on demand. The Equal Rights Amendment, with its vague language, threatened to do further damage to the traditional family, as did the rising sentiment toward so-called homosexual rights. Most Americans were shocked, but kept hoping someone would do something about all this moral chaos.

Organizing the Moral Majority

Facing the desperate need in the impending crisis of the hour, several concerned pastors began to urge me to put together a political organization that could provide a vehicle to address these crucial issues. Men like James Kennedy (Fort Lauderdale, Florida), Charles Stanley (Atlanta, Georgia), Tim La Haye (San Diego, California), and Greg Dixon (Indianapolis, Indiana), began to share with me a common concern. They urged that we formulate a nonpartisan political organization to promote morality in public life and to combat legislation that favored the legalization of immorality. Together we formed the Moral Majority, Inc. Today Moral Majority, Inc., is made up of millions of Americans, including 72,000 ministers, priests, and rabbis, who are deeply concerned about the moral decline of our nation, the traditional family, and the moral values on which our nation was built. We are Catholics, Jews, Protestants, Mormons, Fundamentalists—blacks and whites—farmers, housewives, businessmen, and businesswomen. We are Americans from all walks of life united by one central concern: to serve as a special-interest group providing a voice for a return to moral sanity in these United States of America. Moral Majority is a political organization and is not based on theological considerations. We are Americans who share similar moral convictions. We are opposed to abortion, pornography, the drug epidemic, the breakdown of the traditional family, the establishment of homosexuality as an accepted alternate life-style, and other moral cancers that are causing our society to rot from within. Moral Majority strongly supports a pluralistic America. While we believe that this nation was founded upon the Judeo-Christian ethic by men and women who were strongly influenced by biblical moral principles, we are committed to the separation of Church and State.

Here is how Moral Majority stands on today's vital issues:

1. We believe in the separation of Church and State. Moral Majority, Inc., is a political organization providing a platform for religious and non-religious Americans who share moral values to address their concerns in these areas. Members of Moral Majority, Inc., have no common theological premise. We are Americans who are proud to be conservative in our approach to moral, social, and political concerns.

2. We are pro-life. We believe that life begins at fertilization. We strongly oppose the massive "biological holocaust" that is resulting in the abortion of one and a half million babies each year in America. We believe that unborn babies have the right to life as much as babies that have

been born. We are providing a voice and a defense for the human and civil rights of millions of unborn babies.

3. We are pro-traditional family. We believe that the only acceptable family form begins with a legal marriage of a man and woman. We feel that homosexual marriages and common law marriages should not be accepted as traditional families. We oppose legislation that favors these kinds of "diverse family form," thereby penalizing the traditional family. We do not oppose civil rights for homosexuals. We do oppose "special rights" for homosexuals who have chosen a perverted life-style rather than a traditional life-style.

4. We oppose the illegal drug traffic in America. The youth in America are presently in the midst of a drug epidemic. Through education, legislation, and other means we want to do our part to save our young people from death on the installment plan through illegal drug addiction.

5. We oppose pornography. While we do not advocate censorship, we do believe that education and legislation can help stem the tide of pornography and obscenity that is poisoning the American spirit today. Economic boycotts are a proper way in America's free-enterprise system to help persuade the media to move back to a sensible and reasonable moral stand. We most certainly believe in the First Amendment for every one. We are not willing to sit back, however, while many television programs create cesspools of obscenity and vulgarity in our nation's living rooms.

6. We support the state of Israel and Jewish people everywhere. It is impossible to separate the state of Israel from the Jewish family internationally. Many Moral Majority members, because of their theological convictions, are committed to the Jewish people. Others stand upon the human and rights of persons as a premise for support of the state of Israel. Support of Israel is one of the essential commitments of Moral Majority. No anti-Semitic influence is allowed in Moral Majority, Inc.

7. We believe that a strong national defense is the best deterrent to war. We believe that liberty is the basic moral issue of all moral issues. The only way America can remain free is to remain strong. Therefore we support the efforts of our present administration to regain our position of military preparedness with a sincere hope that we will never need to use any of our weapons against any people anywhere.

8. We support equal rights for women. We agree with President Reagan's commitment to help every governor and every legislature to move quickly to ensure that during the 1980s every American woman will earn

as much money and enjoy the same opportunities for advancement as her male counterpart in the same vocation.

9. We believe ERA is the wrong vehicle to obtain equal rights for women. We feel that the ambiguous and simplistic language of the Amendment could lead to court interpretations that might put women in combat, sanction homosexual marriages, and financially penalize women and deserted wives.

10. We encourage our Moral Majority state organizations to be autonomous and indigenous. Moral Majority state organizations may, from time to time, hold positions that are not held by the Moral Majority, Inc., national organization.

Facing the Opposition

We have been labeled by our critics as arrogant, irresponsible, and simplistic. They accuse us of violating the separation of Church and state. However, the National Council Churches (NCC) has been heavily involved in politics for years, and virtually no one has complained. Since many moral problems, such as abortion, require solutions that are both legal and political, it is necessary for religious leaders to speak on these matters in order to be heard.

What Moral Majority Is Not

1. We are not a political party. We are committed to work within the multiple-party system in this nation. We are not a political party and do not intend to become one.

2. We do not endorse political candidates. Moral Majority informs American citizens regarding the vital moral issues facing our nation. We have no "hit lists." While we fully support the constitutional rights of any special-interest group to target candidates with whom they disagree, Moral Majority, Inc., has chosen not to take this course. We are committed to principles and issues, not candidates and parties.

3. We are not attempting to elect "born-again" candidates. We are committed to pluralism. The membership of Moral Majority, Inc., is so totally pluralistic that the acceptability of any candidate could never be based upon one's religious affiliation. Our support of candidates is based upon two criteria: (a) the commitment of the candidate to the principles that we espouse; (b) the competency of the candidate to fill that office.

4. Moral Majority, Inc., is not a religious organization attempting to control the government. Moral Majority is a special-interest group of

millions of Americans who share the same moral values. We simply desire to influence government—not control government. This, of course, is the right of every American, and Moral Majority, Inc., would vigorously oppose any Ayatollah type of person's rising to power in this country.

5. We are not a censorship organization. We believe in freedom of speech, freedom of the press, and freedom of religion. Therefore while we do not agree that the Equal Rights Amendment would ultimately benefit the cause of women in America, we do agree with the right of its supporters to boycott those states that have not ratified the amendment. Likewise, we feel that all Americans have the right to refuse to purchase products from manufacturers whose advertising dollars support publications and television programming that violate their own moral code.

6. Moral Majority, Inc., is not an organization committed to depriving homosexuals of their civil rights as Americans. While we believe that homosexuality is a moral perversion we are committed to guaranteeing the civil rights of homosexuals. We do oppose the efforts of homosexuals to obtain special privileges as a bona fide minority. And we oppose any efforts by homosexuals to flaunt their perversion as an acceptable life-style. We view heterosexual promiscuity with the same distaste which we express toward homosexuality.

7. We do not believe that individuals or organizations that disagree with Moral Majority, Inc., belong to an immoral minority. However, we do feel that our position represents a consensus of the majority of Americans. This belief in no way reflects on the morality of those who disagree with us or who are not involved in our organizational structures. We are committed to the total freedom of all Americans regardless of race, creed, or color.

Out of the Pew and into the Precinct

Many Christians are raising the question of whether or not they should be involved in politics at all. Some raise the question of the separation of Church and State; others feel that politics is the devil's arena and Christians should stay out; and others say politics requires compromising and Christians should not compromise. Many liberal church people are also claiming that Evangelicals are violating the separation of Church and State. Recently Richard Dingman said: "As one who has held local public office for ten years and worked in congress for ten years, it is my opinion that it is not only proper for Christians to become involved, but it is absolutely biblical and absolutely necessary."

The recent emergence of the Fundamentalists and Evangelicals into politics in no way violates the historical principles of the nation. The incorporation of Christian principles into both the structure and the basic documents of our nation is a matter of historical fact. The doctrine of the separation of Church and State simply means that the state shall not control religion and religion shall not control the state. It does not mean that the two may never work together.

* * *

EDITOR: *Falwell here discussed at length several issues, some of which were not mentioned in the enumerated items above. These included humanism in the public schools, sex education in the public schools, pornography, racial injustice, world hunger, ethical issues, selective breeding, genetic engineering, and euthanasia. Then, he made an appeal to fundamentalists, which is found below. This appeal was necessary because fundamentalists had a history of theological and cultural separatism that kept them from entering politics beyond voting. Notice how similar Falwell's language is to Carl F. H. Henry's argument in the previous chapter. Falwell was calling fundamentalists to political and social action in the same way Henry did in 1947. Notice also the clear distinction he draws between fundamentalists and evangelicals. Ironically, Falwell's move into politics nudged him closer to evangelicalism and away from fundamentalism. In the final fifteen years of his life he usually referred to himself as an evangelical.*

AN APPEAL TO FUNDAMENTALISTS

I have always made it clear that I am a Fundamentalist—big F! A Fundamentalist is one who believes the Bible to be verbally inspired by the Holy Spirit and therefore inerrant and absolutely infallible. True Fundamentalists believe in the deity of Jesus Christ. They readily accept His virgin birth, sinless life, and vicarious death. They believe in His literal resurrection, His ascension into heaven, and His second coming. A Fundamentalist believes in evangelism and discipleship through the local church as the proper fulfillment of the Great Commission of our Lord.

I am also a separatist. We practice separatism from the world and all of its entanglements. We refuse to conform to the standards of a sinful society. We practice personal separation as well as ecclesiastical separation. Most of us are "independents" in our associations. We are at our best when we are free from hierarchical structures that would tie us down to denominational mediocrity. We are our own people. We are not intimidated by academic degrees or ecclesiastical positions. We do our own thinking and we do not care what liberals think about anything!

However, we are not without our weaknesses. We tend to be negative and pessimistic. For too many years now, we have been sitting back waiting for apostasy to take over at any moment, and have nearly let the country go down the drain. We have been irresponsible as Christian citizens. We have almost totally avoided the political process and the social life of our country. We have neglected reaching the whole person for the cause of Christ. We have blasted the Liberals and derided the Evangelicals for their feeble attempts at the social application of the Gospel, while doing almost nothing ourselves.

We love to extol the virtues of our fidelity to the faith. We pride ourselves that we are not as others who have compromised. Yet our lack of capacity for honest self-criticism has often left us hiding behind our honorary degrees while attacking the value of education. Our emphasis on belonging to the right group causes us at times to overlook our own sins. We have just as many failures in our ranks as do the Evangelicals—maybe more. We cannot be blinded by our tendency to use our people to build our churches, instead of using our churches to build our people.

In spite of our weaknesses, we have much to offer our Evangelical brethren that they need. We preach the Bible with authority and conviction. Where they hesitate and equivocate, we loudly thunder: "Thus saith the Lord!" Where they are overly theoretical and impractically idealistic, we have become practical evangelists and experts at church growth. While the Evangelicals are always defining and redefining, we are out building great churches to the glory of God. We are experts at preaching the Gospel to the lost. We have the highest percentage of converts and the fastest-growing churches in America.

✳ ✳ ✳

AN APPEAL TO EVANGELICALS

The Evangelical Movement has been a vital part of this country for two centuries. Evangelical pastors have provided mature and stable leadership for the churches of America. They have demonstrated the love of Christ to their congregations and have been expositors and defenders of the Christian faith. Where others have been extreme, they have remained balanced.

They have attempted to apply the truth of the Gospel to the needs of society. In general, the Evangelical Movement has been faithful to the fundamental doctrines of the Christian faith.

In reality, there is little difference theologically between Fundamentalists and Evangelicals. We both hold to a strong belief in the inspiration and inerrancy of the Bible. We bold to the deity of Christ and to the necessity of personal salvation. Though Evangelicalism tends to be tolerant of varying viewpoints, the vast majority of evangelical pastors tell me that they are concerned about the drift of so-called Young Evangelicals to the left. They do not like the current trend within the movement, which is getting dangerously close to moderate Liberalism.

The lines are not clearly drawn today among Evangelicals. The movement is so broad that it at times takes in everything from Bible churches to Charismatic Catholics. Theologically it extends from Josh McDowell to Helmut Thielicke. Philosophically it includes strong inerrancy defenders such as Norman Geisler and John W. Montgomery. It has provided the conservative movement in general with such able social critics as Harold O. J. Brown. But at the same time it unfortunately includes some who are ready to deny their fundamentalist heritage and exchange their theological birthright for a mess of socioacademic pottage!

We appeal to our evangelical brethren to stand with us for the truth of the Gospel in this hour when America needs us most. Stop looking down your theological and ecclesiastical noses at your fundamentalist brethren. As the English theologian James Barr has already pointed out, non-Evangelicals view Evangelicals and Fundamentalists alike anyhow. We have so much in common. Only the radicals among us (to the left and to the right) divide us. I say it is time we denied the "lunatic fringe" of our movements and worked for a great conservative crusade to turn America back to God. We do not need an organic unity. Such is not necessary in order to achieve a mutual appreciation and respect.

We appeal to you to acknowledge your fundamentalist roots. Stop being intimidated by what others think. Stop worrying about academic credibility and social acceptability. If Evangelicals have one glaring weakness, it is that you are too concerned what the world thinks about you. You are hesitant to speak up on vital issues for fear of what the intellectual elite may think. Let them think what they wish. They have been wrong before, and they will be wrong again!

* * *

Evangelicals need to reaffirm the foundation. Come back to the fundamentals of the Christian faith and stand firm on that which is essential.
Throw down the anchor of truth and stop drifting with every new wave of
religious fad that comes along. Stop trying to accommodate the Gospel to
the pitiful philosophies of unregenerate humankind. You have the truth,
and the truth shall set you free.

You talk much of love, but often you have only words of bitter contempt for those of us who call ourselves Fundamentalists. Do not be embarrassed because we believe the same things you do. Acknowledge us.
Accept us as Bible-believing brethren who love the same Christ you love.
Let us work to reach the world for Christ.

We conservative Fundamentalists and Evangelicals can be used of God
to bring about a great revival of true Christianity in America and the
world in our lifetime.

EDITOR: *Although the specter of government regulation of private schools
in 1970s was initially important in energizing evangelicals and fundamentalists to get involved in politics, by the 1980s no issue was as important
as abortion. The prolife movement within the Christian Right made abortion an evangelical litmus test in the political realm. Below is an essay by
one of conservative evangelicalism's most reasoned defenders of the prolife
position.*

Geisler, Norman. "The Bible, Abortion, and Common Sense." *Fundamentalist Journal* (May, 1985): 24–27. Used by permission.

* * *

Common-Sense Answers to Arguments for Abortion

Here are the arguments used by abortionists to justify this mass slaughter
of innocent lives, and some common-sense answers to them.

No one knows when human life begins. If no one knows when life begins, it might begin at conception. And if it does begin at that point then
abortion is murder. Can we justify killing something that might be human? Should we shoot at a moving object in the woods if we are not sure
whether it is a human being? Neither should we kill babies if we are not
sure they are human.

Actually, we *do* know when life begins. It begins at conception. A male sperm with 23 chromosomes is not a human being, nor is a female ovum with its 23 chromosomes. But when they unite into 46 chromosomes the result is a human being. This is a medical fact. Genetically this fertilized ovum is a human being with its own life-long characteristic code and identity. From this point on it is simply a matter of its growth, not of its kind.

The mother has the right to control her own body. The baby is not part of the mother's body. It is an individual human being with its own separate body. To be sure, the mother is "feeding" the unborn baby, but does a mother have the right to stop feeding her baby after it is born? This would be murder by starvation. Likewise, to cut off the source of life for an unborn is also wrong.

Even if the unborn baby were part of the mother's body, she would not have the right to do anything she wants to her body. For example, she does not have the moral right to mutilate her own body by cutting off a hand or a foot. Nor does she have the right to kill her body by committing suicide.

The unborn is not really human until it is born. If a baby is not human before it is born then what is it? It certainly is not a mineral or vegetable. It is not an animal. Cows give birth to cows and horses to horses. No one has any difficulty identifying an unborn dog as a dog or an unborn pig as a pig. Why should there be any question about an unborn human?

Does this mean they are only human if they change their location and move outside the womb? The difference between babies that are born and those that are unborn is not their nature; it is simply their size and location. Certainly accidental or circumstantial characteristics such as size or place do not determine whether someone is human.

Babies are not conscious personal beings. This objection assumes one must have consciousness to be human. But if consciousness determines humanness then sleeping adults are not human. Further, if consciousness is the test for humanness then all who lapse into a coma lose their humanity. The logical conclusion from this would be that killing unconscious people would not be murder. Perhaps all murderers should simply knock out their victims before they shoot them!

Furthermore, babies *are* conscious before they are born. By one and a half months after conception they have a brain wave of their own, which they keep for their entire life. The absence of a brain wave is considered a sign of human death. Why then is the presence of this brain wave not considered a sign of life? And as early as 3 months they react to stimuli. They can consciously sense pressure and pain.

Self-consciousness—not consciousness—distinguishes a human's ability from an animal's, for higher animals are conscious too. However, self-consciousness does not occur until a child is about a year and a half old. So by the abortionist's logic infanticide up to that age could be considered justifiable "abortion!"

Every child has a right to a meaningful life. What are the criteria for a meaningful life, and who decides whether a life is "meaningful"? This kind of reasoning has already gone so far that some courts have convicted parents for having children they knew by prenatal tests would be deformed.

This rationale for abortion assumes that this deformed human being will be given another chance under better circumstances if we kill him now. This is not so. Taking the life of this unborn is taking the only chance this human being will ever have to live. This particular baby will never get a better chance at life. So the real choice is not between a projected *imperfect* life and a better one. It is between the life they actually have and *none at all!* Everyone has a right to the life he actually has. To take away this right by abortion is to take away the only life he has.

This same logic will lead to murdering larger deformed human beings who live elsewhere (i.e., outside the womb). The logic of abortionists leads to infanticide and euthanasia. Even some pro-abortionists (such as Joseph Fletcher) admit that the two issues are logically tied together. In fact, there is greater justification for taking a life one already *knows* is deformed than to take one that prenatal tests simply indicate *might* be deformed. It is better to have an aborted child than to have an abused one. This assumes that non-abortion of unwanted babies leads to abuse. Statistically, just the opposite is the case. For child abuse cases have increased as abortions have gone up. Apparently the disregard for human life reflected in the acceptance of abortion is extended from the pre-birth to post-birth attitude toward offspring.

This objection wrongly assumes that abortion is not a great abuse. Actually, abortion is one of the worst abuses that can be given to a human being.

If we can murder the unborn to avoid potential abuse, why not murder the born who are undergoing *actual* abuse? Or, to put it the other way, if we protect the born who are undergoing child abuse, how much more should we protect the unborn who are even more defenseless? Abortion is child abuse of the worst kind.

We must stop overpopulation or we will all starve. The claim that we must choose either abortion or overpopulation is false. There are other alternatives. Birth control can limit overpopulation without murder. So the real choice is to control population by killing innocent lives or else without killing them. Here as elsewhere an ounce of prevention is worth a pound of cure.

We cannot legislate morality. If this is so, we should get rid of the legislated morals we now have on the books. We could start by rescinding prohibitions against murder, cruelty, child abuse, incest, and rape. For all of these are cases of legislating morals. We could also eliminate antislavery laws and all civil rights legislation. These also legislate moral behavior. But this would be clearly wrong, and few abortionists would suggest that we do away with any of these laws. But if this is the case, why should we not have laws to protect the moral rights of unborn humans?

Further, the present abortion-on-demand law legislates morality. For it says in effect that taking an unborn human life is morally right, legislating morality is impossible (and undesirable) to avoid. The aim of all good legislation should be to put into law what is morally just and right. And by no stretch of the imagination is it right to take away an innocent human being's right to life. For the right to life is the right to all other rights. Without life there is no right to anything else.

No mentally retarded child should be brought into this world. Interestingly, no organization of parents with mentally retarded children has endorsed abortion-on-demand. Many families I have known with Down's Syndrome children regard them with real joy because of their unfeigned love. Retarded children are human; killing them is killing humans. Just because the unborn are smaller (and defenseless) does not justify killing them. Again, the logic by which abortionists justify therapeutic abortions would also justify infanticide.

Why should a rape victim be forced to bear a child she did not will to have? Rape is one of the worst indignities a person can suffer. One must have great compassion for rape victims. However several things must be kept in mind. First, there is no way to become unraped. Becoming unpregnant (via abortion) does not make one unraped. Second, justice is not served to the rape victim by punishing the unborn baby resulting from the rape.

Two wrongs do not make a right. The guilt of a murder on top of the indignity of the rape will not help the mother. Rape is not a crime for the victim. But killing an innocent life of the unborn is a crime.

Although conception seldom occurs from rape, the few babies who are conceived by rape also have the right to live.

Who has not been blessed by the gospel music of the famous black singer Ethel Waters. Yet her mother was a rape victim at the age of 13. Should she have aborted Ethel? Why should we punish the innocent product of a rape. Let's punish the guilty producer of the rape—the rapist!

People are going to have abortions anyway so we may as well legalize them. Should we legalize rape and child-abuse since people are going to commit these atrocities anyway? Should we add incest and cruelty to the list because people persist in them? Legalizing an evil does not make it morally right.

Legalizing an activity does not necessarily curb its abuse. Sometimes it aids it. Such has been the case with abortion in the United States. On the other hand, changing the law can help change the attitude toward an activity, as the laws abolishing slavery has shown. Laws cannot in themselves force people to be good. But enforcing good laws can help restrain people from doing evil.

Legalizing abortion will save the lives of mothers by making abortions safer. Statistics show that most abortions still occur outside hospitals. The Supreme Court has consistently struck down laws demanding that abortion mills meet even minimal standards of health. In fact if a cattle truck parked at a curb and posted a sign abortions performed here not only would the government not stop the enterprise, it would not even insist that the abortionists sterilize their instruments!

Furthermore, legalizing abortion has not saved lives; it has lost lives—16 million in the first 12 years since the Supreme Court ruled permissible. Even if sterile conditions were guaranteed by the government for all abortions this would simply assure sanitary conditions for the slaying. Knowing it was a clean killing is surely a small consolation for the victim.

We should not project our morality on others. If this is so, why are the abortionists projecting their morality on the unborn? They are saying to the unborn in effect, "My moral belief is that you should not live." This is not a projection of morality but a projection of immorality. In fact, we must project our morality into the abortion situation. If those who are able to project morality to protect the innocent do not do so, who will?

Projecting our moral beliefs on others is not wrong, but destroying the moral rights of others is wrong. Abortion takes away the moral right of the innocent to live.

Abortion is the solution to unwanted pregnancies. Adoption is a better solution. Giving one's child to a stranger is difficult, but that is easier than killing it. On the date the aborted child was to be born the mother often suffers depression. This depression sometimes [occurs] for years later on the child's birthday. Sometimes the feelings are so strong the woman becomes suicidal. Most women with unwanted pregnancies mainly need encouragement. Counseling clinics are the solution, not abortion clinics. We should be helping mothers, not killing babies.

No unwanted baby should ever be born. The assumption here is that an unwanted conception will automatically lead to an unwanted baby. Many mothers change their minds when they begin to think more soberly—after the initial trauma of the unplanned pregnancy fades. More change their mind when they feel or see (by ultrasound) life in the womb. And even more mothers change their minds after their babies are born.

Even if the mother does not want to keep the baby, there are many other families who cannot have children and they do want them. Presently there are more who want children than there are children to want.

Just because we do not want someone else to live does not mean we have a right to kill him. We should not place our *wishes* over the *rights* of others, especially the right to live.

Let me relate the story of a young girl who learned she was pregnant. She was engaged, but her fiancee was not the father of the baby. Her family was poor, so another mouth to feed would add to the family hardship. Her family had a good name in the community and she did not want to drag it into the mud. An abortion would have been a quick solution to her problem. But she did not have an abortion. She had the baby, a little boy. She named him Jesus.

EDITOR: *Along with Falwell, religious broadcaster Pat Robertson became a major Christian Right figure in the 1980s. He ran for president in 1988, and then founded the Christian Coalition in 1990. Below he explains why the Christian Right supports Israel. Such support is directly related to the dispensational views encountered in chapter 3. Dispensationalism teaches that Israel will play a special role in end-times prophecy, but Robertson does not delve into dispensationalism because he was speaking to a Jewish audience in Israel. Most of his listeners would have had little interest in the arcane particulars of Christian end-times prophecy. They were, however, interested in the fact that many evangelicals and fundamentalists comprise a large and vocal body of support for Israel. The implications of that support are spelled out briefly in the Hal Lindsey selection found in chapter 3. Below, note the political implications of Robertson's support for Israel and his direct challenge to his Israeli audience to take a harder line against the Palestinians.*

> Robertson, Pat. "Why Evangelical Christians Support Israel." Speech given at the Herzliya Conference, Lauder School of Government, Diplomacy, and Strategy, December 17, 2003. http://www.patrobertson.com/Speeches/Israel-Lauder.asp. Used by permission.

One day in the late 19th Century, Queen Victoria of England reportedly asked her Prime Minister, Benjamin Disraeli, this question: "Mr. Prime Minister, what evidence can you give me of the existence of God?" Disraeli thought for a moment and then replied, "The Jew, your majesty."

* * *

Ladies and Gentleman, evangelical Christians support Israel because we believe that the words of Moses and the ancient prophets of Israel were inspired by God. We believe that the emergence of a Jewish state in the land promised by God to Abraham, Isaac, and Jacob was ordained by God.

We believe that God has a plan for this nation which He intends to be a blessing to all the nations of the earth.

Of course, we, like all right-thinking people, support Israel because Israel is an island of democracy, an island of individual freedom, an island of the rule of law, and an island of modernity in the midst of a sea of dictatorial regimes, the suppression of individual liberty, and a fanatical religion intent on returning to the feudalism of 8th Century Arabia. These facts about modern day Israel are all true. But mere political rhetoric does not account for the profound devotion to Israel that exists in the hearts of tens of millions of evangelical Christians.

You must realize that the God who spoke to Moses on Mount Sinai is our God. Abraham, Isaac, and Jacob are our spiritual Patriarchs. Jeremiah, Ezekiel, and Daniel are our prophets. King David, a man after God's own heart, is our hero. The Holy City of Jerusalem is our spiritual capital. And the continuation of Jewish sovereignty over the Holy Land is a further bulwark to us that the God of the Bible exists and that His Word is true.

And we should clearly take note that evangelical Christians serve a Jew that we believe was the divine Messiah of Israel, spoken of by the ancient prophets, to whom He entrusted the worldwide dissemination of His message to twelve Jewish apostles.

It should be noted that today Christianity, with well over two billion adherents, is by far the fastest growing religion in the world. Within twenty years, that number will swell to three billion. Of these, at least six hundred million are Bible-believing evangelicals and charismatics who are ardent supporters of the nation of Israel. In twenty years, that number will reach one billion. Israel has millions of Christian friends in China, in India, in Indonesia, throughout Africa and South America, as well as North America.

We are with you in your struggle. We are with you as a wave of anti-Semitism is engulfing the earth. We are with you despite the pressure of the "Quartette" and the incredibly hostile resolutions of the United Nations. We are with you despite the threats and ravings of Wahabbi Jihadists, Hezbollah thugs, and Hamas assassins.

We are with you despite oil embargos, loss of allies, and terrorist attacks on our cities.

We evangelical Christians merely say to our Israeli friends, "Let us serve our God together by opposing the virulent poison of anti-Semitism and anti-Zionism that is rapidly engulfing the world."

Having affirmed our support, I would humbly make two requests of our Israeli friends:

First, please don't commit national suicide. It is very hard for your friends to support you, if you make a conscious decision to destroy yourselves.

I hardly find it necessary to remind this audience of the stated objectives of Yasser Arafat, the PLO, Hamas, Hezbollah, and Islamic Jihad. Their goal is not peace, but the final destruction of the State of Israel. At no time do they, or their allies in the Muslim world, acknowledge the sovereignty of Israel over even one square inch of territory in the Middle East. If a Palestinian State is created in the heart of Israel with sovereign power to deploy troops, import modern weapons-even weapons of mass destruction-and operate with full secrecy and diplomatic immunity, the ability of the State of Israel to defend itself will be fatally compromised.

The slogan "land for peace" is a cruel chimera. The Sinai was given up. Did that bring lasting peace?-No. Southern Lebanon was given up. Did that bring lasting peace?-No. Instead Hezbollah rode tanks to the border of Israel shouting, "On to Jerusalem!" Now, as many as 10,000 rockets aimed at Metulla, Qiryat Shemona, and all of Northern Israel have been put in place throughout Southern Lebanon.

Arafat was brought up at the knees of the man who yearned to finish the work of Adolf Hitler. How can any realist truly believe that this killer and his associates can become trusted partners for peace?

I am aware of the deep feelings of many Israelis who yearn for peace. Who long to be free from the terror of the suicide bombers of the intifada. I would draw their attention to the fact that during the Cold War, the American people yearned to be free from the constant threat of a nuclear holocaust. Then, at Reykjavik, Iceland on the occasion of a summit between President Ronald Reagan of the United Sates and Premier Mikhail Gorbachev of the Soviet Union, what seemed like an incredible opportunity for peace was presented to President Reagan by Mr. Gorbachev. An offer was made for hitherto undreamed of reductions in nuclear weapons. Gorbachev's offer included everything the U.S. arms negotiations had wanted, except one thing. The condition for the Russian offer was to be the agreement by the United States to abandon the so-called "star wars" Strategic Defense Initiative.

Mr. Reagan carefully considered the offer-then reluctantly said no. Without the Strategic Defense Initiative, there would be no deal. Gorbachev was stunned. Then both leaders, with sadness in their hearts, adjourned the meeting and departed Reykjavik.

Once again, the world was hovering on the brink of nuclear annihilation. The American liberal press was apoplectic at Reagan's decision. But he held firm.

Now we all know that he was right. The Russians could not compete with the United States in a nuclear arms race and Gorbachev knew it. The bluster was over—the threats were over—Reagan had won by standing firm. Soon freedom broke out in Poland—in Hungary—in East Germany. The Berlin Wall came down. The barbed wire fences came down. And Soviet Communism came down.

The world is safe from super power nuclear terror. This terror is no more because one strong leader stood against public opinion—against the advice of many of his own counselors and said no! May the leaders of Israel in 2004 have the courage to look the nations of the world in the eye, and when your national interests demand it—say no!

Second, the world's Christians ask that you do not give away the treasured symbols of your spiritual patrimony.

I read recently in the Wall Street Journal an article written by an American Jewish commentator who remarked that the Temple Mount and what is termed the "Wailing Wall" are "sacred stones and sites," but hardly worth bloodshed.

Just think—the place where the Patriarch Abraham took Isaac to offer him to God. The place bought by King David from Araunah where the Angel of the Lord stood with drawn sword. The place of Solomon's temple. The place of the Holy of Holies. The place where Jesus Christ walked and taught. The very spiritual center of the Jewish worship of the one true God—nothing but a pile of sacred stones—unworthy of sacrifice? What an incredible assertion!

Ladies and gentlemen, make no mistake—the entire world is being convulsed by a religious struggle. The fight is not about money or territory; it is not about poverty versus wealth; it is not about ancient customs versus modernity. No—the struggle is whether Hubal, the Moon God of Mecca, known as Allah, is supreme, or whether the Judeo-Christian Jehovah God of the Bible is Supreme.

If God's chosen people turn over to Allah control of their most sacred sites—if they surrender to Muslim vandals the tombs of Rachel, of Joseph, of the Patriarchs, of the ancient prophets—if they believe their claim to the Holy Land comes only from Lord Balfour of England and the ever fickle United Nations rather than the promises of Almighty God—then in that event, Islam will have won the battle. Throughout the Muslim world the message will go forth—"Allah is greater than Jehovah. The promises of Jehovah to the Jews are meaningless.

"We can now, in the name of Allah, move to crush the Jews and drive them out of the land that belongs to Allah."

In short, those political initiatives that some have asserted will guarantee peace, will in truth guarantee unending struggle and ultimate failure. Those political leaders who only understand the secular dimension of Israel's existence and who cavalierly dismiss the spiritual dimension will find that they receive the mess of pottage of Esau rather than the inheritance of Jacob.

* * *

On Christmas Day in 1974, I had the privilege of interviewing Prime Minister Yitzhak Rabin for my television program, *The 700 Club*. Rabin lamented the fact that after Israeli military victories, the nation had been stopped from achieving a peace treaty.

That was thirty years ago. Israel seemed as isolated and alone then as it does today. As I concluded my interview, I asked Prime Minister Rabin a final question. "What would you want the United States to do now for Israel?"

He replied without hesitation. "Be strong! Be strong!"

That evening I joined for dinner a group of several hundred people who had accompanied me from the United States. We were meeting in the large dining room of the InterContinental Hotel on the Mount of Olives in Jerusalem, whose floor-to-ceiling windows gave a stunning view of the illuminated Temple Mount. As I related to the group the substance of my meeting, I began to recall the feeling of sadness which had come from the Prime Minister—the sense of the isolation of his nation. That evening, I made a solemn vow to God that, despite whatever might happen in the future, I and the organizations I headed would stand in support of Israel and the Jewish people. Ladies and gentlemen, I am proud to say that I have kept that vow each year since 1974.

In closing, I would deliver to Israel in 2004 the message Yitzhak Rabin delivered to the United States on Christmas Day in 1974. For you are the living witnesses that the promises of the Sovereign Lord are true. "Be strong! Be strong!"

He will be with you and so will your evangelical friends.

Thank you, and God bless you!

EDITOR: *While most evangelicals find their political views represented substantially by the Christian Right, there is a strong and articulate minority who comprise the evangelical Left. Ronald Sider and his organization Evangelicals for Social Action have long been leaders in this movement. Among the issues of concern for the evangelical Left are poverty, racial justice, peace, and human life issues including abortion. The abortion issue remains virtually the only point of agreement between the Christian Right and the evangelical Left. Below is a selection on peace written by Sider and Darrel Brubaker. It was also given in a revised form as a speech delivered to Peace Sunday, an interreligious peace rally to protest the nuclear arms race, held in the Rose Bowl in Pasadena, California. The essay is representative of the evangelical Left's views on warfare and foreign policy.*

> Sider, Ronald and Darrel Brubaker. "An Evangelical Witness for Peace." In *Preaching on Peace*. Philadelphia: Fortress, 1982. 25–28. Used by permission.

It is no longer I who live, but Christ who lives in me (Gal. 2:20).

I am honored to be here as President of Evangelicals for Social Action, a national movement of evangelical Christians committed to stopping the nuclear arms race.

I am also honored to be here as an evangelical Christian. We all know that some highly visible and vocal evangelical leaders support President Reagan's massive military buildup. Among evangelical Christians, however, they do not represent a majority. Most evangelical Christians are proud of Billy Graham's courageous peace pilgrimage to Moscow in spite of vigorous opposition from the U.S. State Department. More and more evangelical Christians are coming to the conclusion that nuclear war can never be justified. In fact, President Reagan's pastor, the Rev. Donn Moomaw of Bel Air Presbyterian Church, said in a recent sermon: "Because nuclear weapons are so destructive, so devastating, so final . . . they are morally indefensible. I must be a nuclear pacifist."

I am honored to be here, finally, as a citizen of our diverse, pluralistic society. We come together today as Baptists and Buddhists, Catholics and charismatics, Jews and Jesuits, humanists and Hindus, Muslims and Methodists—to say no to nuclear madness. Each of us has our own way of explaining why our deepest beliefs compel us to oppose the arms race. Because we respect each other's different tradition we need to share with each other the diverse bases of our common concern for peace. Briefly, then, permit me to share why I as an evangelical Christian believe that a decision to continue the nuclear arms race would be one of the most immoral decisions in history.

Christians believe that the good earth, all life, and you and I are the creation of a personal, loving God. We do not believe that persons and nature have resulted from the accidental combination of subatomic matter in a blind materialistic process. If that were true, persons would merely be complex machines, and ethical values—even with respect to peacemaking—would be totally subjective products of blind chance. Certainly the Creator used a gloriously complex evolutionary process stretching over vast geological ages to create the world. But it was not an accident.

The Almighty Creator is an Infinite Person who wants to be in free, loving relationship with finite persons. So the Creator molded you and me in the divine image. That is why I believe that every person is of infinite value. The worth of individuals does not depend on their productivity or usefulness to society. Every person is created in God's image for personal relationship with the Lord of the universe. That is why it is wrong for totalitarians to sacrifice millions of people for the alleged benefit of the state. That is why it is wrong for American and Russian militarists to build megaton weapons that will destroy people by the hundreds of millions.

Not just persons but the earth itself also comes from the Creator's loving hand. As I worked on my book *Nuclear Holocaust and Christian Hope,* my love for the gorgeous beauty of the earth grew deeper and deeper. As I faced the stark reality that human madness might actually destroy our little planet in my lifetime, I fell more deeply in love with the soft gentle breezes, the majestic redwoods, and the purple sunset. Christians believe that the earth is a ring from the Beloved to be cherished and preserved, not an accidental commodity to be exploited and destroyed. To continue down a path that makes nuclear destruction ever more likely does not merely reflect callous contempt for future generations; it also demonstrates a blasphemous affront to the Creator of this gorgeous, fragile planet.

The Creator intended persons to live together in harmonious human society shaping cultures and civilizations of beauty, justice, and peace. But human history is a tragic mixture of good and evil. So often human greed, national pride, and sheer selfishness have led to ghastly conflict. Choosing to deny that we are made for obedient relationship with God, choosing to love ourselves more than our neighbor, we have created an upward spiral of violence. Clubs have given way to cannons; firebombs to 20-megaton nuclear warheads. Today we stand trembling at the precipice, peering fearfully into the nuclear abyss.

Still, my friends, I have hope. I believe that it is possible to obtain nuclear disarmament within the next twenty-five years. The basis of my hope, however, is not primarily the growing antinuclear movement, although I am deeply involved in and highly grateful for that movement. The basis of my hope is God.

Christian faith reminds me that God has taken the initiative to correct all that is evil and unjust in the world. Christians believe that the Creator of the galaxies actually took on human flesh and walked the dusty paths of Palestine as a humble teacher. He taught that we should be peacemakers and love our enemies. He cared for the poor and the weak, the sick and the social outcasts, those whom the powerful always ignore. He said that God loves even the people who have messed up their lives the worst, even those who have fallen into the grossest selfishness and sin. And then he took one incredible additional step: he said he was going to die for precisely those kinds of people.

Jesus' radical acceptance of those who had harmed themselves, their families, and their neighbors was not based on some kind of cheap indulgence. In fact he said that harming other people is not just an awful offense against the neighbor; it is also a terrible affront against the Creator who created neighbors in the divine image. Therefore oppressors and sinners are God's enemies because they disrupt the harmony of God's good creation. But Jesus said God loves even these enemies so much that he would die for them. As God in the flesh, Jesus Christ said he would take all the evil of God's sinful enemies upon himself. Because he loved them, he would take on himself the punishment they deserved for their violence, oppression, and sin. At the cross, God himself suffered the agony of Roman crucifixion for the sake of sinful enemies. That is the foundation of Jesus' call to love our enemies. Jesus knew that the Creator of the galaxies loves his enemies enough to suffer incredible agony for them—that is why he taught his followers to love their enemies also.

But isn't that just utopian drivel? Don't we live in a violent, vicious world where loving our enemies does not work? Didn't Jesus' life end in failure at the cross?

That would be a proper conclusion except for one thing: Jesus did not stay dead. On the third day, he was alive again. On Easter morning the tomb was empty. By raising Jesus from the dead, God proved that Jesus' way of loving his enemies was not naive utopianism, but God's way to peace. By raising Jesus from the dead, God proved the correctness of Jesus' teaching that God was busy restoring the broken beauty of human society.

It is because I know that the peacemaker from Nazareth rose from the dead that I have hope today. It is because I know that the Teacher of peace was God in the flesh that I dare to commit my life to the long, costly struggle for nuclear disarmament.

I don't say that easily. I don't for a minute suppose that I can persist in the long twenty-five-year struggle against nuclear holocaust in my own strength. Let's not kid ourselves. Nuclear disarmament will not happen in a year or two or three, even if—please God—we can one day soon elect a President committed to nuclear disarmament rather than nationalistic superiority. If nuclear disarmament comes at all, if we succeed in avoiding nuclear holocaust, it will happen only after long, exhausting decades of costly struggle.

Why then do I hope to be able to walk that long and weary road? Christians believe that the Risen Lord Jesus now lives in those who open their lives to him. As Paul said, "It is no longer I who live but Christ who lives in me." From personal experience I know that the Risen Jesus lives in me. I know that he calls me to oppose nuclear madness—because creation is a divine gift to be treasured, because every human life is sacred, because

God loves his enemies and calls on me to love my enemies. I cannot do that in my own strength. But I don't have to, because Christ lives in me.

My friends, the task before us is awesome. The next two decades will be the most dangerous in human history. But we can succeed. We can rid the world of the monstrous evil of nuclear weapons. The Creator of the galaxies is on the side of peace. In realistic political terms, nuclear disarmament looks extremely difficult to achieve. But it is not impossible. With God all things are possible. Let's join him to make the planet safe for your children and mine.

EDITOR: *The last two selections in this chapter are paired deliberately to show the contrast between evangelical Left and Christian Right. Along with Sider, Jim Wallis has been a long-time leader of peace and justice evangelicalism. As founder and editor of* Sojourners *magazine he has provided a consistent evangelical voice on issues of peace, justice, and human life. While not using the antiabortion position as a litmus test in politics, Wallis is prolife on abortion. He and other evangelicals of the Left have adopted the "consistent life" or "seamless garment" ethic espoused by some leading Catholic theologians in the twentieth century. Those who hold this view oppose abortion, capital punishment, and war.*

Richard Land of the Southern Baptist Convention's Ethics and Religious Liberty Commission has emerged in the past two decades as one of the most influential voices of the Christian Right. Although not in lock step with Falwell and Robertson and not as visible as James Dobson of Focus on the Family, Land has tremendous influence by virtue of the fact that he is the political spokesperson for America's largest Protestant denomination. In the two selections below, notice that both Wallis and Land seek to claim the vital center of American politics, portraying their adversaries as part of the fringe.

Wallis, Jim. "Why Can't Personal Ethics and Social Justice-Together-Become a Real Political Choice?" *Sojourners*, February 2005. Used by permission.

Why can't we talk about religion and politics? These are the two topics you are not supposed to discuss in polite company. Don't break up the dinner party by bringing up either of these subjects! That's the conventional wisdom. Why? Perhaps it's because these topics are too important and too potentially divisive, or because they raise issues of core values and ultimate concerns that make us uncomfortable.

All over the country I feel the hunger for a fuller, deeper, and richer conversation about religion in public life, about faith and politics. It's a discussion that we don't always hear in America today. Sometimes the most strident and narrow voices are the loudest, and more progressive, prophetic, and healing religion often gets missed. But the good news is about how all that is changing.

Abraham Lincoln had it right. Our task should not be to invoke religion and the name of God by claiming God's blessing and endorsement for all our national policies and practices—saying, in effect, that God is on our side. Rather, as Lincoln put it, we should worry earnestly whether we are on God's side.

Those are the two ways that religion has been brought into public life in American history. The first way—God on our side—leads inevitably to triumphalism, self-righteousness, bad theology, and, often, dangerous foreign policy. The second way—asking if we are on God's side—leads to much healthier things, namely penitence and even repentance, humility, reflection, and accountability. We need much more of all those, because they are often the missing values of politics.

Martin Luther King Jr. did it best. With his Bible in one hand and the Constitution in the other, King persuaded, not just pronounced. He reminded us all of God's purposes for justice, for peace, and for the "beloved community" where those who have been left out and left behind get a front-row seat. And he brought religion into public life in a way that was always welcoming, inclusive, and inviting to all who cared about moral, spiritual, or religious values. Nobody felt left out of the conversation.

The values of politics are my primary concern. Of course, God is not partisan. God is not a Republican or a Democrat. When either party tries to politicize God or co-opt religious communities to further political agendas, it makes a terrible mistake. The best contribution of religion is precisely not to be ideologically predictable nor loyally partisan. Both parties, and the nation, must let the prophetic voice of religion be heard. Faith must be free to challenge both the Right and the Left from a consistent moral ground.

"God's politics" are therefore never partisan nor ideological. But God's politics challenge everything about our politics. God's politics remind us of the people our politics always neglect-the poor, the vulnerable, the left behind. God's politics challenge narrow national, ethnic, economic, or cultural self-interest, reminding us of a much wider world and the creative human diversity of all those made in the image of the creator. God's politics remind us of the creation itself, a rich environment in which we are to be good stewards, not mere users, consumers, and exploiters. And

God's politics plead with us to resolve, as much as possible, the inevitable conflicts among us without the terrible destruction of war. God's politics always remind us of the ancient prophetic prescription to "choose life, so that you and your children may live," and challenge all the selective moralities that would choose one set of lives and issues over another. This challenges both the Right and the Left, offering a new vision for faith and politics in America and a new conversation of personal faith and political hope.

People concerned about social change and hungry for spiritual values can actually combine those two quests. Too often politics and spirituality have been separated, polarized, and even put into competition with one another. We have been buffeted by private spiritualities that have no connection to public life and a secular politics showing disdain for religion or even spiritual concerns. That leaves spirituality without social consequences and a politics with no soul. Political discourse that is disconnected from moral values quickly degenerates. How might we change our public life with the values that many of us hold most dear? How can we connect a genuinely "prophetic" spirituality to the urgent need for social justice? This is the connection the world is waiting for.

Prophecy is not future telling, but articulating moral truth. The prophets diagnose the present and point the way to a just solution. The "prophetic tradition," in all of the world's great religions, is just what we need to open up our contemporary political options, which are, honestly, grossly failing to solve our most pressing social problems. The competing ideological options, from which we are forced to choose, are perhaps at their lowest ebb in compelling the involvement of ordinary citizens in public life. It is not that people just don't care, but that they feel un-represented and unable to vote for anything that expresses their best values. That is a serious political crisis, and we need better options.

What would it mean to evaluate the leading current political options by the values of the prophets? Most importantly, what would happen if we asserted that *values* are the most important subject for the future of politics? What if we proposed a "prophetic politics"?

After the 2002 mid-term elections, I attended a private dinner for Harvard Fellows in Cambridge, Massachusetts. Our speaker was a Republican political strategist who had just won all the major senatorial and gubernatorial election campaigns in which he was involved. Needless to say, he was full of his success and eager to tell us about it. This very smart political operative said that Republicans won middle-class and even working-class people on the "social" issues, those moral and cultural issues that Democrats don't seem to understand or appreciate. He even suggested that passion on the social issues can cause people to vote against their economic self-interest. Since the rich are already with us, he said, we win elections.

I raised my hand and asked the following question. "What would you do if you faced a candidate that took a traditional moral stance on the social and cultural issues? They would not be mean-spirited and, for example, blame gay people for the breakdown of the family, nor would they criminalize the choices of desperate women backed into difficult and dangerous corners. But the candidate would be decidedly pro-family, pro-life (meaning they really want to lower the abortion rate), strong on personal responsibility and moral values, and outspoken against the moral pollution throughout popular culture that makes raising children in America a countercultural activity. And what if that candidate was also an economic populist, pro-poor in social policy, tough on corporate corruption and power, clear in supporting middle-class and working families in health care and education, an environmentalist, and committed to a foreign policy that emphasized international law and multilateral cooperation over pre-emptive and unilateral war? What would you do?" I asked. The Republican strategist paused for a long time, and then said, "We would panic!"

Virtually every time I'm out speaking on "prophetic politics" during any election season, somebody asks the question, "How can I vote for what I've just heard?" Some very interesting polling in the last few years shows how increasingly important voters' perceptions of "values" are to their electoral behavior. And most voters feel they can't really vote for their values. In the polling, the values question now goes beyond traditional family and sexual matters to also include matters such as "caring for the poor." The problem is that politics is still run by ideological polarities that leave many people feeling left out.

There are now three major political options in our public life. The first political option in America today is *conservative* on everything—from cultural, moral, and family concerns to economic, environmental, and foreign policy issues. Differences emerge between aggressive nationalists and cautious isolationists, between corporate apologists and principled fiscal conservatives, but this is the political option clearly on the ascendancy in America, with most of the dominant ideas in the public square coming from the political Right.

The second political option in contemporary America is *liberal* on everything—both family/sexual/cultural questions and economic, environmental, and foreign policy matters. There are certainly differences among the liberals (from pragmatic centrists to green leftists), but the intellectual and ideological roots come from the Left side of the cultural and political spectrum-and today most from the liberal/left find themselves on the defensive.

The third option in American politics is *libertarian*-meaning liberal on cultural/moral issues and conservative on fiscal/economic and foreign policy. The "just leave me alone and don't spend my money option" is growing quickly in American life.

I believe there is a *fourth option* for American politics, which follows from the prophetic religious tradition we have described. It is "traditional" or "conservative" on issues of family values, sexual integrity and personal responsibility, while being very "progressive," "populist," or even "radical" on issues like poverty and racial justice. It affirms good stewardship of the earth and its resources, supports gender equality, and is more internationally minded than nationalist-looking first to peacemaking and conflict resolution when it come to foreign policy questions. The people it appeals to (many religious, but others not) are very strong on issues such as marriage, raising kids, and individual ethics, but without being "right-wing," reactionary, mean-spirited, or scapegoating against any group of people, including gays and lesbians. They can be pro-life, pro-family and pro-feminist, all at the same time. They think issues of "moral character" are very important, both in a politician's personal life and in his or her policy choices. Yet they are decidedly pro-poor, pro-racial reconciliation, critical of purely military solutions, and defenders of the environment.

At the heart of the fourth option is the integral link between personal ethics and social justice. And it appeals to people who refuse to make the false choice between the two.

Who are these people? Many are religious: Catholics, black and Latino Christians, evangelicals who don't identify with the Religious Right, and members of all our denominational churches who want to put their faith into practice. They are Jews and Muslims who are guided by an active faith and not just a personal background. They are people who do not consider themselves "religious," but rather "spiritual," and would be drawn to a fourth option in politics. And they are people—religious, spiritual, or not—who consider themselves shaped by a strong sense of *moral* values and long for a political commitment that reflects those values.

As I travel the country, I find many people who share this perspective. Still, it is not yet a viable political option. It should be. As one who has called for a new "moral politics" that transcends the old categories of both the secular Left and the Religious Right, I believe it is time to assert a clear "fourth" political option. In a recent conversation, columnist E. J. Dionne of the *Washington Post* said there was a huge constituency of "non-right wing Christians" and other morally concerned people in the country who need to get organized. Like E. J., they are moderate to conservative on personal moral questions while very progressive on social justice.

Recent polling shows that the more religious voters are, the more likely they are to vote for conservatives. Given how negatively much of the political Left seems to regard religion and spirituality, this is not surprising. But what if a new political option regarded personal ethics as important as social justice and saw faith as a positive force in society-for progressive social change. I think the fourth option could be a real winning vision and believe that many are very hungry for it. While the political elites and many special interest groups resist the "personal ethics/social justice" combination (perhaps because it threatens many special interests), countless ordinary people would welcome it.

What we need is nothing less than "prophetic politics." We must find a new moral and political language that transcends old divisions and seeks the common good. Prophetic politics finds its center in fundamental "moral issues" such as children, diversity, family, community, citizenship, and ethics (others could be added such as nonviolence, tolerance, fairness, etc.) and tries to construct national directions to which many people across the political spectrum could agree. It would speak directly to the proverb "Without a vision, the people perish," and would offer genuine political vision that rises out of biblical passages from prophetic texts. Our own ancient prophetic religious traditions could offer a way forward beyond our polarized and paralyzed national politics and be the foundation for a fourth political option to provide the new ideas politics always needs.

Simply put, the two traditional options in America (Democrat and Republican, liberal and conservative) have failed to capture the imagination, commitment, and trust of a majority of people in this country. Neither has found ways to solve our deepest and most entrenched social problems. Record prosperity hasn't cured child poverty. Family breakdown is occurring across all class and racial lines. Public education remains a disaster for millions of families. Millions more still don't have health insurance, or can't find affordable housing. The environment suffers from unresolved debates, while our popular culture becomes more and more polluted by debased and violent "entertainment." In local communities, people are more and more isolated, busy, and disconnected. Our foreign policy has become an aggressive assertion of military superiority in a defensive and reactive mode, seeking to protect us against growing and invisible threats, instead of addressing the root causes of those threats. The political Right and Left continue at war with each other, but the truth is that these false ideological choices themselves have run their course and become dysfunctional.

Prophetic politics would not be an endless argument between personal and social responsibility, but a weaving of the two together in search of the common good. The current options are deadlocked. Prophetic politics wouldn't assign all the answers to the government, the market, or the churches and charities; but rather patiently and creatively forge new civic partnerships where everyone does their share and everybody does what they do best. Prophetic politics wouldn't debate whether our strategies should be cultural, political, or economic; but show how they must be all three, led by a moral compass.

Perhaps most important, prophetic politics won't be led just by elected officials, lawyers, and their financial backers. Look for community organizers, social entrepreneurs, nonprofit organizations, faith-based communities, and parents to help show the way forward. Pay particular attention to a whole generation of young people forged in community service. They may be cynical about politics but are vitally concerned with public life. The politics we need now will arise more from building social and spiritual movements than merely lobbying at party conventions. And ultimately it will influence the party conventions, as successful movements always do.

The prophetic role that churches are undertaking is illustrative of the larger public vocation that may now be required. That role may become more clear in the wake of the election. Without a vision, Democrats had nothing to offer the American people as an alternative to the vision of the Bush administration.

With the Republicans offering war overseas and corporate dominance at home, and the Democrats failing to offer any real alternatives, who will raise a prophetic voice for social and economic justice and for peace? Never has there been a clearer role for the churches and religious community. We can push both parties toward moral consistency and their best-stated values, over the unprincipled pragmatism and negative campaigning that both sides too often engaged in during the recent election.

The courage many church leaders showed in opposing the war in Iraq is an early sign of that prophetic role. So is the growing unity across the spectrum of the churches on the issue of poverty. The truth is that there are more churches committed to justice and peace than churches that belong to the Religious Right. It's time the voice of those congregations be heard and their activism be mobilized to become the conscience of American politics in a time of crisis.

We've seen other moments in recent history when the churches emerged as the leading voice of political conscience and opposition. Certainly there were key times in the struggle against apartheid in South Africa, in El Salvador during the 1980s, in the people power revolution that ousted dictator Ferdinand Marcos of the Philippines, and in the opposition to communist rule in Poland when the churches became the critical public voice for both political challenge and change.

Even in democracies, churches have responded to that same prophetic vocation. In New Zealand during the 1990s, when conservative forces ripped that society's long-standing social safety net to pieces, it was the churches-in partnership with the indigenous Maori people—who led marches, ignited public protest, and helped restore key programs in health care, housing, and social services. During the Thatcher years in Britain, it was again church leadership that reminded the nation of its responsibilities to impoverished urban communities, to the ethics of the common good over private gain, to social justice, and to peace. And, of course, in the United States, black churches provided the moral foundation and social infrastructure for the powerful civil rights movement that changed our society.

In a bitterly divided nation, we face historic challenges. But the political "tie" that the nation is caught in might be a moment of opportunity. It shows that the old options and debates have created a deadlock. This very crisis could open the way for some new and creative thinking and organizing. And that could be very good news indeed. Our political leaders must learn the wisdom that the way to reach common ground is to move to higher ground. And we citizens should start by showing the way.

Perhaps the most mistaken media perception of our time is that religious influence in political life only equates to the politics of the Religious Right. The biggest story that the mainstream media has yet to discover is how much that reality is changing. My prediction is that moderate and progressive religious voices will shape politics in the coming decades far more significantly than will the Religious Right.

History teaches us that the most effective social movements are also spiritual ones-movements that change people's thinking and attitudes by an appeal to moral and religious values. Those movements change the cultural and political climate, which then makes policy changes more possible, palatable, and, yes, democratic. Perhaps the best example of doing it right, as we have said, is the American civil rights movement, which was led by ministers who appealed directly to biblical faith. I believe that will be the more-likely pattern for future movements that combine faith and politics, replacing the more politically conformist model of the Religious Right.

To move away from the bifurcating politics of liberal and conservative, Left and Right, would be an enormously positive change and would open up a new "politics of solutions." Right now, Washington responds to a problem or crisis in two ways. First, politicians try to make us afraid of the problem, and, second, they look for somebody to blame for it. Then they watch to see whose political spin succeeded, either in the next poll or the next election. But they seldom get around to actually solving the problem. The media make everything worse by assuming that every political issue has only two sides instead of multiple angles to view and solve the problem. Addicted to conflict as their methodology, the media always seem to want to pitch a fight between polarized views instead of convening a public discussion to find serious answers.

The answer is to put values at the center of political discourse and, in every public debate, ask what kind of country and people we really want to be. We would find new agreements across old political boundaries and new common ground among people who agree on values and are ready to challenge the special interests on all sides who are obstructing the solutions most Americans would support. Ideologies have failed us; values can unite us, especially around our most common democratic visions.

Land, Richard. "Toward a Paradigm of Religious Faith." *Liberty* 102:5 (September/October 2007): 1–5. Used by permission.

For the past few years I have been writing a book entitled *The Divided States of America? What Liberals and Conservatives Are Missing in the God-and-Country Shouting Match.*[1] The book, published this past April, is the product of almost a half century of reflection and study about an issue that matters deeply to me as an American committed to the Baptist faith tradition.

I might describe the book as an equal opportunity offender. It has two whole chapters explaining how both liberals and conservatives have taken a wrong fork in the road when it comes to the role of religious faith in

America. I outline how both "factions" should, and should not, act in this ongoing American story. The shorthand version of those two chapters is that conservatives much too often assume that God is on their, or America's, side and that liberals much too often assume that God doesn't have a side in the perplexing issues that face us as a country—vital issues such as the sanctity of all human life from conception to natural death and at all points within those parameters.

* * *

American Exceptionalism

The second subject of *The Divided States of America?* that has drawn the most impassioned and sustained response from readers is my firm belief that America does have a special role to play in the world as the proponent and defender of freedom and human rights.

My formulation of this American "exceptionalism" is both shared by millions of Americans—and often misunderstood by liberals and conservatives alike. I well remember being with Jim Wallis on a panel discussion at Chautauqua in 2005. Jim was asked by someone in the audience to outline the points on which he and I agree and disagree. Jim explained that we both believe that religious faith has a vital, indeed an invaluable, role to play in American society—as opposed to the secularists who disagree vehemently with both of us on that score. We have substantial disagreement, he allowed, about *how* religious faith should be "played out in American society and also in foreign policy" (*Divided States*, p. 30).

Jim went on to say that he does not believe in American "exceptionalism," which he then defined as an American-imposed hegemony and empire. I responded that while I do believe in American "exceptionalism," I did not recognize what I believed from Jim's description.

American "exceptionalism," as I and millions of other Americans understand it, is not a doctrine of pride, privilege, and prejudice, which allows America to be judged internationally by a lower standard than other nations. Instead, it is a "doctrine of obligation, responsibility, sacrifice, and service in the cause of freedom" (*Divided States*, p. 31).

Jim Wallis then asked me for my scriptural justification for such a belief. I cited Luke 12:48: "From everyone who has been given much, much will be required; and to whom they entrusted much, of him they will ask all the more" (NASB)—to whom much is given, much is required.[2]

America as a nation, and the American people as a people have been wonderfully blessed with an abundance of natural resources as well as a remarkable heritage of freedom, the rule of law, and "government of the people, by the people, for the people."

There was either a fortuitous or a providential set of circumstances in the development and rise of America. I, of course, believe there was more providence than mere good fortune involved in the bountiful blessings experienced by America. Blessings, by definition, are undeserved and unmerited—that is why they are called "blessings." Such undeserved and unearned favor invokes obligation.

Most people of a more liberal persuasion find such beliefs anathema and reject any claim of America being "exceptional"—in blessings or anything else. Unfortunately, far too many conservatives assume that such blessings mean that America is God's new "chosen nation."

I summarized my argument for American "exceptionalism" as follows: "What liberals and conservatives are both missing is that America has been blessed by God in unique ways—we are not just another country. But neither are we God's special people. I do not believe that America is God's chosen nation . . . we are not the new Israel. We do not have 'God on our side.' We are not God's gift to the world.

"America does not have a special claim on God. Millions of Americans do, however, believe God has a special claim on them—and their country" (*Divided States*, p. 192).

This means that having been undeservedly given so much, we have an obligation and a responsibility to be the proponent and friend of freedom for all people. We have no right to impose freedom on others, but we do have an obligation to help those who desire it to achieve it whenever possible.

We are not just another country with interests—we are also a cause, and that cause is to be FREEDOM.

* 8 *

Social Positions: Gender and Race

EDITOR: *The question of gender has vexed evangelicals for well over a century and shows no sign of abating anytime soon. From at least the early nineteenth century to the present evangelicals have been divided over the propriety of women preachers, women deacons, and women holding other church offices. In addition to the role of women in churches, evangelicals also debate whether or to what degree wives must be submissive to their husbands. The majority has usually argued from the plain and literal interpretation of certain New Testament passages that spiritual authority in the churches is for men only, but there has always been a strong minority report affirming the full participation of women in all ministerial roles.*

The first selection in this chapter comes from A. J. Gordon and is representative of the minority argument over the past century. Gordon was an evangelical pastor and missions leader who pastored a prominent church in Boston from 1869 until his death in 1895. He founded a missions training school that was the forerunner of Gordon College and Gordon-Conwell Seminary, two evangelical institutions that thrive to this day. Among evangelicals he was a leading proponent of women's suffrage and women in ministry, believing that women as well as men could experience the power of the Holy Spirit that would make them effective proclaimers of the Gospel. His 1894 article, excerpted below, is something of a classic defense of women in ministry.

Gordon, Adoniram Judson, "The Ministry of Women," *Missionary Review of the World.* Vol. 7 (December 1894), 910–21.

The occasion for writing the following article is this: at a recent summer convention a young lady missionary had been appointed to give an account of her work at one of the public sessions. The scruples of certain of the delegates against a woman's addressing a mixed assembly were found to be so strong, however, that the lady was withdrawn from the program, and further public participation in the conference confined to its male constituency.

The conscientious regard thus displayed for Paul's alleged injunction of silence in the church on the part of women deserves our highest respect. But with a considerable knowledge of the nature and extent of women's work on the missionary field, the writer has long believed that it is exceedingly important that that work, as now carried on, should either be justified from Scripture, or if that were impossible, that it be so modified as to bring it into harmony with the exact requirements of the Word of God. For while it is true that many Christians believe that women are enjoined from publicly preaching the Gospel, either at home or abroad, it is certainly true that scores of missionary women are at present doing this very thing. They are telling the good news of salvation to heathen men and women publicly and from house to house, to little groups gathered by the wayside, or to large groups assembled in the zayats. It is not affirmed that the majority of women missionaries are engaged in this kind of work, but that scores are doing it, and doing it with the approval of the Boards under which they are serving. If any one should raise the technical objection that because of its informal and colloquial character this is not preaching, we are ready to affirm that it comes much nearer the preaching enjoined in the great commission than does the reading of a theological disquisition from the pulpit on Sunday morning, or the discussion of some ethical or sociological question before a popular audience on Sunday evening.

But the purpose of this article is not to condemn the ministry of missionary women described above, or to suggest its modification, but rather to justify and vindicate both its propriety and authority by a critical examination of Scripture on the question at issue.

In order to reach a right understanding of this subject, it is necessary for us to be reminded that we are living in the dispensation of the Spirit—a dispensation which differs most radically from that of the law which preceded it. As the day of Pentecost ushered in this new economy, so the prophecy of Joel, which Peter rehearsed on that day, outlined its great characteristic features. Let us briefly consider this prophecy:

17 And it shall be in the last days, saith God,
I will pour, forth of my Spirit upon all, flesh:
And your sons and daughters shall prophesy,
And your young men shall see visions,
And your old men shall dream dreams:
18 Yea, and on my servants and on my handmaidens in those days

Will I pour forth of my Spirit: and they shall prophesy.
[19] And I will show wonders in the heaven above,
And signs on the earth beneath;
Blood, and fire, and vapor of smoke:
[20] The sun shall be turned into darkness,
And the moon into blood.
Before the day of the Lord come,
That great and notable day:
[21] And it shall be, that whosoever shall call on the name of the Lord shall be
saved.
(Acts 2: 17-21, R. V.)

It will be observed that four classes are here named as being brought into equal privileges under the outpoured Spirit:

1. Jew and Gentile: "All flesh" seems to be equivalent to "every one who" or "whosoever" named in the twenty-first verse. Paul expounds on this phrase to mean both Jew and Gentile (Rom. 10:13): "For there is no difference between the Jew and the Greek. . . . For whosoever shall call upon the name of the Lord shall be saved."

2. Male and female: "And your sons and your daughters shall prophesy."

3. Old and young: "Your young men shall see visions, and your old men shall dream dreams."

4. Bondmen and Bondmaidens (*vide* R. V. margin): "And on my servants and on my handmaidens in those days will I pour forth My Spirit, and they shall prophesy."

Now, evidently these several classes are not mentioned without a definite intention and significance; for Paul, in referring back to the great baptism through which the church of the New Covenant was ushered in, says "For in one Spirit were we all baptized into one body, whether Jews or Greeks, whether bond or free" (1 Cor. 12: 13, R. V.). Here he enumerates two classes named in Joel's prophecy; and in another passage he mentions three "for as many of you as were baptized into Christ did put on Christ; there can be neither Jew nor Greek; there can be neither bond nor free; there can be neither male nor female; for ye are all one in Christ Jesus" (Gal. 3:28, R. V.).

We often hear this phrase, "neither male nor female," quoted as though it were a rhetorical figure; but we insist that the inference is just, that if the Gentile came into vastly higher privileges under grace than under the law, so did the woman; for both are spoken of in the same category.

Here, then, we take our starting-point for the discussion. This prophecy of Joel, realized at Pentecost, is the Magna Charta of the Christian Church. It gives to woman a status in the Spirit hitherto unknown. And, as in civil legislation, no law can be enacted which conflicts with the constitution, so in Scripture we shall expect to find no text which denies to woman her divinely appointed rights in the New Dispensation.

* * *

If, now, we turn to the history of the primitive Church, we find the practice corresponding to the prophecy. In the instance of Philip's household, we read: "Now this man had four daughters which did prophesy" (Acts 21:9); and in connection with the Church in Corinth we read: "Every woman praying and prophesying with her head unveiled" (I Cor. 11: 5); which passage we shall consider further on, only rejoicing as we pass that "praying" has not yet, like its yoke-fellow, "prophesying," been remanded exclusively to the apostolic age.

Having touched thus briefly on the positive side of this question, we now proceed to consider the alleged prohibition of women's participation in the public meetings of the Church, found in the writings of Paul.

We shall examine, first, the crucial text contained in 1 Tim. 2: 8-11:

"I desire therefore that the men pray in every place, lifting up holy hands without wrath and disputing. In like manner, that women adorn themselves in modest apparel, with shamefacedness and sobriety; not with braided hair and gold or pearls or costly raiment; but (which becometh women professing godliness) through good works. Let a woman learn in quietness with all subjection. But permit not a woman to teach, nor to have dominion over a man, but to be in quietness, etc." (R. V.).

This passage has generally been regarded as perhaps the strongest and most decisive, for the silence of women in the Church. It would be very startling, therefore, were it shown that it really contains an exhortation to the orderly and decorous participation of women in public prayer. Yet, such is the conclusion of some of the best exegetes.

By general consent the force of *boulomai*, "I will," is carried over from the eighth verse into the ninth: "I will that women" (*vide* Alford). And what is it that the apostle will have women do? The words, "in like manner," furnish a very suggestive hint toward one answer, and a very suggestive hindrance to another and common answer. Is it meant that he would have the men pray in every place, and women, "in like manner," to be silent? But where would be the similarity of conduct in the two instances?

Or does the intended likeness lie between the men's "lifting up holy hands," and the women's adorning themselves in modest apparel? So unlikely is either one of these conclusions from the apostle's language, that, as Alford concedes, "Chrysostom and most commentators supply *proseuchesthai*, 'to pray,' in order to complete the sense." If they are right in so construing the passage—and we believe the *hosautos*, "in like manner," compels them to this course—then the meaning is unquestionable, "I will therefore that men pray everywhere, lifting up holy hands, etc. In like manner I will that women pray in modest apparel, etc."

In one of the most incisive and clearly reasoned pieces of exegesis with which we are acquainted, Wiesinger, the eminent commentator, thus interprets the passage, and as it seems to us, clearly justifies his conclusions. We have not space to transfer his argument to these pages, but we may, in a few words, give a summary of it, mostly in his own language. He says:

"1. In the words 'in every place' it is chiefly to be observed that it is public prayer and not secret prayer that is spoken of.

"2. The *proseuchesthai*, 'to pray,' is to be supplied in verse 9, and to be connected with 'modest apparel', so that this special injunction as to the conduct of women in prayer corresponds to that given to men in the words 'Lifting up holy hands'. This verse, then from the beginning refers to prayer: and what is said of the women in verses 9 and 10 is to be understood as referring primarily to public prayer.

"3. The transition in verse 1 I from *gunaikas* to *gune* shows that the apostle now passes on to something new— viz., the relation of the married woman to her husband. She is to be in quietness rather than drawing attention to herself by public appearance; to learn rather than to teach; to be in subjection rather than in authority."

In a word, our commentator finds no evidence from this passage that women were forbidden to pray in public assemblies of the Church: though reasoning back from the twelfth verse to those before, he considers that they may have been enjoined from public teaching. The latter question we shall consider further on.

The interpretation just given has strong presumption in its favour, from the likeness of the passage to another which we now consider: "Every man praying or prophesying, having his head covered, dishonoureth his head. But every woman praying or prophesying with her head unveiled dishonoureth her head" (1 Cor. 11:4-5).

By common consent, the reference is here to public worship; and the decorous manner of taking part therein is pointed out first for the man and then for the woman. "Every woman praying or prophesying." Bengel's terse comment: "Therefore women were not excluded from these duties," is natural and reasonable. It is quite incredible, on the contrary, that the apostle should give himself the trouble to prune a custom which he desired to uproot, or that he should spend his breath in condemning a forbidden method of doing a forbidden thing. This passage is strikingly like the one just considered, in that the proper order of doing having been prescribed first for the man, and then for the woman, it is impossible to conclude that the thing to be done is then enjoined only upon the one party and forbidden to the other. If the "in like manner" has proved such a barrier to commentators against finding an injunction for the silence of women in 1 Tim. 2:9, the unlike manner pointed out in this passage is not less difficult to be surmounted by those who hold that women are forbidden to participate in public worship. As the first passage has shown to give sanction to woman's praying in public, this one points not less strongly to her habit of both praying and prophesying in public.

We turn now to the only remaining passage which has been urged as decisive for the silence of women—viz., 1 Cor. 14: 34-35: "Let the women keep silence in the churches; for it is not permitted unto them to speak: but let them be in subjection, as also saith the law. And if they would learn anything, let them ask their own husbands at home: for it is shameful for a woman to speak in the church."

Here, again, the conduct of women in the Church should be studied in relation to that of men if we would rightly understand the apostle's teaching. Let us observe, then, that the injunction to silence is three times served in this chapter by the use of the same Greek word, *sigato*, twice on men and once on women, and that in every case the silence commanded is conditional, not absolute. "Let him keep silence in the church" (verse 28), it is said to one speaking with tongues, but on the condition that "there be no interpreter." "Let the first keep silence" (verse 30), it is said of the prophets, "speaking by two or three"; but on condition that "a revelation be made to another sitting by."

"Let the women keep silence in the church," it is said again, but it is evidently on the condition of their interrupting the service with questions, since it is added "for it is not permitted them to speak, . . . and if they would learn anything, let them ask their husbands at home." This last clause takes the injunction clearly out of all reference to praying or prophesying, and shows—what the whole chapter indicates—that the apostle is here dealing with the various forms of disorder and confusion in the church; not that he is repressing the decorous exercise of spiritual gifts, either by men or women. If he were forbidding women to pray or to prophesy in public, as some argue, what could be more irrelevant or meaningless than his direction concerning the case, "If they will learn anything, let them ask their husbands at home"?

In fine, we may reasonably insist that this text, as well as the others discussed above, be considered in the light of the entire New Testament teaching—the teaching of prophecy, the teaching of practice, and the teaching of contemporary history—if we would find the true meaning.

* * *

On the whole, we may conclude, without overconfidence, that there is no Scripture which prohibits women from praying or prophesying in the public assemblies of the Church; that on the contrary, they seem to be exhorted to the first exercise by the word of the apostle (1 Tim. 2:9); while for the prophesying they have the threefold warrant of inspired prediction (Acts 2:17), of primitive practice (Acts 21:9), and of apostolic provision (1 Cor. 11:4).

As to the question of teaching, a difficulty arises which is not easy to solve. If the apostle, in his words to Timothy, absolutely forbids a woman to teach and expound spiritual truth, then the remarkable instance of a woman doing this very thing at once occurs to the mind (Acts xviii.26)— an instance of private teaching possibly, but endorsed and made conspicuously public by its insertion in the New Testament.

In view of this example, some have held that the statement in 1 Tim. 2:9, with the entire paragraph to which it belongs, refers to the married woman's domestic relations, and not to her public relations; to her subjection to the teaching of her husband as against her dogmatic lording it over him. This is the view of Canon Garratt, in his excellent observations on the "Ministry of Women." Admit, however, that the prohibition is against public teaching; what may it mean? To teach and to govern are the special functions of the presbyter. The teacher and the pastor, named in the gifts to the Church (Eph. 4:11), Alford considers to be the same; and the pastor is generally regarded as identical with the bishop. Now there is no instance in the New Testament of a woman being set over a church as bishop and teacher. The lack of such example would lead us to refrain from ordaining a woman as pastor of a Christian congregation. But if the Lord has fixed this limitation, we believe it to be grounded, not on her less favored position in the privileges of grace, but in the impediments to such service existing in nature itself.

It may be said against the conclusion which we have reached concerning the position of women, that the plain reading of the New Testament makes a different impression on the mind. That may be so on two grounds; first, on that of traditional bias; and second, on that of unfair translation. Concerning the latter point, it would seem as though the translators of our common version wrought, at every point where this question occurs, under the shadow of Paul's imperative. "Let your women keep silence in the churches."

Let us take two illustrations from names found in that constellation of Christian women mentioned in Rom. 16: "I commend unto you Phoebe, our sister, which is a servant of the church which is at Cenchrea." So, according to the King James version, writes Paul. But the same word *diakonos*, here translated "servant", is rendered "minister" when applied to Paul and Apollos (1 Cor. 3:5), and "deacon" when used of other male officers of the Church (1 Tim. 3:10, 12, 13). Why discriminate against Phoebe simply because she is a woman? The word "servant" is correct for the general unofficial use of the term, as in Matt. xxii.10; but if Phoebe were really a functionary of the Church, as we have a right to conclude, let her have the honour to which she is entitled. If "Phoebe, a minister of the Church at Cenchrea," sounds too bold, let the word be transliterated and read "Phoebe, a deacon"—a deacon, too, without the insipid termination "ess," of which there is no more need than that we should say "teacheress" or "doctoress." This emendation "deaconess" has timidly crept into the margin of the Revised Version, thus adding prejudice to slight by the association which this name has with High Church sisterhoods and orders. It is wonderful how much there is in a name! "Phoebe, a servant", might suggest to an ordinary reader nothing more than the modern church drudge, who prepares sandwiches and coffee for an ecclesiastical sociable. To Canon Garratt, with his genial and enlightened view of women's position in apostolic times, "Phoebe, a deacon," suggests a useful co-laborer of Paul, "traveling about on missionary and other labors of love."

Again, we read in the same chapter of Romans, "Greet Priscilla and Aquila, my helpers in Christ Jesus." Notice the order here: the woman's name put first, as elsewhere (Acts 18:18; 2 Tim. 4:19). But when we turn to that very suggestive passage in Acts 18:26, we find the order reversed, and the man's name put first: "Whom, when Aquila and Priscilla had heard, they took him and expounded unto him the way of the Lord more perfectly." Yet this is conceded to be wrong, according to the best manuscripts. Evidently to some transcribes or critic, the startling question presented itself:

"Did not Paul say, 'I suffer not a woman to teach, nor to usurp authority over a man'?" But, here a woman is actually taking the lead as theological teacher to Apollos, an eminent minister of the Gospel, and so far setting her authority as to tell him that he is not thoroughly qualified for his work! This will never do: "if the woman cannot be silent, she must at least be thrust into the background." And so the order is changed, and the man's name has stood first for generations of readers. The Revised Version has rectified the error, and the woman's name now leads.

* * *

To follow still further the list of women workers mentioned in Rom. 16, we read: "Salute Tryphaena and Tryphosa, who labour in the Lord. Salute Persis the beloved, which laboured much in the Lord" (verse 12). What was the work in the Lord which these so worthily wrought? Put with this quotation another: "Help those women which laboured with me in the Gospel"; (Phil. 4:3). Did they "labour in the Gospel" with the one restriction that they should not preach the Gospel? Did they "labor in the Lord" under sacred bonds to give no public witness for the Lord? "Ah! but there is that word of Paul to Timothy, 'Let the women learn in silence,'" says the plaintiff. No! It is not there. Here again we complain of an invidious translation. Rightly the Revised Version gives it: "Let a woman learn in quietness" (*hesuchia*), an admonition not at all inconsistent with decorous praying and witnessing in the Christian assembly. When men are admonished, the King James translators give the right rendering to the same word: "That with quietness they work and eat their own bread" (1 Thess. 3:12), an injunction which no reader would construe to mean that they should refrain from speaking during their labour and their eating.

As a woman is named among the deacons in this chapter, so it is more than probable that one is mentioned among the apostles. "Salute Andronicus and Junia, my kinsmen, and my fellow-prisoners, who are of note among the apostles" (verse 7). Is Junia a feminine name? So it has been commonly held. But the *en tois apostolois*, with which it stands connected, has led some to conclude that it is Junias, the name of a man. This is not impossible. Yet Chrysostom, who, as a Greek Father, ought to be taken as a high authority, makes this frank and unequivocal comment on the passage; "How great is the devotion of this woman, that she should he counted worthy of the name of an apostle!"

These are illustrations which might be considerably enlarged, of the shadow which Paul's supposed law of silence for women has cast upon the work of the early translators—a shadow which was even thrown back into the Old Testament, so that we read in the Common Version: "the Lord gave the word; great was the company of those that published it" (Psalm 68:11); while the Revised correctly gives it: "The Lord giveth the word: the women that publish the tidings are a great host."

＊　＊　＊

How slow are we to understand what is written! Simon Peter, who on the Day of Pentecost had rehearsed the great prophecy of the new dispensation, and announced that its fulfillment had begun, was yet so holden of tradition that it took a special vision of the sheet descending from heaven to convince him that in the body of Christ "there can be neither Jew nor Gentile." And it has required another vision of a multitude of missionary women, let down by the Holy Spirit among the heathen, and publishing the Gospel to every tribe and kindred and people, to convince us that in the same body, "there can be no male or female." It is evident, however, that this extraordinary spectacle of ministering women has brought doubts to some conservative men as to "whereunto this thing may grow." Yet, as believers in the sure word of prophecy, all has happened exactly according to the foreordained pattern, from the opening chapter of the new dispensation, when in the upper room "these all continued with one accord in prayer and supplication, with the women, and Mary the mother of Jesus, and with His brethren," to the closing chapter, now fulfilling, when "the women that publish the tidings are a great host."

The new economy is not as the old; and the defendants in this case need not appeal to the examples of Miriam, and Deborah, and Huldah, and Anna the prophetess. These were exceptional instances under the old dispensation; but she that is least in the kingdom of heaven is greater than they. And let the theologians who have recently written so dogmatically upon this subject consider whether it may not be possible that in this matter they are still under the land and not under grace; and whether, in sight of the promised land of world-wide evangelization, they may not hear the voice of God saying: "Moses, my servant, is dead; now, therefore, arise and go over this Jordan."

EDITOR: *John R. Rice was an influential separatist fundamentalist, a real fundamentalist as opposed to a neoevangelical. He ministered in Dallas, Texas, from 1932 to 1940, founding his periodical* Sword of the Lord *in 1934. He moved his newspaper and ministry to Wheaton, Illinois, for many years, before settling in Murfreesboro, Tennessee, where his Sword of the Lord Ministries continues to this day. He wrote widely on many theological, social, and political issues, and is remembered as a controversial figure because of his opposition to theological modernism, Catholicism, Communism, and the civil rights movement.*

The selection below is from a famous book Rice authored and is representative of the fundamentalist view of women. Notice Rice's effort to interpret the Bible literally, but note also that the underlying issues are the authority of God and rebellion against God. Most significantly for our understanding of fundamentalism, he brings the entire discussion eventually around to evangelism, the emphasis of which was highlighted in chapter 1. This is representative of most fundamentalist preachers. When they discuss politics and social conditions, they often are not directly addressing those issues but are actually setting the stage for the evangelistic message that sinners need to repent and be saved. Readers will need to stay with this selection to its conclusion to see how Rice utilizes this strategy.

Rice, John R. *Bobbed Hair, Bossy Wives, and Women Preachers: Significant Questions for Honest Christian Women Settled by the Word of God.* Wheaton: Sword of the Lord Publishers, 1941. 66–79, 84–91. Used by permission.

BOBBED HAIR, THE SIGN OF WOMAN'S REBELLION AGAINST HUSBAND, FATHER AND GOD

Now at last we come to the question of bobbed hair. Do not confuse the subject of bobbed hair with the general subject of woman's dress and use of cosmetics. The question of whether a Christian woman bobs her hair is of infinitely more importance than whether she paints her face or her lips or her fingernails.

A Christian woman ought to dress "in modest apparel" (1 Tim. 2:9), and that command would make every earnest Christian woman careful not to expose her body unduly to the lustful gaze of evil men, nor to tempt clean-hearted, good men. But we are not discussing the clothes here.

Surely we will all agree that a Christian woman who does not live as the world lives and does not follow the world's ideals should not make too much effort to look like worldly women. Of wicked Queen Jezebel we are told that "she painted her face, and tired her head . . . " (II Kings 9: 30). The Bible does not give detailed instructions about lipstick and rouge and painted fingernails. But the most spiritual Christians among women usually feel that they cannot go to the extremes that worldly women follow in painting the face, in use of lipstick, in plucking the brows, and in other unnatural fads. Great numbers of the most spiritual women feel that to follow such a pattern is worldliness and hinders a Christian woman's influence. Besides, the women of the best taste know that they are only temporary fads and do not aid real beauty.

Yet the Bible does not expressly forbid the use of rouge. Spiritually-minded women should prayerfully consider their influence and try to please God. I cannot speak with Bible authority on the question of painted faces as I can on the question of bobbed hair: As to whether a woman should use paint at all, or how much, she must try to have the Spirit's leadership and not be offensive; the Bible gives no explicit directions. But on the matter of bobbed hair, the Bible is so clear that nothing is left to a woman's judgment as to whether she should have bobbed hair or long hair. The Bible expressly teaches that a woman should have long hair and gives a very beautiful and forceful reason for the command.

Let us examine again I Corinthians, chapter 11, verses 3 to 9: "³But I would have you know, that the head of every man is Christ; and the head of the woman is the man; and the head of Christ is God. ⁴Every mean praying or prophesying, having his head covered, dishonoureth his head. ⁵But every woman that prayeth or prophesieth with her head uncovered dishonoureth her head: for that is even all one as if she were shaven. ⁶For if the woman be not covered, let her also be shorn: but if it be a shame for a woman to be shorn or shaven let her be covered. ⁷For a man indeed ought not to cover his head, forasmuch as he is the image and glory of God: but the woman is the glory of the man. ⁸For the man is not of the woman; but the woman of the man. ⁹Neither was the man created for the woman; but the woman for the man."

The above Scripture tells us that since the man is the head of the woman, and there is a fundamental difference between men and women, that difference should be symbolized in the ways men and women wear their hair. Throughout the Bible it is stressed that men and women are different. A man is not like a woman. A woman is not like a man. It is a sin for a woman to try to appear like a man, and it is likewise a sin for a man to try to appear like a woman. God has one place for a man and a different place for a woman. For this cause in Deuteronomy 22:5 we are commanded. "The woman shall not wear that which pertaineth unto a man, neither shall a man put on a woman's garment: for all that do so are abomination unto the Lord thy God." It is a sin for women to appear masculine. It is equally a sin for men to appear effeminate. In fact, I Corinthians 6:9,10 names some of the unrighteous that "shall not inherit the kingdom of God." And among the adulterers and fornicators and drunkards and thieves and covetous and extortioners, God put the effeminate. To be effeminate is a horrible sin in God's sight. And the first sin with which God chided Adam, after the fall, was this: "Because thou hast hearkened unto the voice of thy wife. . . . "

* * *

Man is made in the image of God. God is a masculine God. The masculine pronoun is used of God everywhere in the Bible. That foolish and unscriptural title given by a woman preacher, Mrs. Mary Baker Eddy, "Our Father-Mother God," dishonors God: God is not effeminate. God is not feminine, but masculine. And man is made in the image of God. On the other hand, a woman is not made so much in the image of God, but in the image and as a mate to man. So the Scripture says: "For a man indeed ought not to cover his head, forasmuch as he is the image and glory of God: but the woman is the glory of the man."

Blessed is the woman that remembers this; her glory is in being a help to a man, and in submission to her husband or her father. And long hair is the mark of this submission, the mark of this femininity.

* * *

In this passage of Scripture, comparing verse 6 with verse 15 we find that God mentions three ways for a woman's hair to be worn. It maybe "shaved," that is, all cut off, or "shorn," that is, cut with shears or scissors, or it may be "long." Women often sincerely inquire how long hair must be to be counted long. The answer is that if it is not shaven and not shorn, it is long. God does not say how many inches long hair should be, but simply indicates that it should be left uncut, the symbol of a devout Christian woman who is not in rebellion against God and against her husband.

* * *

These days men have come to feel that if a woman will not fill a woman's place, she shall not have a woman's protection and respect and reverence. Men desert their wives as never before in the world. Very few men nowadays feel reverently about a woman's body. Boys who have dates with these bobbed-haired, smoking, strong-willed, modern girls, expect to kiss them and fondle them as they please, or to kick them out of the car to walk home. The man who marries a modern woman these days marries a woman who expects to vote like a man, smoke like a man, have her hair cut like a man, and go without restrictions and without chaperons and obey nobody. A man who marries such a woman, I say, does not expect to support her. The modern girl is very often expected to work and help make a living.

In I Peter 3:7 husbands are commanded to give "honour unto the wife, as unto the weaker vessel." When women cease to admit that they are the weaker vessels as God's Word says they are, then they lose this honor that men through the centuries have delighted to give to women. How many men now rise to give a seat on the streetcar to a woman? I am told that not long ago a man on the streetcar rose and offered his seat to a woman, and she was so surprised she fainted! When she recovered consciousness she said, "Thank you!" and then he fainted! I say, the honor, the deference, the courtesy, the protectiveness that practically all men, good and bad, once offered to good women, has almost disappeared!

I remember a time when every good woman, that is everyone who was not a harlot, received the utmost respect from practically every man. In circles of only ordinary culture, the worst men never took God's name in vain in the presence of women, and no gentleman ever smoked in the presence of a woman without her express permission. But today the masculine, rebellious woman has lost the reverence and respect good women once inspired in all men.

Oh, women, what you have lost when you lost your femininity! When you bobbed your hair, you bobbed your character, too. Your rebellion against God's authority as exercised by husband and father, has a tendency, at least, to lose you all the things that women value most. If you want reverence and respect from good men, if you want protection and a good home and love and stedfast [sic] devotion, then I beg you to take a woman's place! Dress like a woman, not like a man. Have habits like a woman. No woman ever gained by cursing and smoking and beer drinking and a rowdy life. And if you want God to especially bless you when you pray, then have on your head a symbol of the meek and quiet spirit which in the sight of God is of such great price.

* * *

The Horrible Sin of Rebellion

I hope you have seen by this time that my subject does not primarily deal with anybody's hair, whether a woman's should be long or a man's short. I am really dealing with the question of rebellion against God and His authority. It will be no trouble for you, dear woman, to let your hair grow, if you first settle the real question: Are you willing today to surrender absolutely to the will of God and to His authority in your life? You can be subject to your husband if first you wholly submit to God.

But may I speak here not only to women but to men and to every reader. Will you face this question of surrender today? Will you confess your rebellion and forsake it today, and repent of it? Will you start out today to try to follow the will of God? First of all, there is the will of God as expressed in the Bible. Will you today take the Bible as the rule of your life? Will you honestly seek to know the will of God and to do it, as expressed in the precious Word of God?

Perhaps today God speaks to you also by the Holy Spirit. There is some personal leading, some clear path marked out by the Spirit that you ought to take. Or there is some sin that you should give up, or some work you should begin. Will you follow the leading of God, no matter where it leads? Will you bow your will to His will today? Will you say as the Saviour said to His Father, "Nevertheless, not my will but thine be done"?

"The powers that be are ordained of God" (Rom. 13:1). Will you begin today to obey the law of the land, as carefully and meticulously as if God had spoken these laws from Heaven? Will you recognize the authority of God in the government?

It may be that your boss is rough, inconsiderate, perhaps incompetent. Perhaps you are a Christian and he is not. But will you say today by God's grace, "I will be a good Christian in obeying orders as if they were from Christ"?

Many a young man or woman, many a boy and girl will read this message. You are a Christian, perhaps, but you find it hard to submit to the will of your father or your mother. And yet it is the will of God. The authority of the father and mother is the authority of God. Will you submit to it today? I would pray God to give me such a surrendered heart, and start out to do His will in the home.

In schools, in churches, in business, in homes there should be a new dedication of Christians to lives of obedience. Christians should submit themselves to their own government, to their bosses, to their teachers, to their fathers and to their husbands.

＊ ＊ ＊

It may be God has called you to preach. You have in mind a great and happy career. So had I. It may be already that the future seems to promise glowing and wonderful things, success, prosperity, friends or even fame. So it seemed to me that night in 1921 in the Pacific Garden Mission in Chicago. I was a graduate student in the University of Chicago. I had a contract as a college teacher for the following year. The future looked oh, so bright! But when I led a drunken bum to the Lord, God seemed to speak to my heart and to say that that was the way of joy and usefulness for me. And so with some trembling and many doubts and fears, I gave myself up to do the will of God wherever it led me; to poverty, to obscurity, to sickness, to the loss of friends, to hard life, and then to an obscure grave. I say, I faced it all in my heart, but I took the long took and with all my heart I presented my body as a living sacrifice to God. I said with Isaiah, "Here am I, send me" (Isa: 6:8). Will you surrender to the call of God today? Perhaps God does not call you to preach, but He calls you to come out and be separate. He wants you to leave the worldly ways. He wants you to leave the primrose path you have been traveling. He wants you to come out and be separate and touch not the unclean thing. He wants you to give up certain friends, certain ways of living, and put yourself on the altar as an out-and-out Christian. Is that too hard for, you?

＊ ＊ ＊

Some person will read this, I am sure, who is unsaved. You have never taken Christ into your heart to be your Saviour and Lord. You have never repented of your sins. You have never been born again. You are not a child of God.

And may I ask you why? Have you ever analyzed it? Do you know why today you are outside the arms of God's wing mercy? Do you know why He has never kissed away your tears and forgiven all your sins? Do you know why you do not have the song of rejoicing in your heart and a consciousness that you are God's own child, with a blessed home in Heaven, and with a new heart in your breast?

I will tell you why. There is only one thing that keeps you from God, and that is a rebellious heart that is not willing to surrender to Jesus Christ. You remember the Saviour told a parable of certain people who sent word after their lord, "We will not have this man to reign over us" (Luke 19:14). So it is that every person in the world who is unsaved has simply refused to submit his rebellious will, his stubborn heart, to the will of the Lord Jesus.

One day every knee shall bow to Christ and every tongue shall confess that He is Lord, to the glory of God the Father, we are told (Phil. 2:10, 11). That must be sometime. Why not let it be now before your soul is damned and lost forever?

* * *

I hope you who read this will have a heart-searching time. I hope that children will submit themselves anew to their parents. I hope that men who work under bosses will be such Christians that they will submit themselves to their bosses; as Christians ought to. I hope that wives will submit themselves to their husbands for Jesus' sake. But oh, the most important thing is that you who read this today and are unconverted will here and now submit yourself to Jesus Christ. Give Him your heart. Surrender your will. Trust Him as your own Saviour and do it today!

When the heart fully trusts in Jesus Christ and takes Him as Lord and Master, then it will be easy to settle whether wives shall obey husbands, and whether women shall have long hair. CHRIST OUGHT TO BE FIRST IN YOUR LIFE! Will you make Him first today?

If you will take Christ as your own Saviour and surrender wholly to Him, I hope you will write me and let me know!

In St. Paul, Minnesota, I closed a Sunday afternoon message on the subject discussed in this book. As I recall, I did not give an invitation, but dismissed the congregation and went into an adjoining room. From the back of the auditorium, a young man, eighteen, who had been breaking his mother's heart with gambling and drinking, came out into the room where I was. With tears running down his face, he held out both hands and said, "Brother Rice, today I am ready to meet my Saviour. I give Him my heart today!" I had been preaching on bobbed hair, but he saw that fundamentally what was wrong in his heart was rebellion against Jesus Christ. Bobbed hair is the sin of rebellion against God and that same rebellion was his sin. And he surrendered there. And that is what is wrong with you if you are not saved. The principal thing is not the hair, it is the heart. When the heart gets right, it doesn't take long to get the hair right. If you surrender with all your soul to Jesus Christ, it will not be hard then to surrender to those whom God has put over you in authority.

I suggest that you have a quiet time alone. Don't you want to close the door to your room and get down on your knees and confess your sins to Christ, and say to Him today as Paul did, "Lord, what wilt thou have me to do?" Trust Him for forgiveness and give Him all of your heart and all of your life. What sweet peace you will have! And what, eternal blessings will be yours after taking Christ into your heart as your own Saviour and own Lord.

If you will take Christ as Saviour, will you not write and tell me so? You may write in your own words, or take the form of this letter here. But above all, mean it in your heart and tell others and set out to live for God after you have trusted Him as Saviour.

MY DECISION FOR CHRIST

Evangelist John R. Rice
Wheaton, Illinois

Dear Brother Rice:

I have read the book, *Bobbed Hair, Bossy Wives and Women Preachers.* I see that the heart of all sin is rebellion against God. I have been led to see myself a sinner. Here and now I confess my sin to Christ and surrender to His will. I trust Him to forgive me, and I take Him as my Saviour and my Lord. I claim Him as mine today and by His grace, I will try to live for Him the rest of my days.

Signed . . . .
Address . . . .
. . . .

EDITOR: *Today, there are two national evangelical organizations that address gender issues: Christians for Biblical Equality (CBE) and the Council on Biblical Manhood and Womanhood (CBMW). The CBE espouses the egalitarian position, arguing that all offices in churches should be equally open to both men and women. The CBMW argues for the complementarian position, which holds that men and women were created differently in order to complement each other. The CBMW, therefore, holds that ordained ministry offices that carry spiritual authority are reserved for men only. Below are the official statements of each organization. Notice that each group argues its position from scripture, another testament to the importance of biblical authority for evangelicals, even when they cannot agree on precisely what the Bible teaches.*

> Christians for Biblical Equality. "Men, Women and Biblical Equality," 1989. http://www.cbeinternational.org/new/about/biblical_equality.shtml.   Used by permission.[1]

The Bible teaches the full equality of men and women in Creation and in Redemption (Gen 1:26-28, 2:23, 5:1-2; 1Cor 11:11-12; Gal 3:13, 28, 5:1).

The Bible teaches that God has revealed Himself in the totality of Scripture, the authoritative Word of God (Matt 5:18; John 10:35; 2Tim 3:16; 2Peter 1:20-21). We believe that Scripture is to be interpreted holistically and thematically. We also recognize the necessity of making a distinction between inspiration and interpretation: inspiration relates to the divine impulse and control whereby the whole canonical Scripture is the Word of God; interpretation relates to the human activity whereby we seek to apprehend revealed truth in harmony with the totality of Scripture and under the guidance of the Holy Spirit. To be truly biblical, Christians must continually examine their faith and practice under the searchlight of Scripture.

Biblical Truths

Creation

1. The Bible teaches that both man and woman were created in God's image, had a direct relationship with God, and shared jointly the responsibilities of bearing and rearing children and having dominion over the created order (Gen 1:26-28).

2. The Bible teaches that woman and man were created for full and equal partnership. The word "helper" (*ezer*), used to designate woman in Genesis 2:18, refers to God in most instances of Old Testament usage (e.g. 1Sam 7:12; Ps 121:1-2). Consequently the word conveys no implication whatsoever of female subordination or inferiority.

3. The Bible teaches that the forming of woman from man demonstrates the fundamental unity and equality of human beings (Gen 2:21-23). In Genesis 2:18, 20 the word "suitable" (*kenegdo*) denotes equality and adequacy.

4. The Bible teaches that man and woman were co-participants in the Fall: Adam was no less culpable than Eve (Gen 3:6; Rom 5:12-21; 1Cor 15:21-22).

5. The Bible teaches that the rulership of Adam over Eve resulted from the Fall and was therefore not a part of the original created order. Genesis 3:16 is a prediction of the effects of the Fall rather than a prescription of God's ideal order.

Redemption

6. The Bible teaches that Jesus Christ came to redeem women as well as men. Through faith in Christ we all become children of God, one in Christ, and heirs to the blessings of salvation without reference to racial, social, or gender distinctives (John 1:12-13; Rom 8:14-17; 2Cor 5:17; Gal 3:26-28).

Community

7. The Bible teaches that at Pentecost the Holy Spirit came on men and women alike. Without distinction, the Holy Spirit indwells women and men, and sovereignly distributes gifts without preference as to gender (Acts 2:1-21; 1Cor 12:7, 11, 14:31).

8. The Bible teaches that both women and men are called to develop their spiritual gifts and to use them as stewards of the grace of God (1Peter 4:10-11). Both men and women are divinely gifted and empowered to minister to the whole Body of Christ, under His authority (Acts 1:14, 18:26, 21:9; Rom 16:1-7, 12-13, 15; Phil 4:2-3; Col 4:15; see also Mark 15:40-41, 16:1-7; Luke 8:1-3; John 20:17-18; compare also Old Testament examples: Judges 4:4-14, 5:7; 2Chron 34:22-28; Prov 31:30-31; Micah 6:4).

9. The Bible teaches that, in the New Testament economy, women as well as men exercise the prophetic, priestly and royal functions (Acts 2:17-18, 21:9; 1Cor 11:5; 1Peter 2:9-10; Rev 1:6, 5:10). Therefore, the few isolated texts that appear to restrict the full redemptive freedom of women must not be interpreted simplistically and in contradiction to the rest of Scripture, but their interpretation must take into account their relation to the broader teaching of Scripture and their total context (1Cor 11:2-16, 14:33-36; 1Tim 2:9-15).

10. The Bible defines the function of leadership as the empowerment of others for service rather than as the exercise of power over them (Matt 20:25-28, 23:8; Mark 10:42-45; John 13:13-17; Gal 5:13; 1Peter 5:2-3).

Family

11. The Bible teaches that husbands and wives are heirs together of the grace of life and that they are bound together in a relationship of mutual

submission and responsibility (1Cor 7:3-5; Eph 5:21; 1Peter 3:1-7; Gen 21:12). The husband's function as "head" (*kephale*) is to be understood as self-giving love and service within this relationship of mutual submission (Eph 5:21-33; Col 3:19; 1Peter 3:7).

12. The Bible teaches that both mothers and fathers are to exercise leadership in the nurture, training, discipline and teaching of their children (Exod 20:12; Lev 19:3; Deut 6:6-9, 21:18-21, 27:16; Prov 1:8, 6:20; Eph 6:1-4; Col 3:20; 2Tim 1:5; see also Luke 2:51).

Application

Community

1. In the church, spiritual gifts of women and men are to be recognized, developed and used in serving and teaching ministries at all levels of involvement: as small group leaders, counselors, facilitators, administrators, ushers, communion servers, and board members, and in pastoral care, teaching, preaching, and worship.

In so doing, the church will honor God as the source of spiritual gifts. The church will also fulfill God's mandate of stewardship without the appalling loss to God's kingdom that results when half of the church's members are excluded from positions of responsibility.

2. In the church, public recognition is to be given to both women and men who exercise ministries of service and leadership. In so doing, the church will model the unity and harmony that should characterize the community of believers. In a world fractured by discrimination and segregation, the church will dissociate itself from worldly or pagan devices designed to make women feel inferior for being female. It will help prevent their departure from the church or their rejection of the Christian faith.

Family

3. In the Christian home, husband and wife are to defer to each other in seeking to fulfill each other's preferences, desires and aspirations. Neither spouse is to seek to dominate the other but each is to act as servant of the other, in humility considering the other as better than oneself. In case of decisional deadlock they should seek resolution through biblical methods of conflict resolution rather than by one spouse imposing a decision upon the other.

In so doing, husband and wife will help the Christian home stand against improper use of power and authority by spouses and will protect the home from wife and child abuse that sometimes tragically follows a hierarchical interpretation of the husband's "headship."

4. In the Christian home, spouses are to learn to share the responsibilities of leadership on the basis of gifts, expertise, and availability, with due regard for the partner most affected by the decision under consideration.

In so doing, spouses will learn to respect their competencies and their complementarity. This will prevent one spouse from becoming the perennial loser, often forced to practice ingratiating or deceitful manipulation to protect self-esteem. By establishing their marriage on a partnership basis, the couple will protect it from joining the tide of dead or broken marriages resulting from marital inequities.

5. In the Christian home, couples who share a lifestyle characterized by the freedom they find in Christ will do so without experiencing feelings of guilt or resorting to hypocrisy. They are freed to emerge from an unbiblical "traditionalism" and can rejoice in their mutual accountability in Christ. In so doing, they will openly express their obedience to Scripture, will model an example for other couples in quest of freedom in Christ, and will stand against patterns of domination and inequality sometimes imposed upon church and family.

We believe that biblical equality as reflected in this document is true to Scripture.

We stand united in our conviction that the Bible, in its totality, is the liberating Word that provides the most effective way for women and men to exercise the gifts distributed by the Holy Spirit and thus to serve God.

Council on Biblical Manhood and Womanhood. "The Danvers Statement." Wheaton: The Council on Biblical Manhood and Womanhood, 1988. http://www.cbmw.org/about/danvers.php. Used by permission.

The "Danvers Statement" summarizes the need for the Council on Biblical Manhood and Womanhood (CBMW) and serves as an overview of our core beliefs. This statement was prepared by several evangelical leaders at a CBMW meeting in Danvers, Massachusetts, in December of 1987. It was first published in final form by the CBMW in Wheaton, Illinois in November of 1988.

Rationale

We have been moved in our purpose by the following contemporary developments which we observe with deep concern:

1. The widespread uncertainty and confusion in our culture regarding the complementary differences between masculinity and femininity;

2. the tragic effects of this confusion in unraveling the fabric of marriage woven by God out of the beautiful and diverse strands of manhood and womanhood;

3. the increasing promotion given to feminist egalitarianism with accompanying distortions or neglect of the glad harmony portrayed in Scripture between the loving, humble leadership of redeemed husbands and the intelligent, willing support of that leadership by redeemed wives;

4. the widespread ambivalence regarding the values of motherhood, vocational homemaking, and the many ministries historically performed by women;

5. the growing claims of legitimacy for sexual relationships which have Biblically and historically been considered illicit or perverse, and the increase in pornographic portrayal of human sexuality;

6. the upsurge of physical and emotional abuse in the family;

7. the emergence of roles for men and women in church leadership that do not conform to Biblical teaching but backfire in the crippling of Biblically faithful witness;

8. the increasing prevalence and acceptance of hermeneutical oddities devised to reinterpret apparently plain meanings of Biblical texts;

9. the consequent threat to Biblical authority as the clarity of Scripture is jeopardized and the accessibility of its meaning to ordinary people is withdrawn into the restricted realm of technical ingenuity;

10. and behind all this the apparent accommodation of some within the church to the spirit of the age at the expense of winsome, radical Biblical authenticity which in the power of the Holy Spirit may reform rather than reflect our ailing culture.

Purposes

Recognizing our own abiding sinfulness and fallibility, and acknowledging the genuine evangelical standing of many who do not agree with all of our convictions, nevertheless, moved by the preceding observations and by the hope that the noble Biblical vision of sexual complementarity may yet win the mind and heart of Christ's church, we engage to pursue the following purposes:

1. To study and set forth the Biblical view of the relationship between men and women, especially in the home and in the church.

2. To promote the publication of scholarly and popular materials representing this view.

3. To encourage the confidence of lay people to study and understand for themselves the teaching of Scripture, especially on the issue of relationships between men and women.

4. To encourage the considered and sensitive application of this Biblical view in the appropriate spheres of life.

5. And thereby

* to bring healing to persons and relationships injured by an inadequate grasp of God's will concerning manhood and womanhood,
* to help both men and women realize their full ministry potential through a true understanding and practice of their God-given roles,
* and to promote the spread of the gospel among all peoples by fostering a Biblical wholeness in relationships that will attract a fractured world.

Affirmations

Based on our understanding of Biblical teachings, we affirm the following:

1. Both Adam and Eve were created in God's image, equal before God as persons and distinct in their manhood and womanhood (Gen 1:26-27, 2:18).

2. Distinctions in masculine and feminine roles are ordained by God as part of the created order, and should find an echo in every human heart (Gen 2:18, 21-24; 1 Cor 11:7-9; 1 Tim 2:12-14).

3. Adam's headship in marriage was established by God before the Fall, and was not a result of sin (Gen 2:16-18, 21-24, 3:1-13; 1 Cor 11:7-9).

4. The Fall introduced distortions into the relationships between men and women (Gen 3:1-7, 12, 16).

* In the home, the husband's loving, humble headship tends to be replaced by domination or passivity; the wife's intelligent, willing submission tends to be replaced by usurpation or servility.
* In the church, sin inclines men toward a worldly love of power or an abdication of spiritual responsibility, and inclines women

to resist limitations on their roles or to neglect the use of their gifts in appropriate ministries.

5. The Old Testament, as well as the New Testament, manifests the equally high value and dignity which God attached to the roles of both men and women (Gen 1:26-27, 2:18; Gal 3:28). Both Old and New Testaments also affirm the principle of male headship in the family and in the covenant community (Gen 2:18; Eph 5:21-33; Col 3:18-19; 1 Tim 2:11-15).

6. Redemption in Christ aims at removing the distortions introduced by the curse.

* In the family, husbands should forsake harsh or selfish leadership and grow in love and care for their wives; wives should forsake resistance to their husbands' authority and grow in willing, joyful submission to their husbands' leadership (Eph 5:21-33; Col 3:18-19; Tit 2:3-5; 1 Pet 3:1-7).
* In the church, redemption in Christ gives men and women an equal share in the blessings of salvation; nevertheless, some governing and teaching roles within the church are restricted to men (Gal 3:28; 1 Cor 11:2-16; 1 Tim 2:11-15).

7. In all of life Christ is the supreme authority and guide for men and women, so that no earthly submission—domestic, religious, or civil—ever implies a mandate to follow a human authority into sin (Dan 3:10-18; Acts 4:19-20, 5:27-29; 1 Pet 3:1-2).

8. In both men and women a heartfelt sense of call to ministry should never be used to set aside Biblical criteria for particular ministries (1 Tim 2:11-15, 3:1-13; Tit 1:5-9). Rather, Biblical teaching should remain the authority for testing our subjective discernment of God's will.

9. With half the world's population outside the reach of indigenous evangelism; with countless other lost people in those societies that have heard the gospel; with the stresses and miseries of sickness, malnutrition, homelessness, illiteracy, ignorance, aging, addiction, crime, incarceration, neuroses, and loneliness, no man or woman who feels a passion from God to make His grace known in word and deed need ever live without a fulfilling ministry for the glory of Christ and the good of this fallen world (1 Cor 12:7-21).

10. We are convinced that a denial or neglect of these principles will lead to increasingly destructive consequences in our families, our churches, and the culture at large.

EDITOR: *In the 1980s, conservatives in the Southern Baptist Convention took control of their denomination by ousting the so-called moderates from power. By the measure of most scholars the conservatives and moderates are both evangelical. They differ on a variety of issues, however, the most important being whether a belief in the inerrancy of scripture should be required for officials in the denomination and faculty in the Southern Baptist seminaries. The conservatives and moderates also disagree on the roles of women in churches and in marriage. When conservatives gained power in the SBC, they revised the "Baptist Faith and Message," the denominations confession of faith, to include two statements on gender, one disallowing women ministers and the other dealing with the submission of women to their husbands in marriage. It was the first time in the nearly four centuries of Baptist history that a major Baptist confession of faith stipulated specific gender roles within marriage and in churches. Conservatives believe the gender statements are necessary because many evangelicals have followed the culture in affirming the egalitarian gender position. The SBC statement outlining the woman's role in marriage is often referred to as the "submission statement." When passed, the statement gained national attention in leading newspapers across the nation and on network news broadcasts. The statement puts the nation's largest Protestant denomination in line with the complementarian view espoused above by the CBMW.*

Baptist Faith and Message Statement (2000 Version). Southern Baptist Convention. http://www.sbc.net. Used by permission.

VI. The Church

A New Testament church of the Lord Jesus Christ is an autonomous local congregation of baptized believers, associated by covenant in the faith and fellowship of the gospel; observing the two ordinances of Christ, governed by His laws, exercising the gifts, rights, and privileges invested in them by His Word, and seeking to extend the gospel to the ends of the earth. Each congregation operates under the Lordship of Christ through democratic processes. In such a congregation each member is responsible and accountable to Christ as Lord. Its scriptural officers are pastors and deacons. While both men and women are gifted for service in the church, the office of pastor is limited to men as qualified by Scripture.

The New Testament speaks also of the church as the Body of Christ which includes all of the redeemed of all the ages, believers from every tribe, and tongue, and people, and nation.

Matthew 16:15-19; 18:15-20; Acts 2:41-42,47; 5:11-14; 6:3-6; 13:1-3; 14:23,27; 15:1-30; 16:5; 20:28; Romans 1:7; 1 Corinthians 1:2; 3:16; 5:4-5; 7:17; 9:13-14; 12; Ephesians 1:22-23; 2:19-22; 3:8-11,21; 5:22-32; Philippians 1:1; Colossians 1:18; 1 Timothy 2:9-14; 3:1-15; 4:14; Hebrews 11:39-40; 1 Peter 5:1-4; Revelation 2-3; 21:2-3.

XVIII. The Family

God has ordained the family as the foundational institution of human society. It is composed of persons related to one another by marriage, blood, or adoption.

Marriage is the uniting of one man and one woman in covenant commitment for a lifetime. It is God's unique gift to reveal the union between Christ and His church and to provide for the man and the woman in marriage the framework for intimate companionship, the channel of sexual expression according to biblical standards, and the means for procreation of the human race.

The husband and wife are of equal worth before God, since both are created in God's image. The marriage relationship models the way God relates to His people. A husband is to love his wife as Christ loved the church. He has the God-given responsibility to provide for, to protect, and to lead his family. A wife is to submit herself graciously to the servant leadership of her husband even as the church willingly submits to the headship of Christ. She, being in the image of God as is her husband and thus equal to him, has the God-given responsibility to respect her husband and to serve as his helper in managing the household and nurturing the next generation.

Children, from the moment of conception, are a blessing and heritage from the Lord. Parents are to demonstrate to their children God's pattern for marriage. Parents are to teach their children spiritual and moral values and to lead them, through consistent lifestyle example and loving discipline, to make choices based on biblical truth. Children are to honor and obey their parents.

Genesis 1:26-28; 2:15-25; 3:1-20; Exodus 20:12; Deuteronomy 6:4-9; Joshua 24:15; 1 Samuel 1:26-28; Psalms 51:5; 78:1-8; 127; 128; 139:13-16; Proverbs 1:8; 5:15-20; 6:20-22; 12:4; 13:24; 14:1; 17:6; 18:22; 22:6,15; 23:13-14; 24:3; 29:15,17; 31:10-31; Ecclesiastes 4:9-12; 9:9; Malachi 2:14-16; Matthew 5:31-32; 18:2-5; 19:3-9; Mark 10:6-12; Romans 1:18-32; 1 Corinthians 7:1-16; Ephesians 5:21-33; 6:1-4; Colossians 3:18-21; 1 Timothy 5:8,14; 2 Timothy 1:3-5; Titus 2:3-5; Hebrews 13:4; 1 Peter 3:1-7.

EDITOR: *Agnieszka Tennant is an assistant editor for* Christianity Today, *often considered the flagship evangelical magazine. In 2001, she attended meetings of both the CBE and the CBMW and wrote the reports below. While she makes clear her own egalitarian position, notice that she is keen to expose and refute stereotypical charges that are made against both organizations by their opponents.*

Tennant, Agnieszka. "Seahorses, Egalitarians, and Traditional Sex-Role Reversal: A Dispatch from the Christians for Biblical Equality Conference." *Christianity Today* (2001). http://www.christianitytoday.com/ct/2001/128/33.0.html. Used by permission.

A couple of smitten seahorses arrested my attention recently at Chicago's Shedd Aquarium. The male and female fishes entwined their tails, their skins blushing in a love dance. As their bellies arched gracefully, it seemed both of them were pregnant. But only one of them was. The male.

The female seahorse deposits her eggs on her partner's underside, the aquarium volunteer told me. The male then fertilizes them and provides them with food and oxygen. After ten days to several weeks of pregnancy, the male's brood sack bursts forth with tens or hundreds of newborns.

Within a day, the male gets pregnant again. The cycle repeats itself throughout his lifetime, giving the male a few hours to recover between pregnancies. The same faithful female will visit him every morning for several minutes of affection. Leaving her lover in the same one square meter, she travels perhaps a hundred times that area, ignoring all other males. She's back to visit her partner the next morning.

"How endearingly egalitarian!" was my initial thought/gasp, soon followed by its amendment. "Nah! Unless the male for some reason relishes his pregnancies (which could be true; I don't know), his freedoms seem much more limited than the female's." But even if fundamentally unegalitarian, the reversal of the traditional sex roles—not the oppression of the male—brought to mind the men I met at Christians for Biblical Equality (CBE) conference in Dallas at the end of June. In both cases—the seahorses and the egalitarian men—the culturally sanctioned gender-role reversal is warranted by divine endowments. In case of the seahorses, it's their God-ordained anatomy and instincts. In case of egalitarian men, it's their and their spouses' gifts and talents. Even so, both the male seahorses and egalitarian men remain confidently male, hormones and all. Ask the biologists and the egalitarian men's wives.

Some 2,000 members of CBE incorporated in 1988 believe that "the Bible, properly interpreted, teaches the fundamental equality of men and women of all racial and ethnic groups, all economic classes, and all age groups," according to CBE's statement of faith.

To learn more about those teachings, 375 men and women, most of them evangelicals (a lot of them Southern Baptists) flocked to the annual conference in Dallas. They took in the sessions and workshops that expounded the biblical passages often used to support the hierarchical/complementarian gender structures, as well as some of the 100 Bible verses that support women's ministry; they received advice on egalitarian marriage and gender exactness in Bible translations. The words of biblical scholars such as Gordon D. Fee and Catherine Clark Kroeger soothed the wounds of many women who for too long were taught that God didn't want them to use the gifts he apparently gave them. Tears of hurt, freedom, and worship flowed spontaneously.

I'll direct those who want to know more about what CBE stands for to the group's Web site. The conference, however, made me think of what CBE is not. The uninformed as well as some advocates of male headship at home and in the church propagate at least four fallacies regarding CBE. What I learned at the conference seemed to debunk them all.

CBE is an organization for disgruntled women. Approximately 30 percent of the conference attendees were men, including speakers Gordon D. Fee, Dan Gentry Kent, and Richard J. Foster. Contrary to popular understanding, the egalitarian men are not weaklings codependent on their pants-wearing wives. Instead, the men who attended the Dallas conference know what their gifts are, and they know what their wives' gifts are. They are certain about one thing: they don't want anyone to miss out on what God can do when these gifts are put to use. When I asked them who the leader in their marriage was, these mutual submission advocates replied, "Both of us." The "leadership" depends on who has the relevant gift—not gender—that ought to be employed in a given situation. So, whether the men are better at childhood education and their wives at mowing the lawn—or vice versa—they divide the work accordingly.

CBE is just a phase. I've heard it said that the egalitarian stance is just another fad in church history. But while CBE is relatively new (growing in influence since its incorporation in 1988), functional egalitarians, such as deaconess Phoebe (Romans 16:1), Priscilla who taught Apollos "the way of God" (Acts 18:26), Corrie Ten Boom and Salvation Army cofounder Catherine Booth, to name a few, have always been admired for doing the work of the Lord. As the Dallas conference speaker Robin L. Smith has said, the equality of men and women is at the heart of the ongoing work of Christian reconciliation (Gal. 3:26-28). And that's never going away.

One must be a liberal to be an egalitarian. Most of the people attending the conference were evangelicals with high regard for the Scriptures. They wouldn't be egalitarians if they didn't believe that the Bible, if "properly interpreted," espoused their view. CBE's site offers biblical interpretations of the "problem" complementarian passages, as well as the egalitarian verses.

Egalitarians affirm homosexuality. This statement is a cheap shot fired by the complementarian Council on Biblical Manhood and Womanhood. A news release on its Web site attacks CBE by saying that "no significant middle ground exists"—"one must be in a denomination that affirms the biblical, complementarian view, or one must be in a denomination that makes concessions with homosexuality." This unfair rhetoric runs counter not just to what I saw at the conference, but also to CBE's history. Some CBE founders and its prominent members withdrew membership from the Evangelical Women's Caucus International (EWCI) and decided to form CBE after EWCI presented a resolution recognizing "the presence of the Lesbian minority" in EWCI. "We are accused by more liberal groups of being homophobic," one of CBE's founders, Alvera Mickelsen, told me recently. "You can't win."

Any group wishing to disagree with CBE in a productive, respectful manner (as I'm sure CBMW does), would do well to scrupulously search its polemic for false assumptions and weed them out. Reliance on truth does tend to strengthen any argument.

I'll take my own advice as I report on myths about CBMW that need dispelling after I attend their conference in September. You can hold me to it.

Tennant, Agnieszka. "A Different Kind of Women's Lib: A Dispatch from the Council for Biblical Manhood and Womanhood Conference," *Christianity Today*, 1 October 2001. http://www.ctlibrary.com. Used by permission.

Attending a Council for Biblical Manhood and Womanhood (CBMW) conference is not on my usual slate of retreats. Nor is "complementarian marriage seminar" on the tip of my tongue when I think of a weekend in Florida. It's time for full disclosure: I have this bent toward biblical egalitarianism.

But an article on marriage I'm writing took me to the Sunshine State, where I attended a CBMW's Different by Design conference last month. The "design" in the name did not just stand for human anatomy.

At the conference, I met women who couldn't exercise some of their gifts because of their and their husbands' interpretation of the Bible. Women were repeatedly told to submit to their husbands. Men were taught to properly "assume their headship." No one mentioned mutual submission.

Thanks to God only, I managed to bridle my egalivangelistic zeal. I did not corner any unsuspecting couples to prove to them with my borrowed knowledge of Hebrew grammar that the relationship between men and women was "designed" to be an egalitarian one. I resisted sneaking a box of egalitarian marriage guides on the book table. And I worshipped with these people.

You may remember that when I went to a conference held by the egalitarian body of opinion, Christians for Biblical Equality (CBE), several months ago, I wrote an online article addressing some misconceptions about CBE. It's time to do the same for CBMW.

Here are just a few things that surprised me about the CBMW complementarians:

They aim to liberate women. All this time I thought of egalitarian women as oppressed. But the die-hard complementarian ideologues sure didn't sound like it. At times I wondered if I was at a CBE, not CBMW, conference. "We want women to be free to do what God had called them to do," one speaker said. Another said, "We want men and women to be what God had called them to be." Hearing these words gave me a sensation of déjà vu. I heard the same words at the other conference!

One woman told me that complementarian theology is "very liberating." "I'm free to exercise my gifts," she said, adding, "within the context of God's order, of course. When I submit, such a burden is lifted. I want to be in charge, but when I am, it's confusion."

One speaker quoted Paul Vitz, who said that complementarian understanding of the Bible sets women free from the "debilitating anxiety to be both mother and father." Another speaker described wifely submission as "joyful, willing, creative, energetic" (it was a "he" though).

The similarity in language of complementarians and egalitarians reveals a lot about both groups' intentions. At least one of their goals is women's liberation. Their motivation is also the same—faithfulness to God's Word. Both groups ought to celebrate the love for the Scriptures that they have in common. The trouble is, they disagree on what it is that "the Bible says."

They're not chauvinists. "Give undivided attention to what your wife is saying," said one speaker. "She has wisdom, much to communicate and contribute. So many times God gives ideas to women." Now, egalitarians like me may see this statement as patronizing. On the other hand, it can be argued that an "undivided attention" to one's spouse is a type of submission.

I don't know how many times I heard conference speakers exhort husbands to listen, really listen, to their wives, to "drop everything and ask her 'Honey, what's been on your mind lately?'" "Men, we must never communicate to our wives that they are second class citizens," said a speaker. A leader of a workshop on fathering said, "The way we men treat our wives is the number one factor in the development of our sons and daughters."

They know the most important question—and their answer to it. I asked Randy Stinson, CBMW's executive director, if he believes there are happy, fulfilled, good egalitarian marriages out there. He tried hard, and finally told me, "I just think it's the wrong question. The question we ought to be asking is, 'Is it right?' I think more is at stake than personal happiness. We both cannot be right. I say that with a sense of brokenness." I had to agree with him.

People like me need to get it though our heads that complementarian passion about women's roles may be influenced by tradition, but it is mostly rooted in their interpretation of the Bible. They tell women to submit because it's what God wants (in their understanding), not because it's their fancy.

* * *

EDITOR: *In the 1990s, the organization known as Promise Keepers was widely popular among evangelical men. Founded in 1990 by former University of Colorado football coach Bill McCartney, the organization held rallies in packed stadiums across the country. The rallies were often cathartic events that saw men weeping, embracing, and confessing their sins to one another as they pledged to become better husbands and fathers—in short, men worthy of their wives' voluntary submission. McCartney and Promise Keepers also emphasized racial reconciliation (see Promise 6). Below are the Core Values and Seven Promises of the Promise Keepers organization.*

Promise Keepers—Core Values. http://www.promisekeepers.org. Used by permission.

Promise Keepers is a Christ-centered organization dedicated to introducing men to Jesus Christ as their Savior and Lord, and then helping them to grow as Christians. This is mainly accomplished through our Seven Promises and our men's conference ministry. Millions of men have participated since 1990 when PK first began.

Seven Promises of a Promise Keeper

PROMISE 1

A Promise Keeper is committed to honoring Jesus Christ through worship, prayer and obedience to God's Word in the power of the Holy Spirit.

PROMISE 2

A Promise Keeper is committed to pursuing vital relationships with a few other men, understanding that he needs brothers to help him keep his promises.

PROMISE 3

A Promise Keeper is committed to practicing spiritual, moral, ethical, and sexual purity.

PROMISE 4

A Promise Keeper is committed to building strong marriages and families through love, protection and biblical values.

PROMISE 5

A Promise Keeper is committed to supporting the mission of his church by honoring and praying for his pastor, and by actively giving his time and resources.

PROMISE 6

A Promise Keeper is committed to reaching beyond any racial and denominational barriers to demonstrate the power of biblical unity.

PROMISE 7

A Promise Keeper is committed to influencing his world, being obedient to the Great Commandment (see Mark 12:30-31) and the Great Commission (see Matthew 28:19-20).

EDITOR: *Francis Schaeffer was one of the most influential evangelicals of the twentieth century. He spent the first half of his career ministering within militant and separatist fundamentalism, but after breaking with fundamentalism in the early 1950s, he and his wife Edith founded a Christian community in the Swiss Alps called L'Abri, the shelter. In the mid-sixties he began to return to the United States for speaking tours, mostly at Christian colleges, where his message of evangelical cultural engagement became widely popular. His lectures were taped and transcribed and then edited into books, more than twenty being published before his death in 1984. Although remembered today as one of the founders of Christian Right political activism during the last few years of his life, until the late seventies he was viewed by many as an evangelical progressive. He taught that rather than shunning culture and intellectual matters, as fundamentalists often advocated, evangelicals should engage their culture with an informed critique from a Christian perspective. Although Schaeffer never made race or poverty leading issues in his message, the fact that he spoke out on these issues at all was highly significant for young evangelicals who were put off by the conservative and sometimes reactionary politics of their parents and churches. Below is a famous Schaeffer essay that appeared in* Christianity Today.

Schaeffer, Francis A. "Race and Economics." *Christianity Today* (January 4, 1974): 18–19. Used by permission.

If I were writing my early books again (for example, *The God Who Is There* and *The Church at the End of the Twentieth Century*), I would make one change. I would continue to emphasize that previously in Northern European culture (including the United States) the controlling consensus was Christian, and that this is now changed and we live in a post-Christian world. However, in doing this I would point out that previously when the Christian consensus was the controlling factor certain things were definitely sub-Christian.

Christians of all people should have opposed any form of racism. We know from the Bible that all men have a unity because we have a common origin—we had a common ancestor. The "Christian" slave-owner should have known he was dealing with his own kind, and not only because when he had sexual intercourse with his female slave she produced a child, which would not have happened had he performed bestiality with one of his animals: he should have heard the message of a common ancestor not only taught but applied in a practical way in the Sunday-morning sermon. This applies to slavery, but it applies equally to any oppression or feeling of superiority on the basis of race.

Liberal theologians do not believe in the historicity of a common ancestor, and the orthodox, conservatives, or evangelicals all too often did not courageously preach the practical conclusion of the fact of a common ancestor. The evangelical taught the doctrine of loving one's neighbor as oneself but failed to apply the lesson in the context in which Christ taught it, namely, in the setting of race—the Jew and the Samaritan. This lack discredits the Christian consensus and dishonors Christ.

The second point, no less wrong and destructive, is the lack of emphasis on the proper use of accumulated wealth. In a world of fallen, sinful men, the use of wealth has always been a problem that the true Christian should face, but it came to a point of special intensity with the Industrial Revolution and the rise of capitalism. Happily we can look back to some orthodox Christians, especially in England, who as a part of the preaching of the Gospel saw, preached, and stood for the proper use of accumulated wealth. But, to our shame, the majority of the Church, when it was providing the consensus, was silent. Christians failed to see that a failure to preach and act upon a compassionate use of accumulated wealth not only caused the Church to lose credibility with the working man but was actually a betrayal of a very important part of the biblical message. This fault was not only a thing of yesterday: it is often still with us in evangelical circles.

The Bible does clearly teach the right of property, but in both the Old Testament and the New Testament it puts a tremendous stress on the compassionate use of that property.

If at each place where the employer was a Bible- believing Christian the world could see that less profit was being taken so that the workers would have appreciably more than the "going rate" of pay, the Gospel would have been better proclaimed throughout the whole world than if the profits were the same as the world took and then large endowments were given to Christian schools, missions, and other projects. This is not to minimize the centrality of preaching the Gospel to the whole world, nor to minimize missions; it is to say that the other is also a way to proclaim the good news.

Unhappily, at our moment of history, in almost each place where true Christians are now speaking in this area, the tendency is to minimize missions and the preaching of the Gospel and/or to move over to some degree to the left. On the left, the solution is thought to be the state's [sic] becoming stronger in economic matters. But this is not the answer. Yes, the industrial complex is a threat, but why should Christians think that if modern men with their presuppositions use these lesser monolithic monsters to oppress, these same men (or other with the same presuppositions) would do otherwise with the greater monolithic monster of a bloated state?

The answer is where it should have been always, and especially since the Industrial Revolution: namely, in calling for a compassionate use of wealth by others, and especially by the practice of a compassionate use of wealth wherever true Christians are.

We must say we are sorry for the defectiveness of the preaching and the practice in these two areas, and we must make the proper emphasis concerning these an integral part of our evangelicalism.

EDITOR: *One of the young evangelicals influenced by Schaeffer was Jim Wallis, quoted in the previous chapter. Wallis frequently tells of growing up in an evangelical church in the Detroit area during the civil rights era and wondering why the adults in his church supported the war in Vietnam and opposed the civil rights movement. In 1971, while a student at Trinity Evangelical Divinity School in the Chicago area, Wallis and some other students founded a magazine that eventually became known as* Sojourners. *In 1975, the group moved to one of the poorest sections of the Washington, D.C. area and founded a Christian community that also took the name* Sojourners. *For the past thirty years, Wallis, along with Ronald Sider, has been a leading voice on the evangelical Left. Recently, he has served as an informal consultant to the Democratic Party, admonishing party activists to take religion seriously. In the selection below he takes evangelicals to task for often being on the wrong side of racial issues and for failing to speak out on civil rights for minorities.*

Wallis, Jim. "Evangelicals and Race." *Sojourners* 26:2 (March-April 1997): 11–12. http://www.sojo.net. Used by permission.

Something new, real, and potentially very important is happening among several groups of white evangelicals. A deep conviction and growing passion about racial reconciliation is taking root in the very unexpected soil of the white, conservative Christian world.

First, some honesty. White evangelicalism simply has been wrong on the issue of race for a very long time. Indeed, conservative white Christians have served as a bastion of racial segregation and a bulwark against racial justice efforts for decades, in the South and throughout the country.

All during the civil rights struggle, the vast majority of white evangelicals and their churches were on the wrong side—the wrong side of the truth, the Bible, and the gospel. I will never forget the words spoken to me as a white evangelical teen-ager by an elder in my home church when I began to ask questions about our city of Detroit's painfully obvious racism and its divided churches. Without apology he said, "Christianity has nothing to do with racism."

Ever since, when evangelical Christians gathered to draw up their theological concerns, the sin of white racism was nowhere to be found. In recent years, when conservative white Christians began to construct their political agendas, a recognition of racism's reality was absent from the issues list of abortion, homosexuality, tax cuts for the middle class, and, yes, opposition to affirmative action.

But suddenly, all that appears to be changing. One of the first signs was in the National Association of Evangelicals, the country's largest group of evangelical denominations and organizations. New NAE president Don Argue last year called together black and white evangelical leaders and, in a dramatic moment, confessed the sin of racism by white evangelicals, asked forgiveness, and committed the NAE to forge new multiracial relationships to change evangelical institutions. Even initially skeptical black evangelical leaders became convinced that the new direction was for real. Similar declarations of repentance have been made by the Southern Baptist Convention and by white and black Pentecostals at a historic gathering that was dubbed the "Memphis Miracle" (see "The Spirit Speaks," [*Sojourners*] September-October 1995).

Perhaps the most visible white evangelical group now passionately invoking the language of "racial reconciliation" is the Promise Keepers. In their large stadium rallies and in their list of "promises," a commitment to build relationships between white, black, and brown men has become more and more central to the Promise Keepers mission. Black staff and board members of Promise Keepers testify to the sincerity of the efforts, but the real tests are still to come. Several Promise Keeper leaders came to Washington, D.C., and to Sojourners recently to discuss their hopes and plans for advancing the agenda of racial reconciliation.

Clearly, pilgrimages toward racial reconciliation must lead to concrete commitments to racial justice if the journey is to be truly authentic. Sitting around the campfire together singing "Kumbaya" and holding hands will not suffice. Outside the church meeting rooms and stadium rallies where white and black Christians are hugging each other is a nation where racial polarization is on the rise, where the legacy of slavery and discrimination is still brutally present, and where the majority white population is signaling its tiredness with the "issue" of race by voting down long-standing affirmative action policies.

One black evangelical leader privately wonders whether his white evangelical colleagues "who still hold the trump cards will ever be willing to give them up—purse strings and the decision-making power." Will "racial reconciliation" just be "another fad," others ask, or will white evangelicals let that commitment take them to places they have never been before? Will they allow racial reconciliation to transform the evangelical world, or will they stop short of any real changes? "The crowd still looks pretty much the same," observes one closely involved in the process.

The approach that "we are all racists and need to repent" is neither good theology nor honest history. In the deepest and most honest sense, the real issue at stake in American racial history is the idolatry of white supremacy, as Eugene Rivers names it in his important article in this issue. The persistence of white identity itself, with the accompanying assumption of white privilege, is still the major obstacle to real change in the racial climate. Italians, Swedes, Irish, and Germans were never a common ethnic group, but all became "white people" when they arrived in America.

Indeed, the "white race" was and is merely a political construction to supply the ideology for oppression. That is the ideology that must be dismantled if racial progress is to be made in America. And because the ideology of the white race is also an idolatry that challenges our true and common identity as the children of God, its exorcism is a spiritual and theological necessity. Will evangelical Christians demonstrate the faith to overcome racism? That, ultimately, will be the test of racial reconciliation.

EDITOR: *While the conservative leaders of the Southern Baptist Convention resist the egalitarian position on gender, they came out with a bold statement on racial justice at their annual meeting in 1995. The statement was spearheaded by Richard Land, who we met in the previous chapter as one of the most influential voices of the Christian Right. The statement was composed by a commission that consisted of an equal number of white and black Southern Baptists, the descendents of slaves and the descendents of slave owners, as one black leader put it. Many black journalists criticized*

the resolution below because white Southern Baptist leaders almost all op-
pose affirmative action to remedy the injustices caused by racism. Still, the
statement is remarkable in that it calls racism a sin and calls for repentance
on the part of Southern Baptists for their participation in it.

Resolution on Racial Reconciliation on the 150th Anniversary of the
Southern Baptist Convention, June 1995. http://www.sbc.net. Used by
permission.

WHEREAS, Since its founding in 1845, the Southern Baptist Convention has been an effective instrument of God in missions, evangelism, and
social ministry; and

WHEREAS, The Scriptures teach that Eve is the mother of all living
(Genesis 3:20), and that God shows no partiality, but in every nation who-
ever fears him and works righteousness is accepted by him (Acts 10:34-35),
and that God has made from one blood every nation of men to dwell on
the face of the earth (Acts 17:26); and

WHEREAS, Our relationship to African-Americans has been hindered
from the beginning by the role that slavery played in the formation of the
Southern Baptist Convention; and

WHEREAS, Many of our Southern Baptist forbears defended the right
to own slaves, and either participated in, supported, or acquiesced in the
particularly inhumane nature of American slavery; and

WHEREAS, In later years Southern Baptists failed, in many cases, to
support, and in some cases opposed, legitimate initiatives to secure the
civil rights of African-Americans; and

WHEREAS, Racism has led to discrimination, oppression, injustice,
and violence, both in the Civil War and throughout the history of our nation; and

WHEREAS, Racism has divided the body of Christ and Southern Baptists in particular, and separated us from our African-American brothers
and sisters; and

WHEREAS, Many of our congregations have intentionally and/or un-
intentionally excluded African-Americans from worship, membership,
and leadership; and

WHEREAS, Racism profoundly distorts our understanding of Christian morality, leading some Southern Baptists to believe that racial prejudice and discrimination are compatible with the Gospel; and

WHEREAS, Jesus performed the ministry of reconciliation to restore
sinners to a right relationship with the Heavenly Father, and to establish

right relations among all human beings, especially within the family of faith.

Therefore, be it RESOLVED, That we, the messengers to the Sesquicentennial meeting of the Southern Baptist Convention, assembled in Atlanta, Georgia, June 20-22, 1995, unwaveringly denounce racism, in all its forms, as deplorable sin; and

Be it further RESOLVED, That we affirm the Bible's teaching that every human life is sacred, and is of equal and immeasurable worth, made in Gods image, regardless of race or ethnicity (Genesis 1:27), and that, with respect to salvation through Christ, there is neither Jew nor Greek, there is neither slave nor free, there is neither male nor female, for (we) are all one in Christ Jesus (Galatians 3:28); and

Be it further RESOLVED, That we lament and repudiate historic acts of evil such as slavery from which we continue to reap a bitter harvest, and we recognize that the racism which yet plagues our culture today is inextricably tied to the past; and

Be it further RESOLVED, That we apologize to all African-Americans for condoning and/or perpetuating individual and systemic racism in our lifetime; and we genuinely repent of racism of which we have been guilty, whether consciously (Psalm 19:13) or unconsciously (Leviticus 4:27); and

Be it further RESOLVED, That we ask forgiveness from our African-American brothers and sisters, acknowledging that our own healing is at stake; and

Be it further RESOLVED, That we hereby commit ourselves to eradicate racism in all its forms from Southern Baptist life and ministry; and

Be it further RESOLVED, That we commit ourselves to be doers of the Word (James 1:22) by pursuing racial reconciliation in all our relationships, especially with our brothers and sisters in Christ (1 John 2:6), to the end that our light would so shine before others, that they may see (our) good works and glorify (our) Father in heaven (Matthew 5:16); and

Be it finally RESOLVED, That we pledge our commitment to the Great Commission task of making disciples of all people (Matthew 28:19), confessing that in the church God is calling together one people from every tribe and nation (Revelation 5:9), and proclaiming that the Gospel of our Lord Jesus Christ is the only certain and sufficient ground upon which redeemed persons will stand together in restored family union as joint-heirs with Christ (Romans 8:17).

* 9 *

Fundamentalists, Evangelicals, and Catholics

EDITOR: *In the late nineteenth and early twentieth centuries, virtually all Protestants were anti-Catholic in one way or another. Liberals, evangelicals, and fundamentalists agreed that Catholics could not be fully American because of their alleged political allegiance to the pope in Rome. By the end of the century most liberal and evangelical anti-Catholicism had been softened or eliminated leaving only a minority still holding strongly to the old view. In the last quarter of the twentieth century, the so-called culture wars resulted in an alliance between some key evangelicals and traditionalist Roman Catholics. As interpreted by sociologist James Davison Hunter, the culture war pits progressivists against the orthodox. One of the central disagreements between these two camps has to do with the basis of morality. Progressivists view morality as socially constructed and subject to change over time, while the orthodox emphasize a fixed and transcendent moral foundation. Evangelicals and traditional Catholics share in the orthodox view.[1] The leading political issues that have brought the two groups together are abortion and other human life concerns.*

This brief chapter has just three selections: the first is a representative anti-Catholic text from The Fundamentals *(1910–1915); the second is from Carl McIntire, a fundamentalist who was infamous for his vitriolic antimodernism, anticommunism, and anti-Catholicism; and the third is the Evangelicals and Catholics Together statement that was issued in 1994 and signed by several leading evangelical and traditional Catholic thinkers. Note in the first two texts that evangelical and fundamentalist opposition to Catholicism has theological, political, and social components. Conversely, the third selection shows how evangelicals and Catholics more recently have found much common ground in all three areas. Whereas evangelicals once were inclined to highlight the differences between themselves and Catholics, they are now more inclined to emphasize the commonalities between the two groups.*

This is partly because the two share in promoting orthodox Christianity and traditional morality in the face of modern secularism and postmodern relativism. Also important in the coming together of evangelicals and Roman Catholics was the Vatican II council of the 1960s in which the Roman Catholic Church articulated its religious freedom document. From that time forward, it became difficult for Protestants to claim that the Church opposed religious liberty and favored a Catholic takeover of the United States, something the first two authors below claim.

> Medhurst, T. W. "Is Romanism Christianity?" In *The Fundamentals*. Edited by R. A. Torrey, A. C. Dixon, and others. 1910–15. Reprint, Grand Rapids: Baker, 1970.

I am aware that, if I undertake to prove that Romanism is not Christianity, I must expect to be called "bigoted, harsh, uncharitable." Nevertheless I am not daunted; for I believe that on a right understanding of this subject depends the salvation of millions.

One reason why Popery has of late gained so much power in Great Britain and Ireland, and is gaining power still, is that many Protestants look on it now as a form of true Christianity; and think that, on that account, notwithstanding great errors, it ought to be treated very tenderly. Many suppose that at the time of the Reformation, it was reformed, and that it is now much nearer the truth than it was before that time. It is still, however, the same; and, if examined, will be found to be so different from, and so hostile to, real Christianity, that it is not, in fact, Christianity at all.

✳ ✳ ✳

I submit that the teaching of Rome is at least as different from that of the Sacred Writings as that which Paul calls "another gospel;" and that, therefore, his words authorize us to say that Romanism is not Christianity.

FIRST, Christianity consists of what Christ has taught, and commanded in Scripture, but Romanism does not even profess to be founded on Scripture only: it claims a right to depart from what is contained in it—a right to add to Scripture what is handed down by tradition; and both to depart from and add to Scripture by making new decrees. It says that councils and the pope have been empowered by the Holy Spirit to make decrees by which, in reality, the doctrines delivered by Christ are entirely annulled.

✳ ✳ ✳

SECONDLY: Christ commanded us to show "meekness" towards those who oppose us (2 Tim. 2: 25). He says, "Love your enemies, bless those who curse you, do good to those who hate you, and pray for those who use you despitefully and persecute you" (Matt. 5:44).

But Romanism teaches men to hate, and, if they are able, to persecute to the death all those who will not receive it. Its deeds have been diabolical and murderous. It is "drunken with the blood of the saints." It has inscribed on the page of history warnings which appeal to the reason and the feelings of all generations. Such a warning is what is told of the 24th of August, 1572. On that day the Protestants of Paris were devoted to slaughter by members of the Papal Church. For the one offence of being Protestants, thousands were slain. The streets of Paris ran with blood; everywhere cries and groans, were mingled with the clangor of bells, the clash of arms, and the oaths of murderers. The king, Charles IX, stood, it is said, at a window, and, every now and then, fired on the fugitives. Every form of guilt, cruelty, and suffering, made that fearful night hideous and appalling. Never, in any city, which has professedly been brought under the influence of Christianity, was there such a revelling [sic] in blood and crime. You may say, "Why do you recall the atrocities of a time so remote?" I answer, because this deed received the sanction of the Church of Rome as a meritorious demonstration of fidelity to Romish precepts and doctrines. When the tidings of this wholesale murder were received in Rome, the cannon of St. Angelo were fired, the city was illuminated and Pope Gregory XIII and his cardinals went in procession to all the churches, and offered thanksgivings at the shrine of every saint. The Cardinal of Lorraine, in a letter to Charles IX, full of admiration and applause of the bloody deed, said, "That which you have achieved was so infinitely above my hopes, that I should have never dared to contemplate it; nevertheless, I have always believed that the deeds of your Majesty would augment the glory of God, and tend to immortalize your name."

Some say that Rome has ceased to persecute. But this is not the fact; either as to her acts, or rules of action. She asserts that she is unchanged, unchangeable; that she is infallible, and cannot alter, except so far as necessity, or plans for the future, may require; and facts are often occurring which prove that persecution is still approved by her. Rome has little power now; her persecuting spirit is kept in abeyance for a time; but it is still there. When it is free from restraint, it knows no way of dealing with difference of opinion but by the rack, the stake, the thumbscrew, the iron boot, the assassin's dagger, or a wholesale massacre. Let all who value their liberty, all who love the truth as it is in Jesus have no fellowship with such deeds of darkness, nor with those who work them. Let us show that we have no sympathy with such a cruel spirit; and that we love the names and memory of the noble army of martyrs of the Reformation; of those who sealed their faith with their blood; of those who died to release their country and their posterity from the bondage of Rome.

I agree with Dr. Samuel Waldegrave, when he says that, "The Convocation of the English clergy did wisely, when, in the days of Elizabeth, they enacted that every parish church in the land should be furnished with a copy of *Foxe's Book of Martyrs;*" and that it would be well if a copy of it were "in every house, yea, in every hand;" for "Rome is laboring, with redoubled effort, for the subjugation of Britain," and "the people have forgotten that she is a siren who enchants but to destroy."

THIRDLY: As to the sacrifice of Christ, Christianity teaches that He was "offered once for all, to bear the sins of many" (Heb. 9:28); that those who are sanctified by His sacrifice are so "by the offering of the body of Jesus Christ once for all" (10:10); that "by one offering He has perfected forever those who are sanctified," or made holy (10:14): these passages declare that the sacrifice of Christ was offered once for all, never to be repeated. But Rome declares that Christ is sacrificed anew, every time that the Lord's Supper, which she calls "the mass," is celebrated; and that those who administer it are sacrificing priests.

* * *

The Christ of Romanism is one who is sacrificed again and again for the remission of the sins both of the living and the dead; for those alive, and for those in purgatory. Is this the Christ of Christianity?

* * *

FOURTHLY: Christianity is in direct opposition to Romanism as to the mode of a sinner's justification before God.

What say the Scriptures? "By deeds of law shall no flesh living be justified before God" (Rom. 3:20). "Therefore we conclude that a man is justified by faith, without deeds of law" (3:28). "Even David describes the blessedness of the man to whom God imputes righteousness without works" (Rom. 4:6). . . .

The doctrine thus taught by Christianity is that all men are sinners; that without justification there is no hope for any sinner; that we are justified by the imputation of Christ's righteousness alone; and that His righteousness is received through faith.

Now, what says Romanism? It says that the righteousness by which men are justified is that which the Holy Spirit, by the grace of God, through Christ, makes them work out for themselves; that it is received by means of "the sacrament of baptism . . . without which no one was ever justified;" that it is received "in ourselves," when we are renewed by the Holy Spirit; that it is a righteousness "imparted," "infused," "implanted," and not imputed ([Council of Trent] Session 6, chapter 7). Among the declarations of the Council are these: "If any one say that justifying faith is nothing else but confidence in the Divine mercy which remits sin for Christ's sake; or, that this confidence alone is that whereby we are justified; let him be anathema" (Session 6, canon 12). "If any one say that . . . good works are merely the fruits and signs of justification obtained, but not a cause of the increase thereof; let him be anathema" (canon 24). "If any one say that he who is justified by good works, which are done by him through the grace of God and the merit of Jesus Christ, whose living member he is, does not truly deserve increase of grace, eternal life," etc. . . . "let him be anathema" (canon 32). Thus Romanism anathematizes the preaching of true Christianity!

I will mention but one more proof that Romanism is not Christianity, though there are many others which might be given.

FIFTHLY: Christianity says "there is one Mediator between God and men, the man Christ Jesus" (1 Tim. 2:5), who is at the right hand of the Father (Eph. 1:20), where He "ever lives to make intercession" for us (Heb. 7:25). Christianity says that there is but one Mediator; that we cannot draw near to God except through Jesus.

What says Romanism? I quote from "a book of devotion for every day in the month of May" published by Papal authority. "Great is the need you have of Mary in order to be saved! Are you innocent? Still your innocence is, however, under great danger. How many, more innocent than you, have fallen into sin, and been damned? Are you penitent? Still your perseverance is very uncertain. Are you sinners? Oh, what need you have of Mary to convert you! Ah, if there were no Mary, perhaps you would be lost! However, by the devotion of this month, you may obtain her patronage, and your own salvation. Is it possible that a mother so tender can help bearing a Son so devout? For a rosary, for a fast, she has sometimes conferred signal graces upon the greatest of sinners. Think, then, what she will do for you for a whole month dedicated to her service!"

Here you see that Mary is everything; that Jesus Christ is nothing. Romanism teaches also that it is right to ask the intercession of all departed saints (Session 25). How dreadful is it that sinners are thus kept back from Jesus, and are prevented from reaching God through Him.

Popery is emphatically anti-Christian: it is the adversary of Christ in all the offices which He sustains. It is the enemy of His prophetic office; for it chains up that Bible which He inspired. It is the enemy of His priestly office; for, by the mass it denies the efficacy of that sacrifice which He offered once for all on Calvary. It is the enemy of His kingly office; for it tears the crown from His head to set it on that of the Pope. . . .

McIntire, Carl. "Roman Catholic Terror." *Christian Beacon,* 6 September 1945, 8.

There are two stories in this week's issue that deserve lengthy editorial comment. They both relate to the Roman Catholic Church. One is the report of a dispatch from Rome that tells of the possible selection of new Cardinals and of the part the United States will play in the receiving of these additional Cardinals in order that the United States may be brought Closer to the Vatican.

If there is any doubt that the Roman Catholic Church is out to win America, all that needs to be done is to read this report. If there is any doubt that the Roman Catholic Church realizes the tremendous position that the United States holds in the world and that it is determined to use the position of the United States for its own ecclesiastical advancement, all one needs to do is to read this report.

The other story concerns France and the church in Spain. If there is anything that could possibly be more absurd, it is difficult for us to imagine it. For the Roman Catholic Primate to declare that he is for Franco and yet against totalitarianism is absurd. Franco is another Mussolini, another Hitler, and the tide against Fascism in the world has gained such momentum that at this very moment there is a real campaign on, being led by Russia, encouraged by Great Britain, and certainly not being opposed by the United States, to do away with the present Spanish government. In the dire circumstances in which Franco now finds himself, the man whom Franco himself recommended to the Pope to be appointed head of the Roman Catholic Church in Spain and who was appointed by the Vatican now comes to the defense of Franco. How natural!

But he says the church is not shackled. The Roman Catholic Church, of course, is not because it has had all the favor of the State, Franco himself.

But the Protestant Church has been absolutely enslaved. There is freedom for the Roman Church, and none for any other. This is what the Roman Church has always called freedom.

Here the world is given more clear-cut evidence of the essential oneness of Fascism with the whole Roman Catholic totalitarian system itself. The identity of the Church and State in the Roman Catholic doctrine, with the supreme power being in one man, is ecclesiastical and State Fascism all in one bundle in the most disastrous fashion. The world has not forgotten that the Roman pontiff gave his blessing to Mussolini and approved of his conquest of Ethiopia. Protestants were driven out of that land and the Roman Church was established.

The world has not forgotten that, when France fell, Pétain, now a convicted traitor, received the blessing and the encouragement of the Roman Catholic pontiff for his collaborationist policies. And now the Roman Catholic Church comes to the rescue of Franco. The pontiff's letter itself is filled with the most absurd contradictions. If he is against totalitarianism, he should be against Franco.   But he is not against Franco. He is for him, for him so much that he was willing to lift his voice against the tremendous current of world opinion amassed against the Spanish state, the full force of the current being the world's utter hatred of all that Hitler represented and did.

As we enter the postwar world, without any doubt the greatest enemy of freedom and liberty that the world has to face today is the Roman Catholic system. Yes, we have Communism in Russia and all that is involved there, but if one had to choose between the two, the choice, of course, we are only considering here from an ideological standpoint, one would be much better off in a communistic society than in a Roman Catholic Fascist setup. One wonders sometimes if all the antagonism of the Roman Catholic Church to Communism, an antagonism that every real true Christian feels and recognizes to be real, is not being played up especially in the United States at the present time for the purpose of gaining advantage for the Roman Catholics.

This, of course, does not mean that we should be silent in regard to all the errors of Communism, and especially the activities of the modernistic Protestant leaders in the Federal Council of the Churches of Christ in America in their attempt to turn our free society over into a collectivistic, controlled social order similar to that of Soviet Russia.

America has to face the Roman Catholic terror. The sooner the Christian people of America wake up to this danger, the safer will be our land.

Evangelicals and Catholics Together: The Christian Mission in the Third Millennium. *First Things* 43 (May 1994): 15–22. Used by permission.

As the Second Millennium draws to a close, the Christian mission in world history faces a moment of daunting opportunity and responsibility. If in the merciful and mysterious ways of God the Second Coming is delayed, we enter upon a Third Millennium that could be, in the words of John Paul II, "a springtime of world missions" (*Redemptoris Missio*).

As Christ is one, so the Christian mission is one. That one mission can be and should be advanced in diverse ways. Legitimate diversity, however, should not be confused with existing divisions between Christians that obscure the one Christ and hinder the one mission. There is a necessary connection between the visible unity of Christians and the mission of the one Christ. We together pray for the fulfillment of the prayer of Our Lord: "May they all be one; as you, Father, are in me, and I in you, so also may they be in us, that the world may believe that you sent me." (John 17) We together, Evangelicals and Catholics, confess our sins against the unity that Christ intends for all his disciples.

* * *

The love of Christ compels us and we are therefore resolved to avoid such conflict between our communities and, where such conflict exists, to do what we can to reduce and eliminate it. Beyond that, we are called and we are therefore resolved to explore patterns of working and witnessing together in order to advance the one mission of Christ. Our common resolve is not based merely on a desire for harmony. We reject any appearance of harmony that is purchased at the price of truth. Our common resolve is made imperative by obedience to the truth of God revealed in the Word of God, the Holy Scriptures, and by trust in the promise of the Holy Spirit's guidance until Our Lord returns in glory to judge the living and the dead.

The mission that we embrace together is the necessary consequence of the faith that we affirm together.

We Affirm Together

Jesus Christ is Lord. That is the first and final affirmation that Christians make about all of reality. He is the One sent by God to be Lord and Savior of all. . . .

We affirm together that we are justified by grace through faith because of Christ. Living faith is active in love that is nothing less than the love of

Christ, for we together say with Paul: "I have been crucified with Christ; it is no longer I who live, but Christ who lives in me; and the life I now live in the flesh I live by faith in the Son of God, who loved me and gave himself for me" (Galatians 2).

All who accept Christ as Lord and Savior are brothers and sisters in Christ. Evangelicals and Catholics are brothers and sisters in Christ. We have not chosen one another, just as we have not chosen Christ. He has chosen us, and he has chosen us to be his together (John 15). However imperfect our communion with one another, however deep our disagreements with one another, we recognize that there is but one church of Christ. There is one church because there is one Christ and the church is his body. . . .

We affirm together that Christians are to teach and live in obedience to the divinely inspired Scriptures, which are the infallible Word of God. We further affirm together that Christ has promised to his church the gift of the Holy Spirit who will lead us into all truth in discerning and declaring the teaching of Scripture (John 16). We recognize together that the Holy Spirit has so guided his church in the past. In, for instance, the formation of the canon of the Scriptures, and in the orthodox response to the great Christological and Trinitarian controversies of the early centuries, we confidently acknowledge the guidance of the Holy Spirit. In faithful response to the Spirit's leading, the church formulated the Apostles Creed, which we can and hereby do affirm together as an accurate statement of scriptural truth:

[Apostles' Creed is included here]

We Hope Together

We hope together that all people will come to faith in Jesus Christ as Lord and Savior.

* * *

As Evangelicals and Catholics, we pray that our unity in the love of Christ will become ever more evident as a sign to the world of God's reconciling power. Our communal and ecclesial separations are deep and long standing. We acknowledge that we do not know the schedule nor do we know the way to the greater visible unity for which we hope. We do know that existing patterns of distrustful polemic and conflict are not the way. We do know that God who has brought us into communion with himself through Christ intends that we also be in communion with one another. We do know that Christ is the way, the truth, and the life (John 14) and as we are drawn closer to him—walking in that way, obeying that truth, living that life—we are drawn closer to one another.

* * *

We Search Together

Together we search for a fuller and clearer understanding of God's revelation in Christ and his will for his disciples. Because of the limitations of human reason and language, which limitations are compounded by sin, we cannot understand completely the transcendent reality of God and his ways. Only in the End Time will we see face to face and know as we are known (1 Corinthians 13). We now search together in confident reliance upon God's self-revelation in Jesus Christ, the sure testimony of Holy Scripture, and the promise of the Spirit to his church. In this search to understand the truth more fully and clearly, we need one another. We are both informed and limited by the histories of our communities and by our own experiences. Across the divides of communities and experiences, we need to challenge one another, always speaking the truth in love building up the Body (Ephesians 4).

We do not presume to suggest that we can resolve the deep and longstanding differences between Evangelicals and Catholics. Indeed these differences may never be resolved short of the Kingdom Come. Nonetheless, we are not permitted simply to resign ourselves to differences that divide us from one another. Not all differences are authentic disagreements, nor need all disagreements divide. Differences and disagreements must be tested in disciplined and sustained conversation. In this connection we warmly commend and encourage the formal theological dialogues of recent years between Roman Catholics and Evangelicals.

We note some of the differences and disagreements that must be addressed more fully and candidly in order to strengthen between us a relationship of trust in obedience to truth.

* * *

We Contend Together

As we are bound together by Christ and his cause, so we are bound together in contending against all that opposes Christ and his cause.

* * *

Together we contend for the truth that politics, law, and culture must be secured by moral truth. With the Founders of the American experiment, we declare, "We hold these truths." With them, we hold that this constitutional order is composed not just of rules and procedures but is most essentially a moral experiment. With them, we hold that only a virtuous people can be free and just, and that virtue is secured by religion. To propose that securing civil virtue is the purpose of religion is blasphemous. To deny that securing civil virtue is a benefit of religion is blindness.

* * *

More specifically, we contend together for religious freedom. We do so for the sake of religion, but also because religious freedom is the first freedom, the source and shield of all human freedoms. In their relationship to God, persons have a dignity and responsibility that transcends, and thereby limits, the authority of the state and of every other merely human institution.

* * *

The pattern of convergence and cooperation between Evangelicals and Catholics is, in large part, a result of common effort to protect human life, especially the lives of the most vulnerable among us. With the Founders, we hold that all human beings are endowed by their Creator with the right to life, liberty, and the pursuit of happiness. The statement that the unborn child is a human life that—barring natural misfortune or lethal intervention—will become what everyone recognizes as a human baby is not a religious assertion. It is a statement of simple biological fact. That the unborn child has a right to protection, including the protection of law, is a moral statement supported by moral reason and biblical truth.

We, therefore, will persist in contending—we will not be discouraged but will multiply every effort—in order to secure the legal protection of the unborn. Our goals are: to secure due process of law for the unborn, to enact the most protective laws and public policies that are politically possible, and to reduce dramatically the incidence of abortion. We warmly commend those who have established thousands of crisis pregnancy and postnatal care centers across the country, and urge that such efforts be multiplied. As the unborn must be protected, so also must women be protected from their current rampant exploitation by the abortion industry and by fathers who refuse to accept responsibility for mothers and children. Abortion on demand, which is the current rule in America, must be recognized as a massive attack on the dignity, rights, and needs of women.

Abortion is the leading edge of an encroaching culture of death. The helpless old, the radically handicapped, and others who cannot effectively assert their rights are increasingly treated as though they have no rights. These are the powerless who are exposed to the will and whim of those who have power over them. We will do all in our power to resist proposals for euthanasia, eugenics, and population control that exploit the vulnerable, corrupt the integrity of medicine, deprave our culture, and betray the moral truths of our constitutional order.

In public education, we contend together for schools that transmit to coming generations our cultural heritage, which is inseparable from the formative influence of religion, especially Judaism and Christianity. Education for responsible citizenship and social behavior is inescapably moral education. Every effort must be made to cultivate the morality of honesty, law observance, work, caring, chastity, mutual respect between the sexes, and readiness for marriage, parenthood, and family. We reject the claim that, in any or all of these areas, "tolerance" requires the promotion of moral equivalence between the normative and the deviant. In a democratic society that recognizes that parents have the primary responsibility for the formation of their children, schools are to assist and support, not oppose and undermine, parents in the exercise of their responsibility.

We contend together for a comprehensive policy of parental choice in education. This is a moral question of simple justice. Parents are the primary educators of their children; the state and other institutions should be supportive of their exercise of that responsibility. We affirm policies that enable parents to effectively exercise their right and responsibility to choose the schooling that they consider best for their children.

We contend together against the widespread pornography in our society, along with the celebration of violence, sexual depravity, and antireligious bigotry in the entertainment media. In resisting such cultural and moral debasement, we recognize the legitimacy of boycotts and other consumer actions, and urge the enforcement of existing laws against obscenity. We reject the self-serving claim of the peddlers of depravity that this constitutes illegitimate censorship. We reject the assertion of the unimaginative that artistic creativity is to be measured by the capacity to shock or outrage. A people incapable of defending decency invite the rule of viciousness, both public and personal.

We contend for a renewed spirit of acceptance, understanding, and co-operation across lines of religion, race, ethnicity, sex, and class. We are all created in the image of God and are accountable to him. That truth is the basis of individual responsibility and equality before the law. The abandonment of that truth has resulted in a society at war with itself, pitting citizens against one another in bitter conflicts of group grievances and claims to entitlement. Justice and social amity require a redirection of public attitudes and policies so that rights are joined to duties and people are rewarded according to their character and competence.

We contend for a free society, including a vibrant market economy. A free society requires a careful balancing between economics, politics, and culture. Christianity is not an ideology and therefore does not prescribe precisely how that balance is to be achieved in every circumstance. We affirm the importance of a free economy not only because it is more efficient but because it accords with a Christian understanding of human freedom. Economic freedom, while subject to grave abuse, makes possible the patterns of creativity, cooperation, and accountability that contribute to the common good.

We contend together for a renewed appreciation of Western culture. In its history and missionary reach, Christianity engages all cultures while being captive to none. We are keenly aware of, and grateful for, the role of Christianity in shaping and sustaining the Western culture of which we are part. As with all of history, that culture is marred by human sinfulness. Alone among world cultures, however, the West has cultivated an attitude of self-criticism and of eagerness to learn from other cultures. What is called multiculturalism can mean respectful attention to human differences. More commonly today, however, multiculturalism means affirming all cultures but our own. Welcoming the contributions of other cultures and being ever alert to the limitations of our own, we receive Western culture as our legacy and embrace it as our task in order to transmit it as a gift to future generations.

We contend for public policies that demonstrate renewed respect for the irreplaceable role of mediating structures in society—notably the family, churches, and myriad voluntary associations. The state is not the society, and many of the most important functions of society are best addressed in independence from the state. The role of churches in responding to a wide variety of human needs, especially among the poor and marginal, needs to be protected and strengthened. Moreover, society is not the aggregate of isolated individuals bearing rights but is composed of communities that inculcate responsibility, sustain shared memory, provide mutual aid, and nurture the habits that contribute to both personal well-being and the common good. Most basic among such communities is the community of the family. Laws and social policies should be designed with particular care for the stability and flourishing of families. While the crisis of the family in America is by no means limited to the poor or to the underclass, heightened attention must be paid those who have become, as a result of well-intended but misguided statist policies, virtual wards of the government.

Finally, we contend for a realistic and responsible understanding of America's part in world affairs. Realism and responsibility require that we avoid both the illusions of unlimited power and righteousness, on the one hand, and the timidity and selfishness of isolationism, on the other U.S. foreign policy should reflect a concern for the defense of democracy and, wherever prudent and possible, the protection and advancement of human rights, including religious freedom.

* * *

We Witness Together

The question of Christian witness unavoidably returns us to points of serious tension between Evangelicals and Catholics. Bearing witness to the saving power of Jesus Christ and his will for our lives is an integral part of Christian discipleship. The achievement of good will and cooperation between Evangelicals and Catholics must not be at the price of the urgency and clarity of Christian witness to the Gospel. At the same time, and as noted earlier, Our Lord has made clear that the evidence of love among his disciples is an integral part of that Christian witness.

Today, in this country and elsewhere, Evangelicals and Catholics attempt to win "converts" from one another's folds. In some ways, this is perfectly understandable and perhaps inevitable. In many instances, however, such efforts at recruitment undermine the Christian mission by which we are bound by God's Word and to which we have recommitted ourselves in this statement. It should be clearly understood between Catholics and Evangelicals that Christian witness is of necessity aimed at conversion. Authentic conversion is—in its beginning, in its end, and all along the way—conversion to God in Christ by the power of the Spirit.

* * *

Conclusion

Nearly two thousand years after it began, and nearly five hundred years after the divisions of the Reformation era, the Christian mission to the world is vibrantly alive and assertive. We do not know, we cannot know, what the Lord of history has in store for the Third Millennium. It may be the springtime of world missions and great Christian expansion. It may be the way of the cross marked by persecution and apparent marginalization. In different places and times, it will likely be both. Or it may be that Our Lord will return tomorrow.

We do know that his promise is sure, that we are enlisted for the duration, and that we are in this together. We do know that we must affirm and hope and search and contend and witness together, for we belong not to ourselves but to him who has purchased us by the blood of the cross. We do know that this is a time of opportunity—and, if of opportunity, then of responsibility—for Evangelicals and Catholics to be Christians together in a way that helps prepare the world for the coming of him to whom belongs the kingdom, the power, and the glory forever. Amen.

* * *

Notes

INTRODUCTION

1. David Bebbington, *Evangelicalism in Modern Britain: A History from the 1730s to the 1980s* (Grand Rapids: Baker, 1992), 1–17. See also David Bebbington, "Towards an Evangelical Identity" in Brady Steve and Rowdon Harold eds., *For Such a Time As This: Perspectives on Evangelicalism, Past, Present and Future* (London: Scripture Union, 1996), 37–48. Evangelicalism in the English-speaking world was essentially one movement existing on both sides of the Atlantic.

2. The best book on theological modernism is William R. Hutchison, *The Modernist Impulse in American Protestantism* (Durham: Duke University Press, 1992).

3. Quoted in Gillis J. Harp, *Brahmin Prophet: Phillips Brooks and the Path of Liberal Protestantism* (Lanham, MD: Rowman and Littlefield, 2003), 26.

4. George Marsden, *Fundamentalism and American Culture: The Shaping of Twentieth-Century Evangelicalism, 1877–1925* (New York: Oxford University Press, 1980), 117. This is still the standard history of the rise of fundamentalism and was republished in a slightly revised twenty-fifth anniversary edition in 2005.

5. Marsden, *Fundamentalism and American Culture*, 4. See also George Marsden, *Reforming Fundamentalism: Fuller Seminary and the New Evangelicalism* (Grand Rapids: Eerdmans, 1987).

6. The best book on the rise of neoevangelicalism is Joel Carpenter, *Revive Us Again: The Reawakening of American Fundamentalism* (New York: Oxford University Press, 1997).

CHAPTER 1

1. Harold Lindsell, *The Battle for the Bible* (Grand Rapids: Zondervan, 1976).

2. http://www.campuscrusade.com/fourlawseng.htm.

CHAPTER 4

1. The best book on the Scopes trial is *Summer for the Gods: The Scopes Trial and America's Continuing Debate over Science and Religion* (New York: Basic

Books, 1997). For a discussion of the warfare model see David C. Lindberg and Ronald Numbers, "Beyond War and Peace: A Reappraisal of the Encounter between Christianity and Science," *Church History* 55:3 (September 1986), 347. As they put it, there is "mounting evidence that White read the past through battle-scarred glasses, and that he and his imitators have distorted history to serve ideological ends of their own."

CHAPTER 5

1. See Carpenter, *Revive Us Again*.

CHAPTER 7

1. Richard Land, *The Divided States of America? What Liberals and Conservatives are Missing in the God-and-Country Shouting Match* (Nashville: Thomas Nelson, 2007).

2. New American Standard Bible (La Habra, CA: Lockman Foundation, 1995).

CHAPTER 8

1. Christians for Biblical Equality, 122 W. Franklin Ave., Suite 218, Minneapolis, MN 55404. 612-872-6891. cbe@cbeinternational.org.

CHAPTER 9

1. James Davison Hunter, *Culture Wars: The Struggle to Define America* (New York: Basic Books, 1991).

Index